David H. Hesla is an associate professor
of literature and theology in the Graduate
Institute of the Liberal Arts at Emory
University.

THE SHAPE OF CHAOS
An Interpretation of the Art
of SAMUEL BECKETT

► The publication of this book was assisted by the Atkinson Fund.

THE SHAPE OF CHAOS

AN INTERPRETATION OF THE ART OF

SAMUEL BECKETT

david h. hesla

THE UNIVERSITY OF MINNESOTA PRESS · MINNEAPOLIS

Library of Congress Catalog Card Number: 74-167296
ISBN 0-8166-0625-0

Quotations from the following works of Samuel Beckett are reprinted by permission of Grove Press, Inc., New York: *Endgame, A Play in One Act*, translated from the French by the author; copyright © 1958 by Grove Press, Inc. *Happy Days: A Play in Two Acts*, copyright © 1961 by Grove Press, Inc. *How It Is*, translated from the French by the author; copyright © 1964 by Grove Press, Inc. *Krapp's Last Tape and Other Dramatic Pieces*, copyright © 1957 by Samuel Beckett; copyright © 1958, 1959, 1960 by Grove Press, Inc. *More Pricks Than Kicks*, all rights reserved, first published by Chatto & Windus, London, 1934. *Murphy*, first published 1938; first Grove Press edition 1957. *Poems in English*, copyright © 1961 by Samuel Beckett. *Proust*, all rights reserved, first published 1931. *Stories and Texts for Nothing*, copyright © 1967 by Samuel Beckett, all rights reserved; originally published as *Nouvelles et textes pour rien*, copyright © 1958 by Les Editions de Minuit, Paris, France. *Molloy*, a novel translated from the French by Patrick Bowles in collaboration with the author; all rights reserved in all countries by The Olympia Press, Paris, and Grove Press, New York; first Grove Press edition 1955 (originally published by Grove Press as *Three Novels*). *Malone Dies*, a novel translated from the French by the author; copyright © 1956 by Grove Press; first printing, collected works, 1970 (originally published by Grove Press as *Three Novels*). *The Unnamable*, translated from the French by the author; copyright © 1958 by Grove Press, Inc.; first printing, collected works, 1970 (originally published by Grove Press as *Three Novels*). *Waiting for Godot: Tragicomedy in Two Acts*, translated from the original French text by the author; copyright © 1954 by Grove Press. *Watt*, all rights reserved; originally published by The Olympia Press, Paris, 1953; first American edition, 1959; first printing, collected works, 1970.
    Quotations from the following works of Samuel Beckett are reprinted by permission of Faber and Faber Ltd., London: *Embers, Endgame, Happy Days, Krapp's Last Tape*, and *Waiting for Godot*. These works are fully protected by United States and International Copyright.
    Quotations from the following works of Samuel Beckett are reprinted by permission of Calder and Boyars, London: *How It Is, More Pricks Than Kicks, Murphy, Poems in English, Proust and Three Dialogues, Stories and Texts for Nothing, Three Novels: Molloy, Malone Dies, The Unnamable*, and *Watt*. These works are fully protected by United States and International Copyright.
    Lines quoted from "The Circus Animals' Desertion" on page 12 are reprinted with permission of The Macmillan Company, New York; The Macmillan Company of Canada; and A. P. Watt & Sons, Ltd., London, from *Collected Poems* by William Butler Yeats. Copyright 1940 by Georgie Yeats, renewed 1968 by Bertha Georgie Yeats, Michael Butler Yeats, and Anne Yeats.
    Lines quoted from "Sonnette I, 3" on page 206 are reprinted from *Sonnette an Orpheus* by Rainer Maria Rilke with permission of Insel Verlag, Frankfurt am Main. The translation on page 243 is reprinted from *Sonnets to Orpheus* by Rainer Maria Rilke. Translated by M. D. Herter Norton. Copyright 1942 by W. W. Norton & Company, Inc. Copyright renewed 1969 by M. D. Herter Norton. With the permission of the publisher. An alternative translation by J. B. Leishman is available, published by The Hogarth Press, London.
    Lines quoted from "A Se Stesso" on pages 47–48 are reprinted from *Leopardi: Poems and Prose*, edited by Angel Flores. Copyright © 1966 by Indiana University Press. Reprinted by permission of the publisher.
    An early version of Chapter III appeared in *Critique* (Spring 1963).

PREFACE

Sie mögen das Werk auch noch beurtheilen oder ihm Opfer bringen auf welche Art es sey, ihr Bewusstseyn darein legen, — wenn sie sich mit ihrer Kenntniss darüber setzen, weiss er, wie viel mehr seine That als ihr Verstehen und Reden ist; — wenn sie sich darunter setzen und ihr sie beherrschendes Wesen darin erkennen, weiss er sich als den Meister desselben.

People may, moreover, judge the work, or bring it offerings and gifts, or endue it with their consciousness in whatever way they like — if they with their knowledge set themselves over it, he knows how much more his act is than what they understand and say; if they put themselves beneath it, and recognize in it their own dominating essential reality, he knows himself as the master of this.

Hegel [1]

◄ ► This book is an interpretation of the art of Samuel Beckett mainly from the perspective offered by the history of ideas. In preparing it I did not try to lay hands on manuscripts which Beckett has refrained from publishing; and I did not have the privilege of discussing the various poems, plays, and fictional pieces with the author. I have not tried to relate his work to the British and French literary traditions, and I have given pretty short shrift to the works published after 1960.

What I have tried to do is relate him to the Western intellectual tradition, and get at the problems which have preoccupied Beckett as a writer and thinker. Pre-eminent among these problems is the structure of consciousness and its implications for the art of writing. In my view, Beckett's art is finally ontological: it asks the question, What is the being of that entity we call man? In asking it, he has drawn on the ideas of the pre-Socratics, the rationalists of the seventeenth and eighteenth centuries, on Schopenhauer and Bergson, and that group of thinkers collected under the heading "Existentialists." In order to talk about his work I have thought it necessary to draw on these thinkers, as well as on Hegel, Kierkegaard, Heidegger, Sartre, and Edmund Husserl, among others.

For biographical and bibliographical information, as well as for inspiration, I have relied on several early studies. With remarkable perspicacity, Hugh Kenner has touched on nearly every theme, problem, or idea worth serious study. His name for Beckett's typical hero, "the Cartesian Centaur," properly understood, tells us more about Beckett's work all by itself than many full-length essays do. Ruby Cohn's book contains a great deal of information not only about Beckett's use of comic devices but about the whole range of his work; and it was she who, in 1958, published a number of *Perspective* devoted entirely to Beckett. John Fletcher's two books are especially valuable for their treatment of works which Beckett has suppressed, for information which he got in conversations with the writer, and for his comparison of English and French versions of particular texts. Raymond Federman has provided a detailed study of the early fiction, including some of the suppressed works. Josephine Jacobsen and William R. Mueller emphasize existential and religious dimensions of Beckett's art.[2] Chronological bibliographies of Beckett's works are provided by Cohn, Fletcher, and Federman; and Federman and Fletcher are collaborating on a detailed bibliography. I have not thought it necessary, therefore, to include such apparatus in this study.

A second spate of books appeared in the late 1960's and 1970. Unfortunately for me, Lawrence Harvey's extensive study of Beckett's poetry and criticism, and Edith Kern's study of Kierkegaard, Sartre, and Beckett, came too late for me to incorporate their insights into my interpretation.[3]

In quoting from Beckett's work I have occasionally taken the liberty of altering the case of the initial letter in the quotation, and of providing a full stop where there was a weaker stop (usually a comma) or none at all. In citing his work I have used the following editions and abbreviations:

OERH — *Our Exagmination Round His Factification for Incamination of Work in Progress* (Faber and Faber, 1961)
PTD — *Proust and Three Dialogues* (John Calder, 1965)
MPTK — *More Pricks Than Kicks* (Calder and Boyars, 1966)
M — *Murphy* (Grove, 1957)
W — *Watt* (Grove, 1959)
TN — *Molloy, Malone Dies, and The Unnamable: Three Novels* (Grove, 1959)
WFG — *Waiting for Godot* (Grove, 1954)
E — *Endgame* (Grove, 1958)
KLT — *Krapp's Last Tape and Other Dramatic Pieces* (Grove, 1960)
HD — *Happy Days* (Grove, 1961)
HII — *How It Is* (Grove, 1964)
STN — *Stories and Texts for Nothing* (Grove, 1967)

For financial assistance in preparing this book, I thank Cornell College, Mt. Vernon, Iowa, and its revered dean Howard W. Troyer; the National

Endowment for the Humanities; and the Emory University Research Committee. The manuscript, in one or another stage of completion, has been read by many persons. They know who they are, they know that I know, and that I am grateful. From among these many friendly critics I must single out one, however. Professor Gregor Sebba, a true polymath, did what he could to save me from error; and I count it a grace to have served with him on the faculty of the Graduate Institute of the Liberal Arts of Emory University.

The whole staff of the University of Minnesota Press has been uncommonly helpful and cooperative.

This book is for the family, but especially for the three who always right me to the Something — Mary, Maren, and Thor.

When all is said and done, this book is a report on what I have found necessary or helpful or at least interesting to know in order to understand better the art of Samuel Beckett, and in particular the ideas that are a part of that art, and the way it has grown and developed. On the supposition that even books of literary criticism can and should be *dolce* as well as *utile*, I have not always suppressed the merely amusing.

Of critics' interpretations of his work, and of his work itself, Beckett has said, "We have no elucidation to offer of mysteries that are all of their making. My work is a matter of fundamental sounds (no joke intended) made as fully as possible, and I accept responsibility for nothing else. If people want to have headaches among the overtones, let them. And provide their own aspirin."

This book, you might say, is my box of aspirin.

D. H. H.

Emory University
September 1970

TABLE OF CONTENTS

THE SHAPE OF CHAOS
An Interpretation of the Art
of SAMUEL BECKETT

I PROBLEM, THEME, AND STYLE: THE BEGINNINGS

Inquietum est cor nostrum, donec requiescat in te.
Augustine

What a chimera then is man! What a novelty! What a monster, what a chaos, what a contradiction, what a prodigy! Judge of all things, imbecile worm of the earth; depository of truth, a sink of uncertainty and error; the pride and refuse of the universe!

We desire truth, and find within ourselves only uncertainty.
We seek happiness, and find only misery and death.
We cannot but desire truth and happiness, and are incapable of certainty or happiness. The desire is left to us, partly to punish us, partly to make us perceive wherefrom we are fallen.
Pascal

According to some authorities the end proposed by the Sceptics is insensibility [apatheia]; according to others, gentleness.
Diogenes Laertius

Imagine dispassion [apatheia] as the celestial palace of the Heavenly King; and the many mansions as the abodes within this city, and the wall of this celestial Jerusalem as the forgiveness of sins. Let us run, brethren, let us run to enter the bridal hall of this palace. If we are prevented by anything, by some burden or old habit, or by time itself, what a disaster! . . .
John Climacus

Ascendimus ascensiones in corde . . . quoniam sursum imus ad pacem Jerusalem.
Augustine

On a closer examination it seems as though, in the case of a genius, the will to live, which is the spirit of the human species, were conscious of having by some rare chance and for a brief period attained a greater clearness of vision, and were now trying to secure it or at least the outcome of it for the whole species, . . . so that the light which he sheds about him may pierce the darkness and dullness of ordinary human consciousness and there produce some good effect.

Arising in some such way, this instinct drives the genius to carry his work to completion, without thinking of reward or applause or sympathy; to leave all care for his own personal welfare; to make his life one of industrious solitude, and to strain his faculties to the utmost.
Schopenhauer [1]

3

I

◄ ► In the first of three dialogues with Georges Duthuit on modern painters and painting, Samuel Beckett criticizes Tal Coat and Henri Matisse on the grounds that their work is not really so revolutionary as it is thought to be or as it ought to be. It is, in fact, in the tradition of the Italian Renaissance painters who, though they enlarged the field of "the possible," never stirred from that field. Matisse and Tal Coat, in Beckett's opinion, disturb only a "certain order on the plane of the feasible." Duthuit asks, reasonably enough, what other "plane," what other field or order, is available to the painter? To this Beckett replies that there is logically no other,

> Yet I speak of an art turning from it in disgust, weary of its puny exploits, weary of pretending to be able, of being able, of doing a little better the same old thing, of going a little further along a dreary road.
> DUTHUIT. And preferring what?
> BECKETT. The expression that there is nothing to express, nothing with which to express, nothing from which to express, no power to express, no desire to express, together with the obligation to express.[2]

This uncompromising, unreasonable, and desperate pronouncement puts Beckett in what he himself later terms "an unenviable situation." It is the situation of absolute privation, in which the artist is left with nothing but a disoriented yet unrelenting responsibility to do what an artist does — to express, to make, to produce. And yet, for the painter, there is "nothing to paint and nothing to paint with."

Beckett's interlocutor then asks whether it might not be possible for the artist to conceive of the extremity of his situation in such a way as to provide him with the necessary occasion for expression, in which case such painting would be expressive of the impossibility of expressing by means of art. This, however, is not at all what Beckett has had in mind. He refuses to turn tail before "the ultimate penury," and insists that there is more than a difference of degree between being simply short of world and self and being utterly without these commodities. And for Beckett, the modern artist is not simply short of them: the modern artist simply and completely has no expressible world and no expressible self. "Expressionism" as an aesthetic principle for the explication of what goes on in art is therefore no longer a tenable concept, because its assumptions have been invalidated. Expressionism had assumed the presence and availability of both an expressing artistic self and an expressible world or matter, and had assumed that these two terms establish a relation or matrix from which the work of art issued.

But in this warped and hollow time the relation is quite out of joint, for its constitutive terms are either not present or are present but not available to the artist.

It is obvious that for the artist obsessed with his expressive vocation, anything and everything is doomed to become occasion. . . . But if the occasion appears as an unstable term of relation, the artist, who is the other term, is hardly less so, thanks to his warren of modes and attitudes. . . . Two things are established, however precariously: the aliment, from fruits on plates to low mathematics and self-commiseration, and its manner of dispatch. All that should concern us is the acute and increasing anxiety of the relation itself, as though shadowed more and more darkly by a sense of invalidity, of inadequacy, of existence at the expense of all that it excludes, all that it blinds to. (PTD, 124–25)

It is Beckett's thesis that both the "aliment" and "its manner of dispatch" are unavailable, and that the Dutch painter Bram van Velde is the first in the history of painting to "submit wholly to the incoercible absence of terms or, if you like, in the presence of unavailable terms, the first to admit that to be an artist is to fail, as no other dare fail, that failure is his world and the shrink from it desertion" (PTD, 125). If van Velde is the first painter to acknowledge the recent disappearance or unavailability of the two terms of the expressionistic aesthetic — self or "manner" and world or "aliment" — and the first as well to submit to the obligation of failure, then Beckett himself is perhaps the first writer to make the same discovery and to submit to the same discipline.

Nor can Beckett be charged with desertion, with shrinking from the task of failure. It is true, of course, that the logic of his argument, if taken with unqualified seriousness, would seem to require the artist to put away the tools of his trade, whether paint or words, and lapse into an irresponsible but luxurious solipsism. And it is also true that among Beckett's later works are the pantomimes, in which the words of one of the most gifted literary talents of the day are never heard by a theater audience but are translated directly into spectacle, thereby accomplishing what seems to be the rejection of language by language. In spite of this, the novels, plays, and pieces for radio which have been published since the appearance of the dialogue with Duthuit in 1949 are ample evidence of the fact that the force exerted on Beckett by the "obligation to express" has conquered the logic of his own desperate argument, and conquered as well the anxiety which must surely be aroused in an artist who is so conscious of the discrepancy between the demands of art and the limitations of talent that he can foresee only failure.

We should, of course, be grateful that this has been the outcome of the contention within the artist between judgment and the imperative of responsibility. Nonetheless, what Beckett pronounced in 1949 does not harmonize with what he has practiced since; and though it is no doubt impossible to make an accurate reconstruction of the processes of thought and feeling which have liberated Beckett from the apparent impasse documented in the conversation with Duthuit, there is at least one hypothesis which deserves serious attention.

In the course of an interview with Tom F. Driver, Beckett insisted that art must admit into itself what he calls "the mess" or "the confusion": "The confusion is not my invention. We cannot listen to a conversation for five minutes without being acutely aware of the confusion. It is all around us and our only chance now is to let it in. The only chance of renovation is to open our eyes and see the mess. It is not a mess you can make sense of. . . . One can only speak of what is in front of him, and that now is simply the mess." [3]

This is not quite the same thing Beckett said to Duthuit twelve years earlier. There, in one sentence, he had pummelled to fragments the principles of Expressionism, saving only "the obligation to express," and had asserted that there was "nothing to paint with." To Driver, however, Beckett admits — insists, rather — that there is indeed something to "paint": it is the confusion, the mess.

And yet there is an important continuity between the two dialogues. If it is not quite true to say that there is nothing to paint, nothing to write about, it is also not true to say that one can admit chaos into art without irreparably damaging the form or forms of art which have been transmitted by the tradition. To admit the mess into art is to jeopardize the very nature of art; for the mess "appears to be the very opposite of form and therefore destructive of the very thing that art holds itself to be." Beckett is of course acutely aware of the threat to form posed by the admission of "the confusion": "What I am saying does not mean that there will henceforth be no form in art. It only means that there will be new form, and that this form will be of such a type that it admits the chaos and does not try to say that the chaos is really something else. The form and the chaos remain separate. The latter is not reduced to the former. That is why the form itself becomes a preoccupation, because it exists as a problem separate from the material it accommodates. To find a form that accommodates the mess, that is the task of the artist now." [4]

It is at least possible that when, in 1949, Beckett said that there was nothing to paint, he meant that there was only one thing to paint — the chaos; but at that time he could see no way to include the formlessness of chaos within the structure of art. But in the intervening years, he has been experimenting, trying to create or discover the literary structure or process which will admit chaos without enforming and domesticating it. "To find a form that accommodates the mess": this is the task to which Beckett has applied himself over the last forty years; and if we are to come to some understanding of what this immensely gifted writer is and has been about, it will be necessary to try to understand what he means by "the mess," and to follow the ways in which he has permitted chaos to enter the formal structure of his art without destroying it.

II

◄ ► If the relation between form and chaos is the technical problem which the artist must solve, the chaos itself is his continuing theme. By "the chaos," I take him to mean, simply, the absurdity of human existence.

"Absurd": the word is very much in our modern parlance. "Don't be absurd," we say, and mean "Don't be silly." "Isn't that absurd," we say, and mean ridiculous or funny or ugly or unpleasant.

The word comes from the Latin *surdus*, meaning "deaf," but it is also used of musical sounds, where it means "unharmonious," or of other sounds which are dull or faint. Literally speaking, one is "deaf" to a sound which he cannot hear, or can hear but faintly; metaphorically speaking, one is "deaf" to sounds which he cannot make "sense" of. By extension, a person may be "absurd" if he is so stupid as to be unable to "hear" or "understand" what is being said; or a thing or situation may be "absurd" if what it "says" cannot be understood by a person of normal intelligence. Of more relevance is the fact that the Latin *surdus* was used to translate Euclid's *alogos*, the term for irrational numbers. *Alogos* may be translated "irrational," but can also mean "without a name," or "having no name," or, briefly, "The Unnamable." This is of course the title of the third volume of Beckett's trilogy; and Watt was greatly disturbed by the fact that he found himself "in the midst of things which, if they consented to be named, did so as it were with reluctance" (w, 81).

The word, then, does not mean silly or ugly or unpleasant. It means unnamable or unintelligible — unnamable because unintelligible, unintelligible because unnamable. The absurd is impervious to the human Logos, to human speech and reason. Hence the writer's dilemma: his task is to discourse upon the unintelligible, to name the unnamable.

What is absurd is human existence. Why is it absurd? Because *being human* and *existing* are mutually contradictory. One could be a human being if one did not have to exist, and one could exist, though not as a human being. But one cannot exist, and be a human being, in the same place, at the same time.

There are a number of reasons for this.

To be a human being is to be body and mind; but what one needs and wants as body is what, as mind, one neither needs nor wants; and vice versa.

To be a human being is to want to know and to love — that is to say, to become one with — the Other, but the Other is precisely that with which one cannot become one.

To be a human being is to want to say who one is, but who one is, precisely, is what one cannot say.

To be a human being is to want to be self-grounded, but self-grounded is precisely what a human being is not and cannot be.

In other words, man is not congruous with the conditions — the only conditions — provided for his existence. He and his world do not suit with each other, do not make a fit. "Use your head, can't you," screams Hamm, "use your head, you're on earth, there's no cure for that!" (e, 53.)

There is of course a tradition in the West that holds that whatever problems man has result from the fact that he does *not* use his head. If he used his head he would see that this world is the best of all possible worlds, and is exactly adjusted to the support of human existence. This tradition runs from contemporary Marxist and Christian thinkers back through Hegel and the rationalists of the eighteenth and seventeenth centuries, to the medieval Schoolmen, to Aristotle and Plato, to its source in Parmenides. This tradition acknowledges that there are more or less serious flaws in the system, but holds that these can be corrected either now or in the future by the application of reason or faith or science or technology. The ground of this tradition is the principle that Cosmos and Logos are congruent with each other. Thus Parmenides: "Come, I will tell you — and you must accept my word when you have heard it — the ways of inquiry which alone are to be thought: the one that IT IS, and it is not possible for IT NOT TO BE, is the way of credibility, for it follows Truth; the other, that IT IS NOT, and that IT is bound NOT TO BE: this I tell you is a path that cannot be explored; for you could neither recognize that which IS NOT, nor express it."[5] But if nonbeing or "that which is not" cannot be either recognized or expressed, being or "that which is" can be both recognized and expressed; for, according to Parmenides, "It is the same thing to think and to be,"[6] or, put differently, "That which it is possible to think is identical with that which can Be."[7] Being and Thinking are one, and if you use your head you will see that this is so, and will be comforted. You will avoid the fate of those mortals who take the wrong way, "for perplexity in their bosoms steers their intelligence astray and they are carried along as deaf as they are blind, amazed, uncritical hordes, by whom To Be and Not To Be are regarded as the same and not the same, and (*for whom*) in everything there is a way of opposing stress."[8]

Parmenides no doubt had Heracleitus in mind when he criticized "the way of opposing stress," but it was Democritus of Abdera who took up Parmenides' challenge and boldly declared, "Naught exists just as much as Aught."[9] In reality, both atoms and the Void exist, but since man can have knowledge only of the ways in which the atoms impinge upon his senses he can have no knowledge of the void. Truth is a matter merely of human customs and conventions; and Parmenidean certitude gives way to Democritean scepticism: "We know nothing in reality; for truth lies in an abyss."[10] This means that the cosmos and human logos are incongruent, incompatible, unharmonious; and their relation can properly be spoken of as absurd.

The Greeks dealt with the cosmos in terms of being and nonbeing, truth and ignorance. The Hebrews dealt with it in terms of life and death, justice and injustice, happiness and misery: "Man that is born of a woman is of few days, and full of trouble. He cometh forth like a flower, and is cut down: he fleeth also as a shadow, and continueth not. . . . For there is hope of a tree, if it be cut down, that it will sprout again, and that the tender branch thereof will not cease. . . . But man dieth, and wasteth away; yea, man giveth up the ghost, and where is he?" (Job 14:1–2,7,10.) This too is the absurd, for man would live and be happy, and existence gives him suffering and death.

So the idea of the absurd is not a new idea. It goes back, in the West, from Sartre and Camus through Leopardi and Schopenhauer and Pascal and the Christian ascetic and pietistic traditions to the Desert Fathers, to Valentinians and Marcionites and other Gnostics, to Roman Stoicism and Greek Scepticism and Cynicism, to Oriental wisdom literature such as the book of Job and Ecclesiastes. The idea is implicit in every event that merits the adjective "tragic," and when it is born in a person's consciousness he must ask himself Hamlet's question.

And when he asks Hamlet's question, he usually comes up with Hamlet's answer. "The Everlasting's canon" is a principle or value which carries absolute authority, and only such an authority is weighty enough to counterbalance the despair and anguish of the person for whom "the mess" is not a tricky intellectual problem to be solved but an existential fact to be dealt with. Only a very few alternatives to divine law have been found capable of dealing adequately with that fact, however. Human reason is not one of these, for reason, once it finds itself confronted by both being and nonbeing, is capable only of asking the question, not of supplying the answer. But Love has been celebrated, in the Romantic tradition, as the conqueror of all, even of the last foe, death; and in the Stoic tradition, Courage has sometimes been found adequate to carry man through the tribulations of this world. Love, Courage, and God: these have been what Western man has turned to for the strength to endure what otherwise has seemed unendurable.

Yet there also has been a fourth way of dealing with the mess. It lacks the dignity, the pathos, the heroism, the nobility of the other ways, but it too has worked. For consider: man does not "fit" his world. The world is like an overcoat that is much too long, or a pair of boots that are much too small. But the sight of a man tripping over his own overcoat is funny. Incongruity is the basis of the comic, and a metaphysical incongruity is the basis of metaphysical laughter, "the laugh of laughs, the *risus purus*, the laugh laughing at the laugh, the beholding, the saluting of the highest joke, in a word the laugh that laughs — silence please — at that which is unhappy" (w, 48).

Yet laughter is not the final word, either, for in Beckett's world there is no final word. His world is a syzygy, and for every laugh there is a tear, for every position an opposition, for every thesis an antithesis, for every affirmation a negation. His art is a Democritean art, energized precisely by the dialectical interplay of opposites — body and mind, the self and the other, speech and silence, life and death, hope and despair, being and non-being, yes and no.

No, something better must be found, a better reason, for this to stop, another word, a better idea, to put in the negative, a new no to cancel all the others, all the old noes that buried me down here, deep in this place which is not one, which is merely a moment for the time being eternal, which is called here, and in this being which is called me and is not one, and in this impossible voice, all the old noes dangling in the dark and swaying like a ladder of smoke, yes, a new no, that none says twice, whose drop will fall and let me down, shadow and babble, to an absence less vain than inexistence. Oh I know it won't happen like that . . . (stn, 130–31)

Each of his major works is built upon such contraries and oppositions. *Murphy* is built on the opposition of mind and body; *Watt* on the relation between knower and known, lover and beloved; *Waiting for Godot* is built on the contrast between the actuality of the contingent, inauthentic self and the possibility of the self-grounded, authentic self; and in the trilogy the effort to be and say what one is gets opposed by the inadequacy of language, the nihilating effect of time, and the reflexive structure of consciousness.

Therefore, through all the works there sounds the anguished plea for peace — the peace that comes with the coincidence of the opposites, the synthesis of antitheses, the surcease of consciousness, the arrest of the dialectic. This peace is the condition of the soul which the Sceptics and the Desert Fathers called *apatheia*. The pursuit of peace is a spiritual pursuit; and though Beckett must be honored as a superb stylist, expert craftsman, and subtle dialectician, he is perhaps above all to be honored as a master funambulist of the life of the spirit. For all its obscenity and scatology, his art is ascetic, achieved by the elimination of nearly all the equipment poets and playwrights and novelists have been at such pains to invent. There is something importantly monastic, eremitic, about both the art and the man. Without hope of achieving the beatific vision, he has nonetheless renounced the world and climbed the ladder of divine ascent, in imitation of Johannes Climacus:

A monk is a mourning soul that both asleep and awake is unceasingly occupied with the remembrance of death. Withdrawal from the world is voluntary hatred of vaunted material things and denial of nature for the attainment of what is above nature. . . . [The ascent demands] a great toil, very great indeed, with much unseen suffering, especially for those who live carelessly, until by simplicity, deep angerlessness and diligence, we make our mind, which is a greedy kitchen dog addicted to barking, a lover of chastity and watchfulness. . . . Those who enter this contest must renounce all things, despise all things, deride all things, and shake off all things, that they may lay a firm foundation.[11]

. . . .

But I long to know how Jacob saw thee fixed above the ladder. Satisfy my desire, tell me, What are the means of such an ascent? What the manner, what the law that joins together the steps which thy lover sets as an ascent in his heart?[12]

Climacus here is drawing together two biblical images — that of Jacob's ladder (Gen. 28:10–22) and the ladder in the heart (Ps. 84:5 [KJV; 83:6 in the Vulgate]). St. Augustine used the same imagery: in the *Confessions* (XIII, 9) he writes, "Ascendimus ascensiones in corde, et cantamus canticum graduum." And still another spiritual pilgrim, William Butler Yeats, knew the meaning of the tradition, if not the tradition itself:

> Those masterful images because complete
> Grew in pure mind, but out of what began?
> A mound of refuse or the sweepings of a street,
> Old kettles, old bottles, and a broken can,
> Old iron, old bones, old rags, that raving slut
> Who keeps the till. Now that my ladder's gone,
> I must lie down where all the ladders start,
> In the foul rag-and-bone shop of the heart.
> ("The Circus Animals' Desertion")

Teste David cum Sibylla.

The similarities between the vocation of the artist and the vocation of the saint have frequently been remarked, but rarely have they been so exemplified as in the case of Samuel Beckett. In his art he has indeed renounced all things, despised all things, derided all things. Because he has done so, he has seemed to some a sceptic and a cynic, embittered with life and thought and even art itself. But here too the paradoxical Word has been fulfilled, for in losing his art he has found it, by casting away he has been enriched, by descending into the mud of existence he has ascended into a realm of pure poetry.

III

◄ ► But no one, not even Beckett, begins at the top of the ladder. Even he had to start at the bottom, at the beginning, like an old ballocks. For our purposes, the beginning includes an essay on Joyce, "Dante . . . Bruno . Vico . . Joyce," published in *Our Exagmination Round His Factification for Incamination of Work in Progress* (1929); a poem on Descartes, *Whoroscope* (1930); another essay, *Proust* (1931); and a collection of poems, *Echo's Bones* (1935). I shall tarry over this material only long enough to do two things: first, I want to make some comments on the problems that Beckett's learning raises for the critic; and then I want to look at the stories and poems from the point of view of their style, and use one of the poems — "Sanies I" — as the chief example of Beckett's early technique.

Here are three lines from *Whoroscope*:

> Oh Weulles spare the blood of a Frank
> who has climbed the bitter steps,
> (René du Perron . . .)

Descartes' title, "du Perron," derived from a small "seigneurie" in Poitou which belonged to his parents but which they made over to René. "Perron" means a staircase or flight of steps. In 1624 he visited Rome, perhaps to fulfill a vow, and (probably) climbed the steps of the newly completed Basilica of St. Peter's. Descartes' celebrated phrase, "Cogito, ergo sum," and the massive argument which depends from it, is a reworking of a passage from St. Augustine's *Civitas Dei* (XI, xxvi), which begins, "Fallor, ergo sum": "For if I am deceived, I am. For he who is not, cannot be deceived; and if I am deceived, by this same token I am. And since I am if I am deceived, how am I deceived in believing that I am? for it is certain that I am if I am deceived." [13] And in his *Rules for the Direction of the Mind*, Descartes uses another figure from St. Augustine. He explains that his method entails reducing involved and obscure propositions to simpler ones. "But many people either do not reflect on the precept at all, or ignore it altogether, or presume not to need it. Consequently they often investigate the most difficult questions with so little regard to order, that, to my mind, they act like a man who should attempt to leap with one bound from the base to the summit of a house, either making no account of the ladders provided for his ascent or not noticing them." [14] Not an "ascensiones in corde," then, but an "ascensiones in mentem." Descartes is a philosopher, not a spiritual director.

But see how all things hang together, as Molloy paraphrasing St. Paul would say. The image of a ladder or a flight of stairs, so appropriate to the philosopher who would lead mankind from the dark night of the mind by easy steps and clear and distinct ideas to certain knowledge, is already contained in his name; that same image, equally appropriate to the religious life, is found in an important passage in the theologian who supplied the philosopher with one of the fundamental principles of his philosophy. And, as we shall see later, both Hegel and Kierkegaard used the same image, in Kierkegaard's case with explicit reference to Johannes Climacus. In Beckett's work, the ladder has become a kind of crux, and figures in both *Murphy* and *Watt*. Jacqueline Hoefer thought the image came from Wittgenstein, but Beckett told John Fletcher that it really is based on an old Welsh joke.[15] Yet Beckett was acquainted with the image at least four years before the publication of *Murphy*, for he refers to "Augustine's ladder" in "What a Misfortune," a short story included in *More Pricks Than Kicks* (1934). Finally, the image of the ladder suggests itself to the critic as an opening gambit in a discussion of Beckett's work, thereby connecting — and most appropriately in Beckett's case — the intellectual, the spiritual, and the artistic traditions.

There is something paradigmatic about all this. An image, an exotic word, a quotation, an allusion invites and even requires the critic to chase it to its source. In some cases the source is obvious, and a knowledge of it is important for a correct and adequate understanding of a passage or a complete work. The epigraph to the sixth chapter of *Murphy*, "Amor intellectualis quo Murphy se ipsum amat," tells the critic that he had better brush up on his Spinoza; and the epigraph to *Film*, "Esse est percipi," sends him back to Berkeley. The influence of Descartes on Beckett is obvious and pervasive; the Occasionalists Geulincx and Malebranche are significant; and Schopenhauer is a presence in *Proust* and perhaps still in *Murphy*.

Other cases are less obvious. In *Watt* there is a painting of a broken circle and a dot. Is the critic justified in relating this painting to one of the famous definitions of God? That definition reads, "Deus est sphaera cujus centrum ubique." It is to be found in Pascal, Leibniz, Meister Eckhart, and Nicholas of Cusa, among others, and had its origin, according to Georges Poulet, in *The Book of the Twenty-Four Philosophers*, a pseudohermeneutic manuscript of the twelfth century.[16] Supposing the critic does provide this information, how are we advantaged? Do we know more about *Watt* or about Beckett's practice as an artist? Molloy writes, "My knowledge of men was scant and the meaning of being beyond me" (TN, 49). Does the critic then unfold Heidegger's *Sein und Zeit*? After all, the second paragraph of that great work says, "Do we in our time have an answer to the question of what we really mean by the word 'being'? Not at all. So it is fitting that we should raise anew *the question of the meaning of Being.*" [17] Again, is Beckett acquainted with Kierkegaard? Has he studied *L'Etre et le Néant?* While at Trinity did he write a paper on Edmund Husserl?

Beckett is a learned man, and his learning is evident in his art — not only in the tags, quotations, and allusions to intellectual history that are scattered through his work, but in the kinds of problems his characters encounter, the "plots" which organize their thoughts and actions, and the strategies he has used to accommodate art to his understanding of "how it is." But his learning raises serious problems for the literary critic. In the first place, the critic must try to identify the sources and analogues of Beckett's thought in the history of ideas, insofar as time, his own learning, and his scholarly equipment permit him to do so. In his eagerness to find all the sources and trace all the allusions, however, the critic may exceed the limits set by evidence, propriety, and plain common sense. Moreover, the critic must go on to show how the ideas work in this or that particular text; but then he stands in danger of accounting for some detail by referring to a doctrine when he could account for it just as well by referring to a technical problem of plot or characterization or emotional tone. (But what is a plot if not a pre-established harmony?) Finally, there are some themes or ideas which have no single source, or whose source Beckett has suppressed, or which he may have developed himself independently of everyone else. The theory of consciousness which underlies the trilogy is an important example. It is impossible, I think, to say that Beckett simply "took" the theory from, for example, Sartre, although there is much of *Being and Nothingness* in the trilogy. But if Sartre is there in the trilogy, so are Husserl and Hegel, for Sartre's theory is in a sense the resultant of these two thinkers; and where Sartre is, there too is Kierkegaard, or somewhere thereabouts. In this situation, the critic, believing that to understand the trilogy it is necessary or useful to have an acquaintance with theories of consciousness, may spend so much time talking about philosophy that he quite loses sight of the artist and his work, and trades his identity as critic for that of historian of ideas.

I do not know of any simple formula for guarding the critic from these errors. He must, of course, stick as close to the evidence as he can, and he must try to use good sense; but Beckett asks for a certain amount of daring, and I have risked a couple of chancy hypotheses. In doing so, I have taken some comfort from a passage in *The Unnamable* which Beckett must have written with his critics in mind. The question at issue is, as usual, the identity of the speaker, and he speculates, ". . . perhaps I'm a drying sperm in the sheets of an innocent boy, . . . no stone must be left unturned, one mustn't be afraid of making a howler." In what follows, then, I shall turn over what stones I can. The howlers will have to take care of themselves.[18]

Before passing on to the stories and poems, we might pause briefly to remark that it is extraordinarily appropriate that *Whoroscope* should be one of the first things Beckett published; for in retrospect we can see that Descartes' bifurcation of substance into mind and matter — unextended thinking substance and extended, unthinking substance — is one of the fundamental polarities that pervades all of the poet's work. In the *Discourse on the Method* Descartes describes the human body as an automaton, "a machine which, having been made by the hands of God, is incomparably better arranged, and possesses in itself movements which are much more admirable, than any of those which can be invented by man."[19] How admirable Beckett thinks the machine-man is can be assessed from his description of Watt:

Watt's way of walking due east, for example, was to turn his bust as far as possible towards the north and at the same time to fling out his right leg as far as possible towards the south, and then to turn his bust as far as possible towards the south and at the same time to fling out his left leg as far as possible towards the north . . . (w, 30)

Or the pawl-and-grapple movements in *How It Is*:

ten yards fifteen yards semi-side left right leg right arm push pull flat on face imprecations no sound semi-side right left leg left arm push pull flat on face imprecations no sound not an iota to be changed in this description (HII, 40)

The incomparable arrangement of the parts of the human body–machine raises for Descartes a delicate problem: if there were automata which resembled the human body and imitated the actions of men, how could one be sure they were not men in fact? One sure test is that they could never use "speech or other signs as we do when placing our thoughts on record for the benefit of others." He goes on to say, however, that we can easily imagine a machine built so that it can utter words or give some other response: "For instance, if it is touched in a particular part it may ask what we wish to say to it; if in another part it may exclaim that it is being hurt; and so on."[20] Thus Molloy programs his mother:

I got into communication with her by knocking on her skull. One knock meant yes, two no, three I don't know, four money, five goodbye. I was hard put to ram this code into her ruined and frantic understanding, but I did it, in the end. (TN, 18)

Again, from *How It Is*:

with the handle of the opener as with a pestle bang on the right kidney handier than the other from where I lie cry thump on skull silence brief rest jab in arse unintelligible murmur bang on kidney signifying louder once and for all cry thump on skull silence brief rest (HII, 68)

And when Watt's brain develops a short circuit, he inverts the order of the words in the sentence, the letters in the word, the sentences in the period . . . (W, 168).

We shall return to Descartes from time to time, but it suffices for now to remark that, believing as he did in the integrating function of the conarium, he thought mind and matter worked together in sweetest harmony. In Beckett's view, however, they are joined in mortal combat.

Whoroscope was followed in 1931 by a short essay, *Proust*, in 1934 by *More Pricks Than Kicks*, and in 1935 by *Echo's Bones*. The poems and stories are important if only because they raise the problem of style. The language is rich, luxuriant, sensuous. Here are three examples from one of the stories, "A Wet Night."

The Frica is introduced:

Behold the Frica, she visits talent in the Service Flats. In she lands, singing Havelock Ellis in a deep voice, frankly itching to work that which is not seemly. Open upon her concave breast as on a lectern lies Portigliotti's Penombre Claustrali, bound in tawed caul. In her talons earnestly she grasps Sade's Hundred Days and the Anterotica of Aliosha G. Brignole-Sale, unopened, bound in shagreened caul. A septic pudding hoodwinks her, a stodgy turban of pain it laps her horse face. The eyehole is clogged with the bulbus, the round pale globe goggles exposed. Solitary meditation has furnished her with nostrils of generous bore. The mouth champs an invisible bit, foam gathers at the bitter commissures. The crateriform brisket, lipped with sills of paunch, cowers ironically behind a maternity tunic. Keyholes have wrung the unfriendly withers, the osseous rump screams behond the hobble-skirt. Wastes of woad worsted advertise the pasterns. Aie! (MPTK, 26–27)

In the context of the Advent season, the sequence of colors of a neon sign advertising Bovril is depicted:

18   Problem, Theme, and Style

The lemon of faith jaundiced, annunciating the series, was in a fungus of hopeless green reduced to shingles and abolished. Whereupon the light went out, in homage to the slain. A sly ooze of gules, carmine of solicitation, lifting the skirts of green that the prophecy might be fulfilled, shocking Gabriel into cherry, flooded the sign. But the long skirts came rattling down, darkness covered their shame, the cycle was at an end. Da capo. (MPTK, 25)

The Polar Bear ("a big old brilliant lecher") rallies a Jesuit:

"The Lebensbahn" he was saying, for he never used the English word when the foreign pleased him better, "of the Galilean is the tragi-comedy of the solipsism that will not capitulate. The humilities and retro me's and quaffs of sir-reverence are on a par with the hey presto's, arrogance and egoism. He is the first great self-contained playboy. The cryptic abasement before the woman taken red-handed is as great a piece of megalomaniacal impertinence as his interference in the affairs of his boy-friend Lazarus. He opens the series of slick suicides, as opposed to the serious Empedoclean variety. He has to answer for the wretched Nemo and his corates, bleeding in paroxysms of depit on an unimpressed public."
He coughed up a plump cud of mucus, spun it round the avid bowl of his palate and stowed it away for future degustation. (MPTK, 30)

There is no evidence of effort here; composition is a matter of getting out of the way of the words tumbling out of the mind and into place like three-day-old recruits falling in for drill. This is mind brought to boil, an imagination of such high voltage that it threatens to blow its fuse. In his conversation with Duthuit, Beckett referred to the artist's "obligation to express." It may have seemed a saprogenic phrase of the 1890's, but when considered in the light of the tumescent style of the poems and short stories it is an accurate description of the writer's case, if not a prescription for survival.

At the same time, the style of these early works is impersonal. It is a *pasticcio* of slang, local color, quotations, proper nouns, learned allusions, hyperbole and meiosis, technical terms drawn from the history of art, music, literature, philosophy, and medicine. The writer hides himself behind style and a profusion of detail, and when he exposes himself he does so indecently: "This may be premature. We have set it down too soon, perhaps. Still, let it bloody well stand" ("A Wet Night," MPTK, 33).

The poetry shares these aspects of style. From "Serena II":

> in her dreams she trembles again
> way back in the dark old days panting
> in the claws of the Pins in the stress of her hour

> the bag writhes she thinks she is dying
> the light fails it is time to lie down
> Clew Bay vat of xanthic flowers
> Croagh Patrick waned Hindu to spite a pilgrim
>
> · · · · · · · · · · · · · ·
>
> in a hag she drops her young
> the whales in Blacksod Bay are dancing
> the asphodels come running the flags after
> she thinks she is dying she is ashamed

The poems are exceedingly dense, allusive, erudite, autobiographical, and therefore difficult of access. The language is exotic, the syntax fractured, incomplete, ambiguous. John Fletcher has called attention to the presence of such diverse influences as Symbolisme, Surrealism, the traditions of Provençal lyrics, and the Minnesinger's *Tagelied*.[21] Martin Esslin has said that the poetry is compressed "to the point of being in code."[22] He has contributed to the deciphering by showing, for example, that "Malacoda" concerns the death of Beckett's father. The "Huysum" mentioned in the third stanza is a Dutch painter of flowers and butterflies, reproductions of whose paintings were placed on the coffins of the dead as symbols of the resurrection, for the "imago" is the name of the butterfly after it has emerged from its cocoon-coffin. The final word in the poem, however, is "nay": the hope of eternal life, so naively suggested by the butterfly imagery, is bluntly denied. The poem borrows freely from "Draff," the last of the stories in *More Pricks Than Kicks*.

"Sanies I" (the title means fetid pus or discharge) is typical of the poems in the collection. It is full of cruxes and opacities and ambiguities, some of which yield to analysis. The others are occasions for guesswork. The poem is fifty-two unpunctuated lines long, the first forty-two lines being mostly a succession of past and present participles leading to the independent clause "I see" — at which point the author announces wearily, triumphantly, "main verb at last." Another independent clause begins at line 48 ("get along with you now") and runs to the end. As a death in the family was matter for both the story "Draff" and the poem "Malacoda," so too a trip to Portrane furnished both the funeral meats of "Fingal" and the marriage tables of "Sanies I." The short story tells of an excursion made by Belacqua Shuah (the protagonist of *More Pricks Than Kicks*) and his girl Winnie Coates to Portrane, a town perhaps twenty kilometers north of Dublin. After events which twice made Belacqua a sad animal (perphrasis in the original), and he having spied an untended bicycle in the area and she a doctor-friend, they separate, to meet again in an hour at a certain place. She makes for the doctor, he for the machine. "It was a fine light machine, with red tires and wooden rims. . . . He mounted and they flew down the hill and round the corner till they came at length to the stile. . . . The machine was a treat to ride" (MPTK, 14). By the time Winnie and Sholto, her doctor-friend, realize what has happened, Belacqua is "safe in Taylor's public-house in Swords, drinking and laughing in a way that Mr. Taylor did not like" (MPTK, 16). So much for the funeral meats. Now for the poem.

> all the livelong way this day of sweet showers
>   from Portrane on the seashore
> Donabate sad swans of Turvey Swords
> pounding along in three ratios like a sonata
> like a Ritter with pommelled scrotum atra cura on the step
> Botticelli from the fork down pestling the transmission   5
> tires bleeding voiding zeep the highway
> all heaven in the sphincter
> *the* sphincter

The poem, cast in the first person and present tense, describes a bicycle ride, the reflections of the narrator on a recent sexual episode, his re-encountering the girl, and his attitude toward her. It begins with the quasi-Belacqua's itinerary: "from Portrane on the seashore [to] Donabate . . . [to] Swords." I make nothing of "sad swans of Turvey," unless it is a glance in the direction of Jove and Leda, woven by Arachne into her tapestry.[23] The machine is a deluxe model, equipped with a gear shift providing three gear ratios. The bicyclist is like a knight "with pommelled scrotum atra cura on the step." The Latin quotation is from Horace's "Odi profanum vulgus et arceo" (*Odes*, 3, 1, l. 40): "Post equitum sedet atra cura," "behind the horseman sits black care." Beckett uses the Latin tag as a personification of anxiety. In "What a Misfortune," Lucy was "atra cura in the dicky the best part of the way down to Galway" (MPTK, 83); so the phrase in the poem means something like: anxiety with its foot on the pedal ("step"). The German noun may allude to Dürer's famous etching, "Ritter, Tod, und Teufel."

In "Draff," the Smeraldina is described as having "Botticelli thighs" (MPTK, 99), and to be "Botticelli from the fork down" may be supposed to mean that the rider's legs feel as heavy as a Botticelli figure's legs look. As he rides, the tires "bleed," or lose air slowly (the bicycle, like the rider, is subject to decay). "Voiding" can attach to both "tires" and the rider: the tires squeegee the highway clear of the rain; and the rider ingests the road before him and expels it behind him. The italicized article in line 8 calls attention to the fact that, although there are several such contractile muscular structures in the human body, the rider is feeling pleasure in the chief or (as one might say) the fundamental ring. In the Cartesian centaur, atra cura is not incompatible with hyletic ecstasy.

> müüüüüüüde now
> potwalloping now through the promenaders   10
> this trusty all-steel this super-real
> bound for home like a good boy
> where I was born with a pop with the green of the larches
> ah to be back in the caul now with no trusts
> no fingers no spoilt love
> belting along in the meantime clutching the bike
> the billows of the nubile the cere wrack
> pot-valiant caulless waisted in rags hatless
> for mamma papa chicken and ham
> warm Grave too say the word   20
> happy days snap the stem shed a tear

Now tired (*Germanice*, müde), now refreshed, he is bound for home where he was born "with a pop" in the season (April, May) when the larches bloom. The thought of his birth elicits the desire to be back in the womb, where there are no trusts or promises between lover and beloved (the machine, however, is "trusty"), no fingers for sexual exploration, no "spoilt love." (Belacqua [in "Fingal"] expressed the same sentiment in different words: " 'No shaving or haggling or cold or hugger-mugger, no' — he cast about for a term of ample connotation — 'night sweats' " [MPTK, 13].) The caul in Beckett's later works is represented by various kinds of hats — usually a bowler or derby. This equation is beginning to be worked out, in line 18: "caulless . . . hatless."

Line 17 illustrates Esslin's remark on the compression of this poetry, and illustrates as well the problems of punctuation, diction, and syntax the critic must try to solve. Let us assume that the poet knows what he is about, and that we have an accurate text. (The first edition [Paris: Europa Press, 1935], Calder's British, and Grove's American editions print identical texts, so the assumption is reasonable.) "Cere," therefore, is just that, and not "sere" or "sear"; and "wrack" is "wrack" and not "wreck" or "rack." The line, then, must be understood to read so:

the billows of the nubile[,] the cere[, the] wrack . . .

Syntactically, the present participle "clutching" (l. 16) appears to govern this line, just as "bound for" (l. 12) governs not only "home" and the rest of that line but also lines 19 and 20: "bound for home . . . [bound] for mamma [and] papa . . . [bound for the] warm Grave too . . ." But the rider cannot be "clutching the bike" *and* clutching the billows (i.e., "breasts") of the nubile *and* the cere *and* the wrack—not, at least, all at the same time. Rather, the rider contrasts the sensation of clutching the cold, hard "all-steel super-real" bicycle with the remembered feeling of touching the softness and warmth of the "billows." The cere is "The naked wax-like membrane at the base of the beak in certain birds, in which the nostrils are pierced" (OED, s.v.). It is common among parrots and birds of prey—hawks, falcons—and is sometimes soft and swollen. The only meaning I can come up with (and this is one of the guesses) is that the term designates the female's fork. "Wrack" should probably be understood both as rubbish or offal and as the instrument or cause of a disaster. Lines 16 and 17 move, then, by association from the sensation of clutching the hard, wet bicycle to the memory of touching a girl's soft, warm breasts and "cere." "Wrack" becomes an exclamation of disgust, and identifies the girl (or sexuality) as the cause of some disaster.

The rider is bound for home, bound for mamma and papa, bound too for the "warm Grave." The noun carries both its ordinary meaning (cf. l. 33: "hair ebbing[,] gums ebbing[,] ebbing home . . .") and—capitalized and modified by "warm"—the sexual meaning associated with "cere." (The ebbing of gums and hair also signifies the diminution of vital or sexual energy or power—an ebbing, alas, of what in German is called *Kraft*.) In the first sense, line 21 suggests the usual rites of the wake—the toast, the snapping of the stem of the goblets from which the toast is drunk, the official tear. In the sexual sense, however, the line suggests childbirth—the toast drunk to the proud parents, the severing of the umbilical cord, the crying of the newborn infant.

> this day Spy Wedsday seven pentades past
> oh the larches the pain drawn like a cork
> the glans he took the day off up hill and down dale
> with a ponderous fawn from the Liverpool London and Globe　20
> back the shadows lengthen the sycomores are sobbing
> to roly-poly oh to me a spanking boy
> buckets of fizz childbed is thirsty work

for the midwife he is gory
for the proud parent he washes down a gob of gladness   30
for footsore Achates also he pants his pleasure
sparkling beestings for me

These eleven lines compose the crux of the poem. They describe or reflect upon a traumatic sexual incident, but there is a very difficult problem
in identifying the "he" of line 24, determining the amount of time denoted
by "seven pentades," and supplying the appropriate punctuation. To be
quick about it, I understand these lines to be describing three separate incidents. The first is the bicycle trip occurring now, "this day of sweet showers"; the second involves the bicycle rider and a trip he took thirty-five *days*
before "this day"; and the third involves the rider's father and a trip he
took thirty-five *years* earlier. Take the third incident first. On "Spy Wedsday" (the Wednesday before Easter, so named in recollection of Jesus' betrayal by Judas) the rider's father took the day off to go on a bicycle ride
with a "ponderous fawn from the Liverpool London and Globe." They
went to "roly-poly," the result of which was that "to me [the father] a
spanking boy" was born. "Childbed is thirsty work," so "buckets of fizz"
are called for. It is thirsty work for the midwife, and because he is gory the
"fizz" he needs is soapsuds to wash in. It is thirsty work for the father, but
the fizz he wants is beer, to wash down "a gob of gladness." It is also thirsty
work "for me," the newborn; the fizz he needs is "beestings," the first milk
produced by the mother after she has given birth. Finally it is thirsty work
for "footsore Achates." The fizz belonging to Achates is the saliva bubbling
from his mouth as he "pants his pleasure"; for Achates is (Aie!) a dog, the
Kerry Blue bitch that accompanied Belacqua in "Walking Out" (MPTK,
56); that accompanied the couple in *How It Is* (p. 30: "the dog askew on
its hunkers in the heather it lowers its snout to its black and pink penis
too tired to lick it"); and mentioned in "Serena II":

with whatever trust of panic we went out
with so much shall we return
there shall be no loss of panic between
   a man and his dog
bitch though he be . . .

At the same time, these lines must be read as describing a painful and
frightening sexual adventure which the bicycle rider himself experienced
thirty-five *days* (possibly weeks) before the ride he is describing in the rest
of the poem. Like his father before him, the rider took off Spy Wednesday,

and, accompanied by "Achates," went for a bicycle trip with a "ponderous fawn." He and the fawn also went roly-poly, but the experience for the rider was painful and disgusting. As he himself had been "born with a pop," so now his glans penis is "drawn like a cork" from the cere of the fawn. Given this reading, line 31 takes on an ominous tone, for "Achates" is the name of Aeneas' constant companion, "fidus Achates." And while the rider plays Aeneas to the fawn's Dido, he also pants his pleasure for his male companion.

We have then three separate excursions. The first, involving the rider's father and mother, took place thirty-five years before "this day of sweet showers," and resulted in the birth of the rider, "a spanking boy." The second, involving the rider and his girl (and the dog), took place thirty-five days (or weeks) before "this day"; and it too resulted in a birth—that of the rider's psychosexual self, a self which, traumatized by heterosexual experience, is now beginning to incline toward homosexuality. The third trip is the solo excursion described in the rest of the poem, and is in the nature of a celebration honoring not his birthday, of course, that would be too easy, but the day of his conception. The "sweet showers" in the first line may allude to the ingenious disguise used by Jove when he begot Perseus on Danae; but by fixing the day of his conception as "Spy Wedsday," the rider is clearly suggesting that his birth was a betrayal into existence. The rider is thirty-five years old, the age when the artist as such finds himself and is born into his vocation:

> Nel mezzo del cammin di nostra vita
> mi ritrovai . . .

(Beckett himself had the foresight, courage, and sense of ironic humor to be born on Good Friday, the thirteenth of April, 1906.)

> tired now hair ebbing gums ebbing ebbing home
> good as gold now in the prime after a brief prodigality
> yea and suave   35
> suave urbane beyond good and evil
> biding my time without rancour you may take your oath
> distraught half-crooked courting the sneers of these fauns
>   these smart nymphs
> clipped like a pederast as to one trouser-end

Although lines 33–36 can apply equally well to father and son, the "my" of line 37 returns the narrative to the bicycle rider and the present time of "this day of sweet showers." Having tasted of the fruit of the tree of the knowledge of good and evil, he has become like unto the gods, a superman transcending the moral distinctions which apply to the herd. He is not, like Browning's Caliban, "a bitter heart that bides its time and bites" ("Caliban upon Setebos," l. 167), for he is "without rancour."

This tone of self-confidence and equanimity is suddenly disrupted, however, for the rider says he is "distraught" — literally pulled in two directions; for as he rides through the crowd of promenaders he courts not only "these smart nymphs" but the sneers of the young males ("fauns"). On his trouser-leg he wears a metal clip to prevent the cuff from getting caught in the bicycle chain, but the image he uses to describe the way the clip grips his leg clearly indicates the nature of the psychosexual self that was brought into being what time he planted his fawn. He is "half-crooked."

> sucking in my bloated lantern behind a Wild Woodbine   30
> cinched to death in a filthy slicker
> flinging the proud Swift forward
>   breasting the swell of Stürmers
> I see main verb at last
> her whom alone in the accusative
> I have dismounted to love
> gliding towards me dauntless nautch-girl
>   on the face of the waters
> dauntless daughter of desires in the old black and flamingo

He rides along, his half-soaked lantern strapped behind him, smoking a cigarette, his slicker pulled tight against the showers. "Swift" is the tradename of the bicycle, but it puts us also in mind of the bilious, the truly rancorous Dean of St. Paul's. (The tower where, for a second time, Winnie made Belacqua a sad animal, and which was perhaps the scene of the sexual incident described in the poem, was reputed to have been the tower in which Swift kept Stella. Cf. MPTK, 15.) The rider is pushing his way through a sea of soccer players (a Stürmer is a soccer forward) when suddenly he sees among them his Dido, his fawn, "her whom alone . . . I have dismounted to love," the "dauntless nautch-girl."

A nautch-girl is an East Indian or oriental dancing-girl. One of the few places the poet might have come across the word is in Browning's "Fifine at the Fair" (XXXI):

> there was no worst
> Of degradation spared Fifine: ordained from first

To last, in body and soul, for one life-long debauch.
The Pariah of the North, the European Nautch!
This, far from seek to hide, she puts in evidence
Calmly, displays the brand, bids pry without offence
Your finger on the place. . . .

Beckett may have been alluding to the play on "hide and seek" in "Whoroscope" (ll. 29–30) and in both "Fifine" and "Sanies I" fingers are instru-
ments of sexual exploration. In "What a Misfortune," the story of Belacqua's marriage to Thelma bboggs, we encounter "Hermione Nautzsche, a
powerfully built nymphomaniac panting in black and mauve" (MPTK, 76).
Hermione's last name is a conflation of "nautch" and the name of the
author of *Jenseits von Gut und Böse* (cf. "Sanies I," l. 36). In the present
instance, the nautch-girl is confounded with both the spirit of God which
moved on the face of the waters (cf. Gen. 1:2) — the "waters" here being
the "swell" or sea of "Stürmers"—and (even more blasphemously) with
St. Theresa, who, in Richard Crashaw's "The Flaming Heart" is apostro-
phized as the "undaunted daughter of desires" (l. 93). Hermione is ap-
parelled in black and mauve, the nautch-girl in black and flamingo. Black
and some hue of red are for Beckett the colors of sex. The images that are
applied to the girl suggest a combination of religious fervor and sexual
abandon or even depravity; the bicyclist's attitude toward her is a jumble
of fear, attraction, and contempt.

> get along with you now take the six the seven the eight
>   or the little single-decker
> take a bus for all I care walk cadge a lift
> home to the cob of your web in Holles Street   50
> and let the tiger go on smiling
> in our hearts that funds ways home

She apparently asks him for a ride home, but he dismisses her, tells her
to take a tram or a bus, walk, thumb a ride home. He refuses to get caught
again in the web of her allurements. Already half-crooked, he now confirms in a concrete act the attitudes and tendencies which had been growing in him as he reflected on his sexual adventure. "Funds" in the last line
is used in the sense of "unites" or "combines" (cf. "Walking Out," MPTK,
59: "What adverse fate forbad them at this point to fund their ways?").
As for the smiling tiger:

> There was a young lady of Niger,
> Who rode with a smile on a tiger;

> They returned from the ride
> With the lady inside,
> And the smile on the face of the tiger.

The syntax of the last two lines of "Sanies I" is obscure, but "tiger" seems to be the subject of both "go on smiling" and "funds." The rider tells the girl that the two of them should not try to relive or re-enact their love affair, for it is only "in our hearts" or memories that there is any common way for two persons. To try to come together again would be to destroy whatever makes the tiger smile, whatever of good there was about their affair.

If some of the details remain vague, the general point is still clear: the rider dismisses the girl, albeit in a tone more of regret than anger. There is perhaps in this act something of the sentiment expressed in the essay on Proust: "For the artist, who does not deal in surfaces, the rejection of friendship is not only reasonable, but a necessity. Because the only possible spiritual development is in the sense of depth. The artistic tendency is not expansive, but a contraction. And art is the apotheosis of solitude" (PTD, 64). To be is to be alone; to be an artist is to be alone and make something out of it. Of the thirteen poems collected in *Echo's Bones*, not one could be called a "love poem." "Sanies I" seems to be explaining the reason for that fact.

Most of the other poems in the collection are similar to this one. They are autobiographical, cranky, full of low spirits and fancy language:

> quick quick the cavaletto supplejacks for mumbo-jumbo
> vivas puellas mortui incurrrrrsant boves
> oh subito subito ere she recover the cang bamboo for bastinado
> a bitter moon fessade a la mode
> Oh Becky spare me I have done thee no wrong
>   spare me damn thee
> ("Sanies II")

This is a language that will not serve Beckett's matured purpose. That purpose will require a hard, dry, simple language, a Cartesian language, so to speak. And there is a suggestion of that later style even here in *Echo's Bones*. This is the title poem, the last in the collection:

> asylum under my tread all this day
> their muffled revels as the flesh falls
> breaking without fear or favour wind
> the gantelope of sense and nonsense run
> taken by the maggots for what they are

The first poem, "The Vulture," is not flawed by a sophomorism like "breaking without fear or favour wind." Its language is stark and simple:

> dragging his hunger through the sky
> of my skull shell of sky and earth
>
> stooping to the prone who must
> soon take up their life and walk
>
> mocked by a tissue that may not serve
> till hunger earth and sky be offal

I take the vulture to be the poet's mind or imagination, never satiated by what it has already produced; the prone are the characters (or words) on which the artist works his miracle, giving them the vitality to live and move. Yet both the characters (or words) and the artist's mind are mocked by their bodies (standing where it does, the past participle modifies both "the prone" and — in parallel with the two preceding present participles — the vulture). The last line is bivalent: it can be read both as continuing the fifth line — ("may not serve/ till earth and sky be offal") — in which case there is the suggestion that the tissue *will* serve after hunger, earth, and sky have become offal (perhaps with the religious sense of "awful" as well); or it can be read in connection with the participles, in which case it means that the mocked vulture must go on dragging and stooping until it dies.

At the head of the collection, then, a skull poem, and at the end or foot a foot poem, both suggesting the suave new dry style of the works composed in French. In the middle, the guts, liquid, slithering, gorged:

> Ah the banner
> the banner of meat bleeding
> on the silk of the seas and the arctic flowers
> that do not exist.
>   ("Enueg I")

These are not Beckett's words. As John Fletcher has pointed out, they are Rimbaud's: "Le pavillon en viande saignante sur la soie des mers et des fleurs arctiques; (elles n'existent pas)." [24] But in a sense, none of the words in the short stories and poems belong to Beckett. They belong to French surrealists, to Horace or Virgil or Dante, to surgeons and botanists, to the historians of art and philosophy, to Trinity undergraduates and pot-valiant poets. They belong supremely to Beckett's landsman James Joyce, master of those who can, who made the world's words his own, whose art is the art of opulence. Had Beckett continued in the way indicated by "Sanies I" or "A Wet Night," he would have ended up playing Wenceslas' page, performing the Imitatio Jacobi. As it turned out, he discovered or created his own vocation as an artist. He has spoken of it, and contrasted it with Joyce's: "Joyce was a superb manipulator of material — perhaps the greatest. He was making words do the absolute maximum of work. . . . The more Joyce knew the more he could. He's tending toward omniscience and omnipotence as an artist. I'm working with impotence, ignorance. I don't think impotence has been exploited in the past." [25]

The poems and the stories (and the two early novels *Murphy* and *Watt*) do not bespeak impotence and ignorance. They are facile and luxuriant; worst of all they are "expressive." They are to Beckett what strong drink is to some men and women to others — a temptation, a weakness of the flesh, to be overcome only with prayer and fasting and spiritual discipline. They are the Old Adam that must be put away, the sins of youth which a critical graciousness will not remember. They represent, in short, what Beckett must reject if he is to achieve a personal as well as an artistic identity. History records many instances of the conversion of the will, the Bishop of Hippo being a notable instance; and it records not a few instances of the conversion of the intellect — Descartes, for example, found that it was necessary to purge his mind of all received opinion. But Beckett must suffer a conversion of the imagination, and where is the precedent for this?

II THE SPECTATOR AND THE MACHINE: MURPHY

You may look upon life as an unprofitable episode, disturbing the blessed calm of non-existence.

Life is a task to be done. It is a fine thing to say *defunctus est*; it means that the man has done his task.

Schopenhauer

Ce n'est pas parce que les autres sont morts que notre affection pour eux s'affaiblit, c'est parce que nous mourons nous-mêmes.

Proust

When I no longer know anything of external objects, it is because I have taken refuge in the consciousness that I have of myself. If I abolish this inner self, its very abolition becomes an object for an imaginary self which now perceives as an object the self that is dying away. Be it external or internal, some object there always is that my imagination is representing. . . . In this coming and going of our mind between the without and the within, there is a point, at equal distance from both, in which it seems to us that we no longer perceive the one, and that we do not yet perceive the other: it is there that the image of "Nothing" is formed.

Bergson

Sum igitur nudus speculator hujus machinae.

Geulincx[1]

I

◄ ► In *Murphy* (1938), the first of his novels, Beckett recounts the adventures of a young man who, like the Descartes of *Whoroscope*, has fallen out of alignment with the Cartesian universe. There are five main characters in the novel and three minor ones. Murphy (he apparently has no Christian name) is an ex-theological student whose studies and experience have led him to embrace dualism as his ontological principle and indolence as its ethical corollary. Murphy's meager income derives from a fraudulent arrangement with his landlady whereby she sends an exorbitant bill for his room to his uncle in Holland, deducts her "commission" from the payment, and gives him the rest. It is enough to keep him alive and faithful to his values. Murphy loves and is loved by the prostitute Celia (whose surname, Kelly, is never mentioned), and lives with her in an apartment in London. He has fled thence from Ireland to escape Miss Counihan, a Dublin whore, who naively believes him to be hard at work earning enormous sums of money which he will spend on her. Miss Counihan in turn is sought after by Neary, an aging Cork philanderer who does moderately well by running an Academy in which he purveys an eclectic Science made up partly of pre-Socratic philosophy, partly of Gestalt psychology, and partly his own speculation. Wylie is one of Neary's pupils (Murphy is another) and himself an adept confidence man who volunteers to intercede with Miss Counihan on Neary's behalf. Cooper is Neary's man of all work, Mr. Willoughby Kelly is Celia's paternal grandfather, and Mr. Endon is a patient in the mental institution where Murphy eventually finds work. The action takes place in the period between September 12 and October 26, 1935.

Characters and action are subordinate to or expressive of an ontological dualism, however, and though we must pay attention to the former two, we shall do so in order to get at the ways in which the philosophical system operates in the novel.

Thus, the opposition of mind and body establishes a polarity of characters. At one extreme there is the somatic Miss Counihan. "It is superfluous to describe her," Beckett writes, "she was just like any other beautiful Irish girl, except, as noted, more markedly anthropoid" (M, 118). Miss Counihan's cunning being an aspect of her anthropoidal nature, it must be said of her that she aspires to mind, and that only halfheartedly. Her one effort at thought, a rehearsal no doubt of a lesson Murphy had tried to teach her, is ill received by a hostile audience. "There is a mind and there is a body," she begins, but is immediately silenced: " 'Shame!' cried Neary, 'Kick her arse! Throw her out!' " Celia, Murphy's affianced, is also a prostitute. Hence, when she first appears in the novel she is exhibited by means of a list of statistics and Aristotelian accidents: "Head. Small and round. . . . Neck. 13–¾. . . . Hips etc. 35″. . . . Weight. 123 lbs." As a prostitute she is body only, although it is evident as the novel progresses that she alone of Murphy's cohorts and admirers comes to know what Murphy had always known — that existence is a colossal fiasco.

At the other extreme there is Mr. Endon, "a schizophrenic of the most amiable variety." He has withdrawn almost completely from the world of things into the world of his own mind.

The languor in which he passed his days, while deepening every now and then to the extent of some charming suspension of gesture, was never so profound as to exhibit all movement. His inner voice did not harangue him, it was unobtrusive and melodious, a gentle continuo in the whole consort of his hallucinations. The bizarrerie of his attitudes never exceeded a stress laid on their grace. In short, a psychosis so limpid and imperturbable that Murphy felt drawn to it as Narcissus to his fountain. (M, 186)

Neary, Murphy's cicerone into gnosis and a sometime Pythagorean, would appear to have overcome the bifurcated world. On those extreme occasions when the world becomes unendurably oppressive, "as when he wanted a drink and could not get one, or fell among Gaels and could not escape, or felt the pangs of hopeless sexual inclination," Neary can stop his heart. This achievement, and the fact that Neary's tutorial discourses celebrate the harmony of Being, suggest that Neary is the victor in the conflict of mind and matter. In fact he is not, for he is sorely buffeted by the winds of passion, and is hurled from one affair to another. Neary's designs are now upon Miss Dwyer, then upon Miss Counihan, later upon Murphy as an instrument for the accomplishment of his purposes for Miss Counihan, still later upon Murphy himself as an end in himself, and finally upon Celia. Indeed, as a result of contemplating what he expects to be his imminent end, Neary's hair turns white overnight. Extended substance cannot be overcome; it can only be escaped.

No one is so sensible of this truth as Murphy. He has no apprehension of what Neary calls variously the Apmonia, the Isonomy, or the Attunement. It is his fate to be attracted both to the little world of the mind and the big one of bodies — e.g., Celia. The novel opens with Murphy naked, strapped by seven [sic] scarves into a teak rocking chair. "He sat in his chair in this way because it gave him pleasure! First it gave his body pleasure, it appeased his body. Then it set him free in his mind. For it was not until his body was appeased that he could come alive in his mind. . . . And life in his mind gave him pleasure, such pleasure that pleasure was not the word" (M, 2). Murphy's rocking chair is the vehicle for his escape, his destination the little world of his mind. His schizoidal condition is illustrated when he is interrupted in mid-rocking-chair-flight by a telephone call from Celia: "He laid the receiver hastily in his lap. The part of him that he hated craved for Celia, the part that he loved shrivelled up at the thought of her" (M, 8). On this occasion Murphy's body, the part he hates, wins the struggle.

It is the fact of the struggle, however, which so perturbs him, and it is to evade the necessity of having to dwell in a world where the struggle is inevitable that Murphy develops the technique of autohypnosis, of "coming out in his mind," as he calls it. By means of this technique he can escape from the tumult and clangor of what Neary (after William James) calls the "big blooming buzzing confusion" into the peace and freedom of his mind.

Murphy's mind is a remarkable contraption, and a short chapter is devoted to a description of it. The description is preceded by a paraphrase of Spinoza—"Amor intellectualis quo Murphy se ipsum amat"—but the construction of Murphy's little world seems to owe less to Spinoza than to Leibniz. Thus, his mind pictured itself as "a large hollow sphere, hermetically closed to the universe without." This, however, is not an impoverishment for his mind "excluded nothing that it did not itself contain. Nothing ever had been, was or would be in the universe outside it but was already present as virtual, or actual, . . . in the universe inside it." We are reminded of Leibniz' monad, which is absolutely self-contained and has no "windows through which anything may come in or go out"; but which, in spite of this is "a perpetual living mirror of the universe." [2] Moreover, Murphy's mind, being shut off from the universe without, is itself "a closed system, subject to no principle of change but its own, self-sufficient and impermeable to the vicissitudes of the body" (M, 109). In this respect too it is like a monad, for there is no way of explaining how a monad can be altered or changed in its inner being by any other created thing; hence the natural changes of the monad come only from an internal principle; and one created monad cannot have a physical influence upon the inner being of another. [3]

Whereas the general layout of Murphy's mind seems to be based on Leibniz, the inventory of its contents is not. This seems to be original. [4] In his mind there are three zones, the light, the half-light, and the dark. These are related to the actual and virtual of his mind, between which he distinguishes as that of which he has both mental and physical experience (the actual) and that of which he has mental experience only (the virtual). "The mind felt its actual part to be above and bright, its virtual beneath and fading into dark" (M, 108). Each of the three zones has a particular pleasure. In the first or light zone are forms with parallels in the big world, and here the pleasure is reprisal. In this part of his mind he can readjust persons and events in the big world in ways to his liking. "Here the kick that the physical Murphy received, the mental Murphy gave. . . . Here the whole physical fiasco became a howling success" (M, 111). In the second or half-light zone are forms without parallel in the big world, and the pleasure is contemplation. Since there is no macrocosmic counterpart to this zone Murphy does not need to revise or adjust or otherwise pay attention to the big world. In the third or dark zone there is nothing but "a flux of forms, a perpetual coming together and falling asunder of forms." The first zone contains the "docile elements" of the world of the body which he can readjust according to taste, and the second zone contains states of peace. In both of these he is free. But in the third zone he is not simply free but "a mote in the dark of absolute freedom," "a missile without provenance or target." This is the condition of "will-lessness," the highest good Murphy can imagine, and it is in this estate that, increasingly, he longs to dwell.

What prevents him from doing so is his perverse and irrational bondage to Celia. She is determined not to be the breadwinner in their family, and, using Lysistrata's tactic, she forces Murphy to seek employment in the "mercantile gehenna." He does so in spite of his conviction that the result will be that he will lose one or more of the goods that he can lay claim to: if Celia, then only her; if his body, then that and Celia; if his mind, then all three. As he wanders over London doing his best to avoid being hired, Murphy is discovered by Austin Ticklepenny, pot poet and fellow Dubliner. Ticklepenny is a male nurse in a mental institution known as the Magdalen Mental Mercyseat, but his circumstances are such that he must find a substitute. Murphy recalls the horoscope cast for him by one R. K. N. Suk, finds that its prognostications and suggestions jibe with the requirements detailed by Ticklepenny, and accepts the poet's offer. A few days later, Murphy moves out of the flat he shares with Celia and into the MMM. His success as male nurse is immediate and conspicuous.

There is good reason for his success, for he is profoundly sympathetic with his charges. Indeed, so far as Murphy is concerned, the melancholics, the paranoids, the hebephrenics, the hypomanics, and the schizoids, for whose somatic well-being he is responsible, have in their "self-immersed indifference to the contingencies of the contingent world" dealt more intelligently with the primal fact of chaos than their would-be healers. Murphy's experience as a physical and rational being obliged him, indeed, "to call sanctuary what the psychiatrists called exile and to think of the patients not as banished from a system of benefits but as escaped from a colossal fiasco" (M, 177–78). It is no wonder, then, that Murphy's arrival at the Magdalen Mental Mercyseat is in the nature of a homecoming, for "here was the race of people he had long since despaired of finding."

He is especially attracted to Mr. Endon, and on his first tour of night duty he and the schizophrenic play a portentous game of chess. Murphy attempts to engage his opponent, but Mr. Endon refuses. Again and again Murphy puts himself in jeopardy (Kt–QB$_5$, a move which elicits the comment, "High praise is due to White [Murphy] for the pertinacity with which he struggles to lose a piece"), and each time Mr. Endon disdains the offer. At the forty-third move, neither side having lost a piece, Murphy's forces in complete disarray, and Mr. Endon preparing to move his king into its original position, thereby restoring — except for two pawns — each of his pieces to the place where it started, Murphy surrenders. The last note reads, "Further solicitation would be frivolous and vexatious, and Murphy, with fool's mate in his soul, retires." He has encountered a mind nearly as "othertight" as his own is "bodytight," and he subsides into a psychic coma resembling that achieved with the help of his rocking chair.

Murphy began to see nothing, that colourlessness which is such a rare postnatal treat, being the absence (to abuse a nice distinction) not of *percipere* but of *percipi*. His other senses also found themselves at peace, an unexpected pleasure. Not the numb peace of their own suspension, but the positive peace that comes when the somethings give way, or perhaps simply add up, to the Nothing, than which in the guffaw of the Abderite naught is more real. Time did not cease, that would be asking too much, but the wheel of rounds and pauses did, as Murphy with his head among the armies continued to suck in, through all the posterns of his withered soul, the accidentless One-and-Only, conveniently called Nothing. (M, 246)

The trance is rudely cracked by the impingement on Murphy's percipere of "the familiar variety of stenches, asperities, ear-splitters and eye-closers" of the big world. Murphy returns from wherever he has been to discover Mr. Endon gone. After a short search Murphy finds him and returns him to his cell, restores order there, and then, kneeling down beside Mr. Endon, stares deeply into the schizophrenic's eyes.

Kneeling at the bedside, the hair starting in thick black ridges between his fingers, his lips, nose and forehead almost touching Mr. Endon's, seeing himself stigmatised in those eyes that did not see him, Murphy heard words demanding so strongly to be spoken that he spoke them, right into Mr. Endon's face, Murphy who did not speak at all in the ordinary way unless spoken to, and not always even then.

> "the last at last seen of him
> himself unseen by him
> and of himself"

A rest.

"The last Mr. Murphy saw of Mr. Endon was Mr. Murphy unseen by Mr. Endon. This was also the last Murphy saw of Murphy."

A rest.

"The relation between Mr. Murphy and Mr. Endon could not have been better summed up than by the former's sorrow at seeing himself in the latter's immunity from seeing anything but himself."

A long rest.

"Mr. Murphy is a speck in Mr. Endon's unseen."

That was the whole extent of the little afflatulence. (M, 249–50)

Without reluctance and without relief, but apparently in torment of soul because of what he had not seen and what he had said, Murphy retreats to his garret room to have a short rock in his chair. He decides that if he feels better after the rock he will leave the MMM forever. But it is the last time he comes out in his mind. An accident, apparently, severs the long, frayed, and much abused cord which had kept the kite of Murphy's mind tied to the hand of Murphy's body. He dies of severe shock and burns sustained when his residence explodes and burns.

II

◄ ► It is not the consummation for which this seedy solipsist could have wished; for, if he resented his body, Murphy was fairly attached to it — as well as to other such gross bodies as the lovely Celia, ginger cookies, and so on. And while the psychic Murphy had long since voted in favor of the little world, the somatic Murphy insists upon existing in the realm of the fiasco, the realm of figure and ground. Split as he is between body and mind, Murphy is a Cartesian catastrophe. The problem, as Neary once pointed out to this asyndetic hero, is that Murphy's conarium has shrunk to nothing. No worse fate can befall the man who is built according to the specifications of Cartesian philosophy, for it is the function of the conarium, or pineal gland, to mediate between mind and matter, between unextended thinking substance and extended, unthinking substance.

It is likewise necessary to know that although the soul is joined to the whole body, there is yet in that a certain part in which it exercises its functions more particularly than in all the others; and it is usually believed that this part is the brain, or possibly the heart. . . . But, in examining the matter with care, it seems as though I had clearly ascertained that the part of the body in which the soul exercises its functions immediately is in nowise the heart, nor the whole of the brain, but merely the most inward of all its parts, to wit, a certain very small gland which is situated in the middle of its substance and so suspended above the duct whereby the animal spirits in its anterior cavities have communication with those in the posterior, that the slightest movements which take place in it may alter very greatly the course of these spirits; and reciprocally that the smallest changes which occur in the course of the spirits may do much to change the movements of this gland.[5]

Whether Murphy's alarming deficiency is due to atrophy or to shoddy workmanship on the part of his maker, the consequence is the same. Murphy is split, his mind is "bodytight"; for his animal spirits, in passing from the anterior to the posterior cavities of his brain, or vice versa, have no gland to affect or be affected by, and he is incapable of understanding through what channel his mind has its apparent intercourse with his body. "He neither thought a kick because he felt one nor felt a kick because he thought one."

Perhaps the knowledge was related to the fact of the kick as two magnitudes to a third. Perhaps there was, outside space and time, a non-mental non-physical Kick from all eternity, dimly revealed to Murphy in its correlated modes of consciousness and extension, the kick *in intellectu* and the kick *in re*. . . .
However that might be, Murphy was content to accept this partial congruence of the world of his mind with the world of his body as due to some such process of supernatural determination. The problem was of little interest. (M, 109)

Of little interest to Murphy, perhaps, but of considerable to Arnold Geulincx (1624–1669). Geulincx viewed Descartes' acknowledgment of the need for a human factor mediating between body and mind as an intolerable compromise of the logic of the argument of the *Discourse*. Dismayed by Descartes' willingness to negotiate the lucid and beautifully symmetrical structure of both man and the *Discourse*, Geulincx attempted to preserve both man and logic by substituting God for the pineal gland.

Geulincx begins by taking the Cartesian *cogito* and its consequences with absolute seriousness. I am *res cogitans*, said Descartes, unextended thinking substance, whose entire essence or nature is thinking. The being of this thinking needs no place, nor does it depend on anything material, so that this "me" or soul or that in virtue of which I am what I am is entirely distinct from my body.[6] But instead of using the *cogito* as a principle or point of departure for elaborating clear and distinct ideas about God and the soul and "toute la chaîne des autres vérités" which Descartes deduced from these first two, Geulincx uses it to circumscribe the "I" strictly within the realm of thinking. For if it is the case that the *entire* essence or nature of the I is thinking and thinking only, then the I exists or is what it is only in its acts of thinking. Moreover, the realm of thought is pellucid: I not only know, I know *how* I know. Conversely, if I do not know how I know what I think I know, I must conclude that in fact I do not know it. Consequently, the I is, or is active and free and responsible, only when it is engaged in doing something which it knows how to do. But the only act the I knows how to perform is the act of thought. Only in thinking, then, is the I a causal agency — an efficient cause, in the Aristotelian-Scholastic terminology. In such other instances as those in which the I appears to be the cause — as when I command my arm to rise or my feet to walk — the I is not really the cause, for it does not know how it can impart motion to extended, unthinking substance. The general principle which Geulincx derives from the *cogito*, then, is this: *Ego non facio id, quod quomodo fiat nescia.*

If it is impossible for the I to do what it does not know how to do, and if it does not know how it causes the arm to rise, then the I does not in fact cause the arm to rise. The act of thought by which I command my arm to rise is rather, according to Geulincx, the occasion for God himself to impart to my arm the motion of rising. The same holds for an action in the opposite direction: body cannot affect mind, so the sensations which the I feels are not caused by the operation of an external body upon mind but are produced in the mind by God on the occasion of the motion of that body. This in its strictest form is the doctrine of Occasionalism or occasional causation.[7]

The ethical corollary of the doctrine of Occasionalism is obvious. The being of the I is restricted to the act of thinking, and here it is radically free, for not even God can cause me to think or alter what I think or how I think. But the I does not enter into the world of matter and extension, not even into its own body. Indeed, with regard to its body the I is merely the spectator. But since nothing of the I is invested in the realm of *res extensa*, and since it can do nothing by itself to alter what happens in that realm, the I should set no value on it. The world of things does not affect and is not affected by the I, so it is worth nothing to the I. If the world is worth nothing, it is not worth being desired. *Ubi nihil vales, ibi nihil velis.*

Neary may be right. Murphy's inability to coordinate the part of himself that he hates with the part he loves may be due to the fact that his conarium has shrunk to nothing. But in the Geulincxian scheme of things, the conarium is as useful as an appendix, and whether it has shrunk or not is irrelevant. From the Occasionalist point of view such a coordination is God's business, not man's, and Murphy does well to cleave to that which is his to cleave to, namely, his mind. Humility, according to Geulincx, is the fourth and highest of the four cardinal virtues, and it consists in self-knowledge and self-abasement. Murphy knows himself to be split, and does his best to abase himself, though in his case abasement in the full sense of the word lies beyond his powers and he has to settle for appeasement.

Murphy's Geulincxianism accounts not only for his ontological dualism and his attitudes toward his two worlds, but for his attitude toward work as well. Work understood as Celia, say, understands it — that is, in the commercial sense of being some effort on my part for which I am rewarded — is a philosophical impossibility. What work is done is not done by Celia or Murphy or any other human but by God; and though Murphy does not himself put this interpretation on his aversion to work, still his indolence might be thought of as a contribution to the Divine ease.

If Murphy doesn't see himself in this light, it is probably because he can accept Geulincx' doctrine of the bifurcation of being but cannot accept the way in which the Occasionalist puts being back together again. He agrees with the phenomenological analysis, one might say, but disagrees with the theological synthesis. "Disagrees with" is too strong. He simply does not concern himself about the matter: he is content to accept the congruence of his mind and body as owing to some "process of supernatural determination," but the problem is really of little interest to him. Murphy is not a philosopher probing the causes of things, nor a theologian speculating on the ultimate questions. He is a practical man trying to live in a world that makes very little sense, given him and given the world. The fact of his being split is a fact he recognizes and accepts and is even able to exploit by means of coming out in his mind, but the reason for this split is unimportant to him. In other words, Murphy is an Occasionalist without at the same time being a Deist.

But any dualist, even such a stoutly anti-theoretical one as Murphy, needs some principle of mediation and unity; and as the pineal gland, which had served that function for Descartes, was replaced by Geulincx with God, so

God is replaced by Murphy with "the only system outside his own in which he felt the least confidence, that of the heavenly bodies." Murphy is an astrologer.

There is an important difference between the function of the pineal gland in Descartes' system and God in Geulincx', and the function of the heavenly bodies in Murphy's, however. In the two philosophical systems the function is theoretical, in each case serving to explain how mind and body can interact, whereas in Murphy's case the function is practical and normative, telling him how he ought to behave. The stars do not and cannot mix the immiscible or correlate the uncorrelatable. Instead they tell him what he should do in a world where nothing is intrinsically worth doing. From Plato on, values in dualistic systems have always been transcendent, not immanent. For Murphy work is a third-order value, good only as a means of keeping Celia. She in turn is not more than a second-order value, of worth only in the chthonic realm. That whole realm, however, is finally worthless, beatitude lying removed in the transcendent and wholly other realm of mind. Since Murphy must live in the world, however, and since the world has no immanent value, he must seek some transcendent principle which, if it will not automatically confer value on the valueless, will at least give him some reason for choosing one piece of worthlessness instead of another. Since he can find no reason in himself why work should take one form rather than another (all forms being equally valueless), he looks to the celestial system to provide him with the vocational counseling he needs. He calls his horoscope "a corpus of incentives," and once provided with it agrees to abide by it. "The very first fourth to fall on a Sunday in 1936 I begin. I put on my gems and off I go, to custode, detect, explore, pioneer, promote or pimp, as occasion may arise" (M, 34).

Certainly Murphy uses his horoscope to put off still further the grim day when he must seek work. But his belief in the validity of the system of the heavenly bodies is still genuine and is in fact congruent in an important way with the thought of two of Murphy's mentors, Geulincx and Leibniz. What all of them have in common is a view of the universe as a mechanical system which man is helpless, or very nearly so, to alter. What happens in the world happens because God is continuously intervening (Geulincx), or because he wound up the machine at the time of creation and it runs according to plan thereafter (Leibniz), or because of the interaction of the various heavenly bodies (Pandit Suk). The notion of the universe as a machine leads almost inevitably to determinism; and what is astrology, after all, but the technology of determinism, a practical science which since the time of the Babylonian empire has sought to derive from theoretical knowledge concrete benefits for the life of man? And it is for its practical use in helping him get on in the world by providing a mimal set of goals and values that Murphy turns to astrology.

Split into extended, unthinking substance and unextended, thinking substance, determined and determining in its operation, a closed system incapable of being changed by human wish or will—this is the universe Murphy lives in. It is the supreme creation of a small group of men living in the period Alfred North Whitehead has called "the century of genius." By training and temperament they were mathematicians, and the scheme of thought they produced was, in Whitehead's phrase, "framed by mathematicians, for the use of mathematicians." [8] The most striking characteristics of the scheme are its neatness, clarity, precision, and rationality. Above all, rationality: it was created by rational men for the use of rational men. Those who were not rational were offered manuals of self-help to make them so: Descartes provided his *Rules for the Direction of the Mind* and the *Discourse on the Method of Rightly Conducting the Reason*, Spinoza his *De Intellectus Emendatione*. Leibniz wrote a brief tract, "On Universal Synthesis and Analysis, or The Art of Discovery and Judgment," and Nicholas Malebranche's major work is entitled *De la Recherche de la vérité où l'on traite de la nature de l'esprit de l'homme et de l'usage qu'il en doit faire pour éviter l'erreur des sciences*. The way to avoid error is of course to follow reason and not some other guide. Inevitably, Geulincx declares that virtue consists in loving right reason.[9] Spinoza promises that the more the mind rejoices in the divine love, the more it understands, and the more it understands the less is it subject to evil emotions.[10] Indeed, the universe created by the rationalist thinkers is eminently comfortable for those whose lives are innocent of passion.

But this is the point. Man does not live by clear and distinct ideas alone. For all the emending he may subject his intellect to, man lives out of his emotional nature, and knock it on the coxcomb as he will the wanton will not down. Beckett's first novel takes this fact as its premise, and in it Beckett constructs a seventeenth-century universe inhabited by twentieth-century people. Or, to speak in proper nouns, it is a Cartesian cosmos with Proustian inhabitants.

◀ ▶ Not one of the characters in the novel is a mathematician (though Neary is acquainted with Pythagorean language), so none of them knows what to do or how to live in a cosmos created by mathematicians for the use of mathematicians. Each is driven by passion or lured by the goal of the satisfaction of a need, though some needs are less gross than others. Cooper, Neary's man, has only one weakness, and that is an overpowering need for strong drink. Miss Counihan seeks economic support and then some, and expects Murphy to supply her with "the little luxuries to which she was accustomed." Wylie, for his part, will be satisfied by the possession of financial security and Miss Counihan's body, not necessarily in that order of preference. Neary and Celia are a little more complex and difficult to satisfy. Having ricocheted from one unsatisfying affair to another, and having yet to achieve in himself the Apmonia or Attunement which he has so cordially commended to others, Neary looks to Murphy as to "the one and only earthly hope of friendship and all that friendship carried with it" (M, 200). His conception of friendship is very curious, for "he expected it to last." Celia loves Murphy, certainly, but she also needs him to take her off the streets and establish her in middle-class propriety. The nucleus in this atom of conation is of course Murphy himself. "Murphy then is actually being needed by five people outside himself. By Celia, because she loves him. By Neary, because he thinks of him as the Friend at last. By Miss Counihan, because she wants a surgeon [in an obscure and figurative sense]. By Cooper, because he is being employed to that end. By Wylie . . ." (M, 202).

But whether the relations among the several characters is defined in terms of need or desire or even love, the substance of the relations is still passional, and in the world of the novel persons driven by passions and needs are treated as extended bodies in motion through space. Hence, the life of passion is subject to the same kind of mechanical order as the motion of billiard balls on a table or the stars in their courses through the heavens. The life of passion is a closed system, its symbol a circle: "Of such was Neary's love for Miss Dwyer, who loved a Flight-Lieutenant Elliman, who loved a Miss Farren of Ringsakiddy, who loved a Father Fitt of Ballinclashet, who in all sincerity was bound to acknowledge a certain vocation for a Mrs. West of Passage, who loved Neary" (M, 5).

The wily Wylie, who is of them all perhaps the least encumbered with illusion, sets out his own version of the human existence dominated by desire. He takes for his text the fifteenth verse of the thirtieth chapter of Proverbs, which, together with the sixteenth verse, reads as follows:

The horseleach hath two daughters, crying, Give, give. There are three things that are never satisfied, yea, four things say not, it is enough:
The grave; and the barren womb; the earth that is not filled with water; and the fire that saith not, It is enough.

On this text he preaches briefly to Neary: "I greatly fear . . . that the syndrome known as life is too diffuse to admit of palliation. For every symptom that is eased, another is made worse. The horse leech's daughter is a closed system. Her quantum of wantum cannot vary" (M, 57). Neary, as glad to learn as to teach, draws the appropriate conclusion. "From all of which I am to infer . . . correct me if I am wrong, that the possession — *Deus det!* — of angel Counihan will create an aching void to the same amount." And Wylie drives home the point with a final brilliant metaphor: "Humanity is a well with two buckets, . . . one going down to be filled, the other coming up to be emptied."

The "two buckets" hypothesis applies both macrocosmically in the field of interpersonal relations and microcosmically and intrapersonally. In evidence of the former, whatever loss the world sustains by Murphy's death is at least partly recovered by the fact that Cooper, who formerly could neither sit nor remove his hat, can latterly do both. Also, there seems to be a limit to the number of adventurers into the little world of the mind allowed to exist at any given time, so Celia cannot up until Murphy out. In regard to the microcosmic world, Miss Counihan's chagrin at finding Murphy living with Celia is palliated by Wylie's oyster kisses, and her grief at finding Murphy dead is mollified by a check from the hand of the not ungrateful Neary. Here loss is offset by gain, but sometimes it is the other way around. "No sooner had Miss Dwyer, despairing of recommending herself to Flight-Lieutenant Elliman, made Neary as happy as a man could desire, than she became one with the ground against which she had figured so prettily" (M, 48).

The confirmation of the hypothesis, if confirmation there need be, is given in the relationship of Celia and Murphy. She is determined to make a man of him (and so a lady of herself) by requiring him to take work, and she rejects as absurd his contention that if he works he will lose her, his body and her, or his mind, body, and her. Eventually he bends to her will and hits the job-path, and she, having nothing to do during the day, waits for him, rocking in his chair.

She preferred sitting in the chair, steeping herself in these faint eddies [of light] till they made an amnion about her own disquiet, to walking the streets (she could not disguise her gait) or wandering in the Market, where the frenzied justification of life as an end to means threw light on Murphy's prediction, that livelihood would destroy one or two or all three of his life's goods. This view . . . lost something of its absurdity when she collated Murphy and the Caledonian Market. (M, 66–67)

All of Murphy's explanations as to why he could not afford to work, which he quit supplying when he began to look for work, went uncomprehended by Celia when she listened to them. After rocking in the chair, however, she began to get his drift. "Thus in spite of herself she began to understand as soon as he gave up trying to explain."

The crucial scene, however, is that in which Murphy tells Celia that a job is his at last. This announcement "excited her to the extent of an 'Oh.' Nothing more. Not even an 'Oh indeed.'" Her monomaniacal desire for Murphy to get a job is a bucket that has been emptied. At that very moment another bucket is already descending at full clip, this time to bring up the waters of her growing *Todestrieb*.

Although Wylie's hypothesis pretty well explains the mechanics of desire, it fails to account for another of its aspects — its tendency to create its own object. Of the five people who need Murphy, two — Cooper and Wylie — need him mediately, and three need him immediately. But between the Murphy they need and the Murphy who actually exists there is little resemblance. Having been cured of Miss Counihan, as earlier he had been of Miss Dwyer, Neary yearns for Murphy "as though he had never yearned for anything or anyone before," for Murphy now is to Neary "the one and only earthly hope of friendship and all that friendship carried with it" (M, 200). How Neary, who was not more uninsightful than he was ungrateful, could suppose that he could form a permanent friendship with an avowed and practicing solipsist it is hard to imagine — Murphy, of all people, who spoke seldom, and then only when spoken to, and sometimes not even then! As far off the mark as Neary's judgment is, it is still not so bad as that of the two women who claim to love Murphy. Both Celia and Miss Counihan believe Murphy capable of and even eager for gainful employment, the proceeds of which are to go to their support. The first of the horse leech's daughters is simply obtuse. Celia is something else again, and Murphy has his own interpretation of her and her plans for him. "'What do you love?' said Murphy. 'Me as I am. You can want what does not exist, you can't love it. . . . Then why are you all out to change me? So that you won't have to love me, . . . so that you won't be condemned to love me, so that you'll be reprieved from loving me'" (M, 36). Celia does indeed have an image of Murphy as a man of the world, and this encourages her in her efforts to get him to get a job; but this image is the product of her fantasy, not an extrapolation from the facts (M, 65, 66). Of the three who need Murphy not one of them really needs him as he is, but as he might be or ought to be in order to fill some gap or perform some function for the one who needs him. As distinct from the essential Murphy, the Murphy as he is, the Murphy who is needed is a creation of the passions, desires, and imaginations of those who think they need or want him.

Murphy falls into the same trap himself. He is a confirmed essentialist and (therefore?) rationalist. "You do what you are," he says to Celia, "You do a fraction of what you are, you suffer a dreary ooze of your being into doing." Drowning as much as swimming in the mainstream of Cartesianism, he seeks the freedom which comes from living purely in the realm of the mind. But as convinced as he is of the ultimate truth of the respective ethics of Geulincx and Spinoza, he also knows it is not enough to want nothing where he is worth nothing, and not enough to renounce all that lies outside the intellectual love for himself. The rocking chair helps, but neither the chair nor his desire to abnegate desire is enough to set him free from "his deplorable susceptibility to Celia, ginger, and so on." So when he encounters the patients in the MMM, he thinks he has found the virtuous few who have overcome their several deplorable susceptibilities and have achieved in fact, and permanently, what he has sought for and achieved only intermittently. So convinced is he that the patients are happily "immured in mind" and pleased withal at having escaped from the big world into the little, that "the frequent expressions apparently of pain, rage, despair and in fact all the usual . . . Murphy either disregarded or muted to mean what he wanted." So Murphy "saved his facts against the pressure of those current in the Mercyseat," as Celia, Miss Counihan, and Neary save theirs against the pressure of Murphy as he is.

It is the way in which desire operates in the novel that legitimates the use of the adjective "Proustian" in respect of the characters. Indeed, the mechanism of desire which Wylie propounded under the rubric of the horse leech's daughter and the figure of the two buckets Beckett himself had set out in only slightly more prosaic form in his essay on Proust, published eight years earlier than *Murphy*. The theme of that essay is the effect of time, "that double-headed monster of damnation and salvation," upon the desiring, remembering, habit-ridden self. There is no escape from time, Beckett writes. "There is no escape from yesterday because yesterday has deformed us, or been deformed by us. The mood is of no importance. . . . Yesterday is not a milestone that has been passed, but a daystone on the beaten track of the years, and irremediably part of us, within us, heavy and dangerous. We are not merely more weary because of yesterday, we are other, no longer what we were before the calamity of yesterday" (PTD, 13). Since we are not today what we were yesterday, the aspirations of yesterday are not valid for today's ego. We are disappointed when we have achieved the attainment of some desire, when the subject desire is identified with its object. But this is a foolish reaction, for the subject has died, and perhaps died several times, on the way to attaining its desire. "For subject B to be disappointed by the banality of an object chosen by subject A is as illogical as to expect one's hunger to be dissipated by the spectacle of Uncle eating his dinner" (PTD, 14). The effect of time upon a subject, then, is "an unceasing modification of his personality," and the only permanent reality, if there is any such thing, can be apprehended only as "a retrospective hypothesis" (PTD, 15).

If we look for these ideas about time and the self not in *A la recherche* but in *Murphy*, we immediately see them embodied in Neary and Celia. Miss Dwyer is only one in a succession of the objects of Neary's desire which, being attained, dissolves into nullity. She will be followed by Miss Counihan, Murphy, and Celia. His future gives no promise of success, and he seems "doomed to hope unending." And when we read of Neary that "The fire will not depart from his eye, nor the water from his mouth, as he scratches himself out of one itch into the next," we may recall that two of the four things which are never satisfied are "the earth that is not filled with water; and the fire that saith not, It is enough." Celia's relation to Murphy is of course another instance of the same phenomenon. The Celia who drives Murphy into the jaws of a job is not the same person as the Celia who receives the announcement of his being hired with nothing more than an "Oh." In the time between these two events she has been profoundly altered by the suicide of the ex-butler and by the unexpected pleasure she receives from rocking in Murphy's chair.

If the relationship between the subject and object of desire is complicated by the unceasing modification of the subject by his experiences in time, that complication is still further compounded when the object itself is another human being and therefore itself a subject of desire. We might represent such a situation by saying that at any given moment of time (T_1) subject A has certain desires relating to subject B, and subject B has certain desires in relation to subject A. In the course of time (T_2, T_3) the desires of A are subject to modification, as are the desires of subject B, and so at, say, T_4 A's desires are no longer what they were at T_1 nor are B's. Moreover, the change in A is not necessarily related to the change in B or vice versa. So in any relationship in which B is the object of A's desire but B is also a subject with A as the object of desire, there are "two separate and immanent dynamisms related by no system of synchronisation" (PTD, 17).

The structure of the self and its relations to other selves that Beckett sees in Proust is very like what we have seen in Beckett's first novel, and it probably is not surprising to recognize that the thought of Geulincx and Leibniz informs both Beckett's literary criticism and his art. What he sees in Proust and what he constructed in *Murphy* is a truncated version of the rationalists' cosmos, the missing element being of course God. Without God there is no means for integrating the vectors of conation, so he can speak of Proust's novel (and indirectly of his own work) as containing "no system of synchronisation." [11]

If the "subject desire" is in a constant state of flux, it can have no permanent object of desire, for, as we have seen, the subject that could be satisfied by the possession of the object of its desire is not the same subject by the time it possesses that object. The sad conclusion to be drawn from this state of affairs is that, "Whatever the object, our thirst for possession is, by definition, insatiable. At the best, all that is realized in Time . . . can only be possessed successively, by a series of partial annexations — and never integrally and at once" (PTD, 17–18). There is no point, then, in trying to achieve the pleroma of attainment, for it is unachievable.

What one can try to achieve, however, and what all the sages from Brahma to Leopardi have urged, is not the satisfaction of desire but its ablation. As illustration, Beckett quotes from a poem by Giacomo Leopardi, "A se stesso," which in translation reads thus (the passage in italics is what Beckett quotes in the Italian):

> Now, and for ever, you may rest,
> My haggard heart. Dead is that last deception.
> I had thought love would be enduring. It is dead.
> *I know that my hoping, and even*
> *My wishing to be so dearly deceived, have fled.*

Rest, and for ever. The strife
Has throbbed through you, has throbbed. Nothing is worth
One tremor or one beat; the very earth
Deserves no sign. Life
Has shrunk to dregs and rancor; the world is unclean.
Calm, calm. For this
Is the last despair. What gift has fate brought man
But dying? Now, vanquish in your disdain
Nature and the ugly force
That furtively shapes human ill, and the whole
Infinite futility of the universe.[12]

For all his erudition and pretension to erudition, Neary has not learned
the wisdom of the sages, has not in fact arrived even at the penultimate
condition where hope is gone, for he is doomed to hope unending. Murphy,
however, knows that his only unsophisticated pleasure is to be found in the
third zone of his mind, in the condition of will-lessness and the abnegation
of desire. And we might pause briefly to reflect on the paradox that the
quietism to which Leopardi is brought by his conviction that "Amaro e
noia/ La vita, altro mai nulla; e fango e il mondo" is not perceptibly different from the quietism to which Geulincx is brought by his conviction —
set out clearly and distinctly — that:

1. In hoc mundo me extra me nihil agere posse. 2. Omnem Actionem meam,
quatenus mea est, intra me manere. 3. Eam vi divina aliquando extra me dif-
fundi. 4. Eatenus vero non esse meam Actionem, sed Dei. . . . 6. Tantum-
modo spectare me hunc Mundum. 7. Ipsum tamen Mundum non posse se mihi
spectandum exhibere. 8. Solum Deum mihi exhibere illud spectaculum. 9. Idque
modo ineffabili, incomprehensibili; . . . 10. . . . Esse autem me in hoc Mundo
non est aliud, quam me spectare hunc Mundum. . . .

1. In this world I am not able to do anything outside myself. 2. Every action of
mine, insofar as it is mine, remains within me. 3. Such action is sometimes extended beyond me by divine power. 4. To that extent it is indeed not my doing
but God's. . . . 6. I merely view this world. 7. However, this world itself cannot offer itself to my sight. 8. Only God exhibits this sight to me. 9. And this in
an inexpressible, incomprehensible way; . . . 10. . . . But for me to be in this
world is nothing other than for me to view this world. . . .[13]

Leopardi's world is totally divested of God, whereas Geulincx' world is
totally invested by Him. Yet the human result is the same — the total paralysis of man.

There is one other aspect of Beckett's thought concerning man in time
that we must look at, because though it appears first in the essay on Proust

it also gets used in *Murphy* and the later works. "No object prolonged in this temporal dimension tolerates possession," he writes, and means by possession "the complete identification of object and subject." (PTD, 57). All that is active, all that is enveloped in time and space, even the most vulgar and insignificant human creature is "endowed with what might be described as an abstract, ideal and absolute impermeability." The reason is that the object of desire is not enclosed within its little body but is spread out in time and space to all the points of the four dimensions which it has occupied or will occupy. Beckett quotes Proust: "If we do not possess contact with such a place and with such an hour we do not possess that being" whom we desire to possess (PTD, 58).

The impermeability of the other is borne in upon Murphy in his encounter with Mr. Endon. When Murphy peeps through the judas to check on Mr. Endon and sees that he has prepared a game of chess for the two of them to play, Murphy is much gratified, for he believes that Mr. Endon has "recognized the feel of his friend's eye upon him." But Murphy wants their relationship to be closer than this, and wants to believe that Mr. Endon sees not an impersonal friend's eye but the eye of Murphy himself. So Murphy persists in muting the fact, which in this case is that "while Mr. Endon for Murphy was no less than bliss, Murphy for Mr. Endon was no more than chess." What the schizophrenic sees through the judas is neither friend's eye nor Murphy's, but merely "the chessy eye." Mr. Endon is Murphy's ideal of what it means to be immured in mind, but as far as Mr. Endon is concerned Murphy does not exist: "Mr. Murphy is a speck in Mr. Endon's unseen." Beckett camouflages the poignancy of the moment with frigid prose — "The relation between Mr. Murphy and Mr. Endon could not have been better summed up than by the former's sorrow at seeing himself in the latter's immunity from seeing anything but himself" — but the fact is that Murphy is both frightened and saddened by his inability to get through to his patient.

The incident concluded, Murphy heads back to his garret and rocking chair. On the way he undresses, and naked finally, lies down in the grass and tries to get a mental picture of Celia. He fails. Of his mother. In vain. He can summon to his mind's eye no image of any creature he has ever met.

Murphy's inability to visualize a fellow creature suggests that he has distanced himself from the physical world further than he realized. Two things had bound him, though ever so tenuously, to that world. The first was Celia and his body's delight in her. When he removed his chair from their apartment (M, 142, 154) he signaled his intention of leaving her for good. The only other extramental system in which he reposed any trust was the celestial system. His success with the patients at the MMM turns his head, however, and he refuses to attribute his success to the auspicious relationship of the Moon and the Serpent at the hour of his birth. "The more his own system closed around him, the less he could tolerate its being subordinated to any other. Between him and his stars no doubt there was correspondence, but not in Suk's sense. They were *his* stars, he was the prior system. . . . So far as the prophetic status of the celestial bodies was concerned Murphy had become an out-and-out preterist" (M, 182–83). With this statement Murphy casts away the second of the two bonds that had held him to *rem extensam*, and there is nothing left to prevent the withdrawal of himself into himself.

On the Saturday following the Sunday he began work at the MMM Murphy returns to the apartment to get his chair, brings it back, and settles down for a rock. He is surprised by Ticklepenny, the homosexual whose place he is taking as male nurse. Ticklepenny compares Murphy's expression while in his trance with that of a patient who had been in a catatonic stupor for three weeks, and warns Murphy to mind his health, take a pull on himself. The experience with Mr. Endon is another warning, as is his failure to image Celia, his mother, or anyone else. But the warnings come too late and he flees to his fatal chair like Cooper to a bar. He is too far gone to realize that the price of absolute freedom is absolute isolation. As far as concerns the world, even the diminished world of those who need him, Murphy is a lost cause; and between Murphy dead and Murphy escaped into his bodytight mind there is little to choose. Unavailable is unavailable, no matter what its cause or mode.

In the novel the impermeability of the self is rendered almost parabolically by exhibiting it in the form of a schizophrenic, but as we have already remarked, it is an integral part of both Geulincx' Occasionalism and Leibniz' theory of the monad. In each case, though for slightly different reasons, there is no possible way for one self to engage any other self. In the case of the philosophers this is the result of the radical dichotomy of body and mind, whereas for Proust it is a function of man's existence in time. In any event, Beckett draws the only conclusion available to him when he writes in the essay: "We are alone. We cannot know and we cannot be known. 'Man is the creature that cannot come forth from himself, who

knows others only in himself, and who, if he asserts the contrary, lies'"
(PTD, 66). We see this in the novel, as Neary-monad collides with Couni-
han-monad, Murphy-monad with Celia-monad and Endon-monad, no one
understanding Murphy as he is, the system of synchronization nonexistent.
Given the impermeability of self the best that two human beings can hope
for is that, like the tug and its barge tied abreast and floating down the
river, like the two kites in tandem aloft in the wind, a man and his likes
may move in parallel, neither moved by nor moving the other, through the
fifth element, the human element, time.

IV

◀ ▶ Beckett must have written the essay on Proust after having just put
down Schopenhauer's *Die Welt als Wille und Vorstellung*, for the essay is littered with the will-weary philosopher's terms, distinctions, and
values. Proust, Beckett writes, is pure subject, almost exempt from the im-
purity of will, whereas the people whom he describes are "victims of volition" so lacking in self-reflection as to be amoral in the sense that vegetation is amoral about the way it reproduces itself. Proust deplores his lack
of will until he realizes it is not relevant to the artistic experience. For, says
Beckett, "When the subject is exempt from will the object is exempt from
causality (Time and Space taken together). And this human vegetation
is purified in the transcendental aperception [*sic*] that can capture the
Model, the Idea, the Thing in itself" (PTD, 90). Into these two sentences
Beckett has packed Schopenhauer's concept of causality as the union of
time and space, the definition of the artist as the pure will-less subject of
knowledge, and the goal of art as the contemplation of the Idea. Schopenhauer writes: "In the aesthetical mode of contemplation we have found
two inseparable constituent parts — the knowledge of the object, not as individual thing but as Platonic Idea, that is, as the enduring form of this
whole species of things; and the self-consciousness of the knowing person,
not as individual, but as *pure will-less subject of knowledge*."[14] In fact,
the quotation from Calderon — "Pues el delito mayor/ Del hombre es
haber nacido" (PTD, 67) — he probably took from §51 of *Die Welt*, where
Schopenhauer himself quoted it.

The World as Will and Idea ends on this wise:

Before us there is certainly only nothingness. But that which resists this passing into nothing, our nature, is indeed just the will to live, which we ourselves

are as it is our world. . . . But if we turn our glance from our own needy and embarrassed condition to those who have overcome the world, in whom the will, having attained to perfect self-knowledge, found itself again in all, and then freely denied itself, and who then merely wait to see the last trace of it vanish with the body which it animates; then, instead of the restless striving and effort, instead of the constant transition from wish to fruition, and from joy to sorrow, instead of the never-satisfied and never-dying hope which constitutes the life of the man who wills, we shall see that peace which is above all reason, that perfect calm of the spirit. . . . Thus, in this way, by contemplation of the life and conduct of saints, whom it is rarely granted us to meet with in our own experience, but who are brought before our eyes by their written history, and, with the stamp of inner truth, by art, we must banish the dark impression of that nothingness which we discern behind all virtue and holiness as their final goal. . . . Rather do we freely acknowledge that what remains after the entire abolition of will is for all those who are still full of will certainly nothing; but, conversely, to those in whom the will has turned and has denied itself, this our world, which is so real, with all its suns and milky-ways — is nothing.[15]

There is an obvious congruence of this style of philosophy with the ideas and values of the author of *Murphy*. Schopenhauer repeats — as perhaps any world-denier must — Geulincx' division of *Humilitas* into two parts: "perfect self-knowledge" is what Geulincx means by *inspectio sui*, and the free denial of self is what he means by *despectio sui*. In the man of will, who is condemned to "never-satisfied and never-dying hope," we see Neary (whose name is simply a scrambling of the letters in "yearn"); and in Murphy we see one who is at least trying to be one of those saints "whom it is certainly rarely granted us to meet with in our own experience."

Schopenhauer's role in *Murphy* is neither original nor distinctive, however. He serves simply to reinforce the attitudes and values already expressed by Geulincx and Leopardi, or for that matter Democritus of Abdera or Marcus Aurelius or Epictetus or the book of Ecclesiastes or Job or Aeschylus. For, to paraphrase Wylie, once a certain degree of pessimism has been reached, all stoics and cynics talk, when talk they must, the same tripe.

What is more interesting is his role in the essay on *Proust*. Here Beckett takes over Schopenhauer's Idealism and reads *A la recherche* in its terms. Proust, says Beckett, has contempt for "the literature that 'describes,' for the realists and naturalists worshiping the offal of experience, prostrate before the epidermis and the swift epilepsy, and content to transcribe the surface, the façade, behind which the Idea is prisoner" (PTD, 78–79). Only in art can Proust decipher the "baffled ecstasy that he had known before the inscrutable superficies of a cloud, a triangle, a spire, a flower, a pebble," for here the "mystery, the essence, the Idea, imprisoned in matter" can give itself to the artist (PTD, 76). Beckett uses this language to distinguish between Baudelaire's symbolism and Proust's, that of the former being "determined by a concept, therefore strictly limited and exhausted by its own definition" (PTD, 79). Baudelaire's symbolism continually points beyond itself to something else, whereas for Proust "the object may be a living symbol, but a symbol of itself"; hence, "the symbolism of Baudelaire has become the *autosymbolism* of Proust" (PTD, 80).

The influence on Proust of Schopenhauer's theory of music, Beckett flatly declares, is "unquestionable." And he goes on to summarize the philosopher's theory of music. Here is an important passage from that theory.

The (Platonic) Ideas are the adequate objectification of will. To excite or suggest the knowledge of these by means of the representation of particular things (for works of art themselves are always representations of particular things) is the end of all the other arts, which can only be attained by a corresponding change in the knowing subject. Thus all these arts objectify the will indirectly only by means of the Ideas; and since our world is nothing but the manifestation of the Ideas in multiplicity, . . . music also, since it passes over the Ideas, is entirely independent of the phenomenal world. . . . Music is as *direct* an objectification and copy of the whole *will* as the world itself, nay, even as the Ideas, whose multiplied manifestation constitutes the world of individual things. Music is thus by no means like the other arts, the copy of the Ideas, but the *copy of the will itself*, whose objectivity the Ideas are.[16]

The superiority of music results from the fact that it alone of the arts can claim equal status with the Ideas themselves, for as the Ideas are the objectification of the will, so too is music. The other arts, literature included, can objectify the will only indirectly and by reference to the Ideas (this, perhaps, is the ground of Beckett's criticism of Baudelaire's symbolism), but music copies the will itself. So Schopenhauer can go on to say that music "does not therefore express this or that particular and definite joy, this or that sorrow, or pain, or horror, or delight, or merriment, or peace of mind," but expresses such emotions "*themselves*, to a certain extent in the abstract, their essential nature, without accessories, and therefore without their motives."[17] Opera sullies the purity of music with words, thus distracting from the Ideal, and tries to speak a language which is not its own. Because of the universal significance of a melody it is possible to set not only one poem but "other equally arbitrarily selected examples of the universal expressed in this poem corresponding to the significance of the melody in the same degree"; and this is why one melody may have many verses, and is what makes vaudeville possible.[18] All of this Beckett summarizes brilliantly:

Thus . . . opera is a hideous corruption of this most immaterial of all the arts: the words of a libretto are to the musical phrase that they particularize what the Vendôme Column, for example, is to the ideal perpendicular. From this point of view opera is less complete than vaudeville, which at least inaugurates the comedy of an exhaustive enumeration. (PTD, 92)

And Beckett concludes the essay with a panegyric upon the most immaterial of the arts and the Ideal world which it objectifies:

Music is the catalytic element in the work of Proust. It asserts to his unbelief the permanence of personality and the reality of art. . . . The narrator — unlike Swann who identifies the "little phrase" of the Sonata with Odette, spatializes what is extraspatial, establishes it as the national anthem of his love — sees in the red phrase of the Septuor . . . the ideal and immaterial statement of the essence of a unique beauty, a unique world, the invariable world and beauty of Vinteuil, expressed timidly, as a prayer, in the Sonata, imploringly, as an inspiration, in the Septuor, the "invisible reality" that damns the life of the body on earth as a pensum and reveals the meaning of the word: "defunctus." (PTD, 92, 93)

It is not our business to decide the accuracy of Beckett's assessment of the influence of Schopenhauer on Proust, but it is most definitely our business to remark the enthusiasm with which Beckett receives and uses Schopenhauer's Idealism. Certainly it is congruent, as we have remarked, with the Dualism and Weltschmerz that are so conspicuous even in the early works. But we might not have expected Beckett to expound so vigorously a philosophical system which celebrates the unicity and staticity ("a unique world, the invariable world") of the Ideal in the same essay in which he defends a theory of the self as fluid and changing. Is there an Idea of Albertine, or an Idea of Celia? Beckett can insist that for Proust music asserts the "permanence of personality and the reality of art," but everything else he has said in the essay makes us believe that this is a paradox, if not a flat contradiction. For either the Self is One through its various alterations, in which case it is susceptible of being Idealized, or it is Many, in which case it is not. Sooner or later Beckett will have to make up his mind on this score.

We can see in the essay the strategy he will adopt for resolving the problem, however. It is contained in the phrase "the comedy of an exhaustive enumeration." Suppose that by the Ideal one means the totality of experiences which any given person has had and therefore is, and suppose that one seeks to objectify adequately that Ideal in the art of words. The only possible method that offers itself is that of "exhaustive enumeration," the cataloging of all the actual (not possible) moments of the being of the self in all their detail and variety. And as the catalog grows, once comes closer and closer to the adequate objectification of the self. But does one ever finally come to the end, or is the relation between description and event asymptotic, more and more nearly approximating but never touching, seeking for the Unit by the process $\frac{1}{2} + \frac{1}{4} + \frac{1}{8} \ldots$? Does not the pursuit of the Ideal lead to the frustration of Achilles chasing the tortoise, reducing the distance by half, and again by half, and again by half, but never catching the thing itself? And is this not why Beckett said to Duthuit that there is "nothing to express, nothing with which to express, nothing from which to express"? If one has before him the notion of art as defined by Schopenhauer, then indeed the artist, trying to represent the One Ideal in the Many Selves, is doomed to failure. "At the best, all that is realized in Time . . ., whether in Art or Life, can only be possessed successively, by a series of partial annexations — and never integrally and at once," for the action of Time upon the self results in an "unceasing modification of his personality, whose permanent reality, if any, can only be apprehended as a retrospective hypothesis" (PTD, 17–18). This is the fact, the Ideal is the goal. They are as isolated from one another as Murphy's body is from his mind.

We are returned to the primordial immiscibles, to reflect briefly on the concoction that is that native's mind. We recall that his mind is divided into three zones, each with its corresponding pleasure. In the first or light zone are forms with parallel to reality in the big world. The pleasure here is reprisal, and the kick the physical Murphy receives the mental Murphy can give, corrected in direction. Here the foul-smelling Miss Carridge is available for rape by the homosexual Ticklepenny. What is wanted in the way of psychic faculties to construct the scene of revenge? Two things, mainly: some means for imaging Miss Carridge and Ticklepenny — memory or imagination; and some sort of *voluntas* to set those images into the appropriate action. In the second or half-light zone the forms are without parallel in the big world, and the pleasure is contemplation. In this zone some faculty of perception is required to enable Murphy to contemplate the several images offered, but *voluntas* drops out, leaving only enough of itself or some similar faculty to let Murphy choose among the available forms. In the third zone is a "flux of forms, a perpetual coming together and falling asunder of forms. . . . Here there was nothing but commotion and the pure forms of commotion." This is the condition of total will-lessness, and here Murphy is simply "a mote in the dark of absolute freedom."

We are led to speculate on the relation between these three zones and the three parts of the trilogy, the first volume of which appeared in 1951. The first zone does in fact seem to correspond with *Molloy*. The two chief figures in the work, Molloy and Moran, are both possessed of the usual faculties of perception and volition, and can perceive, remember, imagine, and set themselves to tasks given or invented. In *Malone Dies*, the second part of the trilogy, *voluntas* drops out: "I could die to-day, if I wished, merely by making a little effort, if I could wish, if I could make an effort" (TN, 243). But the will does not drop out entirely, and Malone is still able to choose among the creatures of his invention: "Moll. I'm going to kill her." Finally, in *The Unnamable*, will has disappeared entirely, and there is only . . . what? The flux of forms? Pure commotion? Not really, for there is some strange kind of order, and it seems to be imposed by the Unnamable himself.

We would do better to reorganize the relationship along different lines. Murphy active in the big world corresponds to Molloy seeking his mother and Moran seeking Molloy. Murphy quiet in his body, alert in his mind, inventing a new and improved world, corresponds to Malone in his bed, inventing stories about Saposcat and MacMann. Murphy in his Belacqua bliss, contemplating the forms that rise before him, corresponds to the Unnamable watching Malone revolve around him. On this scheme of organization, unfortunately, Murphy in the third zone seems to correspond to nothing at all.

This is not as much of an embarrassment as it might at first appear, however, for it is questionable whether this third zone is capable of sustaining even the minimal life that Beckett in his later work will want to investigate. Certainly the stupor into which Murphy declines following his game of chess with Mr. Endon will not serve Beckett's later purposes. For we are told that in his trance Murphy began to see that void which is "the absence (to abuse a nice distinction) not of *percipere* but of *percipi*," and that he sucked in "the accidentless One-and-Only, conveniently called Nothing." The implication of the description of the last zone of Murphy's mind and of his stupor seems to be that Murphy has eliminated himself (or been eliminated — the mood is irrelevant) from his own experience. But where in the absence of *percipi*, where in the flux of forms — where is Murphy? If there really is nothing but commotion, how does Murphy know that fact? For him to know it he must be there, and not only be there but be *aware that* there is nothing but commotion. Or, to take the trance, can there be an absence of *percipi* which is not also an absence of *percipere*? In what does *percipi* consist if not in an act of *percipere*?

The fact is that neither of these passages is a true account of what Beckett in *Proust* called "the only world that has reality and significance, the world of our own latent consciousness." This is the world Beckett will want to explore in the trilogy and the other later works, but the concept of mind which he seems to have in *Murphy* will not let him into that world. Perhaps the Nothing that Murphy sees is the "content" of the mind of a person sunk as deep in schizophrenia as Murphy is, but as far as concerns art, even such an art as Beckett's, schizophrenia is a dead-end street. Murphy's stupor and the third zone of his mind is a problem for psychotherapy, not a subject for fiction.

Somewhere between 1938 and 1951 Beckett learned this fact, and modified his concept of consciousness accordingly. He might have learned from Henri Bergson, who was one of the first to realize that there is a limit to what of the human self can be eliminated. In *Creative Evolution*, in a section entitled "The Idea of 'Nothing,'" Bergson sets out the only theory of consciousness which can support Beckett's exploration of the "within." Bergson begins by repeating the Cartesian *cogito*: "I am going to close my eyes, stop my ears, extinguish one by one the sensations that come to me from the outer world. Now it is done; all my perceptions vanish, the material universe sinks into silence and the night." He then goes on to report what he finds once these sensations are gone.

I subsist, however, and cannot help myself subsisting. I am still there, with the organic sensations which come to me from the surface and from the interior of my body, with the recollections which my past perceptions have left behind them — nay, with the impression, most positive and full, of the void I have just made about me. How can I suppress all this? How eliminate myself? I can even, it may be, blot out and forget my recollections up to my immediate past; but at least I keep the consciousness of my present reduced to its extremest poverty, that is to say, of the actual state of my body. I will try, however, to do away even with this consciousness itself. I will reduce more and more the sensations my body sends in to me: now they are almost gone; now they are gone, they have disappeared in the night where all things else have already died away. But no! At the very instant that my consciousness is extinguished, another consciousness lights up — or rather, it was already alight: it had arisen the instant before, in order to witness the extinction of the first; for the first could disappear only for another and in the presence of another. I see myself annihilated only if I have already resuscitated myself by an act which is positive, however involuntary and unconscious. So, do what I will, I am always perceiving something, either from without or from within.[19]

This is the truth of the matter. We may in philosophy or fiction eliminate a great deal from consciousness — sense data, memories, received opinion, feelings. What we cannot eliminate is consciousness itself. Consciousness is, and to be is to be conscious. To put it another way, consciousness "goes on." When he comes to realize this, Beckett will be free in the trilogy to explore the weird and still uncharted terrain of consciousness to its farthest reaches.

But before we get to the trilogy, we must go through the story of one who, in the words of the essay on *Proust*, tried to possess an "object prolonged in this temporal dimension," who meant by possession "the complete identification of subject and object," and who failed utterly.

III THE DEFEAT OF THE PROTO-ZETETIC: WATT

All these [men] were called Pyrrhoneans after the name of their master, but Aporetics, Sceptics, Ephectics, and even Zetetics, from their principles, if we may call them such — Zetetics or seekers because they were ever seeking truth, Sceptics or inquirers because they were always looking for a solution and never finding one, Ephectics or doubters because of the state of mind which followed their inquiry, I mean suspense of judgment, and finally Aporetics, or those in perplexity.

Diogenes Laertius

For limited are the means of grasping (*i.e., the organs of sense-perception*) which are scattered throughout the limbs, and many are the miseries that press in and blunt the thoughts. And having looked at (*only*) a small part of existence during their lives, doomed to perish swiftly like smoke they are carried aloft and wafted away. . . . But he (*God*) is equal in all directions to himself and altogether eternal, a rounded Sphere enjoying a circular solitude.

Empedocles

Naught exists just as much as Aught.

Democritus

Determinatio negatio est.

Spinoza

The plan of this story is to be as follows. I want to strike at philosophy by means of a sombre irony. This irony is to consist not in any particular utterance of J[ohannes]. C[limacus]. but in the whole of his life; he being a deeply serious young man who quietly and without fine phrase tried honestly and sincerely to do what philosophy says, and only became unhappy in the attempt.

Kierkegaard

Reine Kritik ist im Grunde nur ein artikuliertes Lachen. Jedes Lachen ist Kritik, die beste Kritik.

Mauthner

Seek, and ye shall find.

Matt. 7:7 [1]

I

◀ ▶ *Watt* and the three nouvelles — *L'Expulsé, Le Calmant, La Fin* — though published later, were completed by 1946,[2] and we may perhaps take this year and these works as the beginning of what has since come to be a

59

new road which Beckett has taken in an immense effort on his part to discover and exploit the forms of literary art which are available to the artist who would take seriously the fact of "the mess."

A measure of the artist's progress may be had by contrasting some of the more obvious characteristics of *Watt* with those of *Murphy*. In the earlier novel, the narration was "omniscient," time and place were specified, characters were reasonably though eccentrically motivated, and their actions produced not wholly unrelated reactions and consequences. In *Watt*, the action occurs some time in history after the development and general use of trams and railways; the place is some place where trams and railways are in use — probably Ireland. Watt, a man about whom little is known, goes, we know not why, to the house of a Mr. Knott, there to serve, first on the ground floor, then on the next. He undergoes certain experiences which he understands poorly or not at all; is replaced, apparently according to some prearranged plan; and after a mortifying experience at the railway station, leaves for the "further end" of the line — that end, as we must infer from the third chapter, being a mental institution. The narrative point of view is similarly distorted and confusing. The novel is told from a point of view which seems at first omniscient. Then, about halfway through (though there have been hints earlier), we learn that the narrator is Watt's friend, and everything he knows about Watt has been told him by Watt himself. Only at the beginning of the third chapter do we discover that the narrator is named Sam, that he is Watt's co-resident in the same institution, and that the novel is a tale told by a psychotic to a psychotic and then retold to us. Beckett has here begun the process of evacuating his artificial world of those tangibles by which the reader usually is able to orient himself in time and space, and of those causal relationships among the incidents of the plot according to which the reader is able to discern the conditions of necessity and probability which, be they ever so strained or extraordinary, determine in part the structural coherence and "meaning" of the story.

The ambiguity of the novel extends to particular incidents and sequences of incidents. Two examples from the early pages of the book are typical. The first series of incidents comprises the two lovers who are making passionate but at the same time disinterested love, and who suddenly disappear (w, 7–9); the activity of the railway porter, which Watt thinks is perhaps "a punishment for disobedience, or some neglect of duty," for the porter is simply rolling cans from one end of the platform to another (w, 24–26); and Watt's ride to Knott's house with his back to his destination (w, 26).

The second series of incidents includes the following: Watt gets off the tram; Nixon comments that Watt is weighed down (w, 19); Watt bumps into the porter and falls; Lady McCann throws a stone and hits Watt's hat; he wipes his face; he is overcome by weakness and sits down; he hears a mixed choir singing (w, 32–35).

In both sequences there seems to be some kind of pattern, but it is elusive. Indeed, the lack of a clear and evident "meaning" to these two sequences puts the reader into much the same position that the incident of the Galls, father and son, put Watt himself. The Galls are piano tuners, and they appear one day while Watt is at work on the ground floor of Knott's house: they announce that they have come to "choon" the piano. As they do so, they make various ominous comments:

> The piano is doomed, in my opinion, said the younger.
> The piano-tuner also, said the elder.

This, says the narrator, was perhaps the "principal incident" of Watt's early days at Knott's house, but it resembled, in a sense, all the other incidents of note in that

> it was not ended, when it was past, but continued to unfold, in Watt's head, from beginning to end, over and over again. . . . It resembled them in the vigour with which it developed a purely plastic content, and gradually lost, in the nice processes of its light, its sound, its impacts and its rhythm, all meaning, even the most literal.
>
> . . . .
>
> This fragility of the outer meaning had a bad effect on Watt, for it caused him to seek for another, for some meaning of what had passed, in the image of how it had passed.
> The most meagre, the least plausible, would have satisfied Watt. . . . (w, 72–73)

The scene quickly ceases to signify for Watt the fact that a piano was tuned, that the two men stood in some familial and professional relation to each other, that judgments were passed, and so on. The scene becomes for him "a mere example of light commenting bodies, and stillness motion, and silence sound, and comment comment."

To return to the two sequences of incidents mentioned above, "meagre," perhaps implausible interpretations do in fact seem to offer themselves. The events in the first sequence — the lovers, the porter, and Watt's trip — are not dissimilar to events in Dante's *Inferno*: Paolo and Francesca (Canto V); the punishment of the misers and the spendthrifts (Canto VII); and the punishment of the sorcerers and diviners (Canto XX). These last have their heads twisted around so that they cannot see where they are going (into the future) but only where they have been (the past); and this is the condition also of Arsene and Erskine, two of Mr. Knott's servants, and generally of those of Knott's retainers who are "little fat shabby . . . men, with a little fat bottom sticking out in front and a little fat belly sticking out behind" (w, 58).

Concerning the second sequence of incidents, Beckett (or Sam) proffers the reader an interpretation when he writes that Watt had become so used to being abused and knocked down that he found the best thing to do was simply to staunch the blood, pick up what had fallen, and continue "as soon as possible, on his way, or in his station" (w, 32). Watt's journey to Knott's house is a fairly close parallel with the Stations of the Cross. Watt's departure from the tram is his first Station, the condemnation to death. Watt is "weighed down" by the cross (the second Station); he falls for the first time; he meets his mother, Lady McCann (MacAnne, i.e., child of Anne, i.e., Mary, the mother of Jesus); he wipes his face with a "sudarium." (He has of course no Veronica to wipe it for him, just as he has no Simon of Cyrene, except possibly for Dum Spiro, editor of *Crux*, "the popular Catholic monthly.") Watt falls again (the seventh Station); and in the singing he meets the women of Jerusalem — indeed, four generations of them: great granma Magrew, granma Magrew, mama Magrew, and Miss Magrew (in the soprano, alto, tenor, and bass voices, respectively).

The reader is driven to these and other interpretations of incidents in the novel because he suffers, like Watt, from an inability to discover any meaning, "even the most literal," in these incidents. The simple fact that when Watt bumps into the porter it is he who falls and not the porter tells us nothing about Watt except that he has not the sense of equilibrium that the porter has. It is not in the "what" that passes that we find significance, but "in the image of how it had passed," in connection with Lady McCann, the use of the sudarium, and so on. But these two series of events are typical of other events in the novel also, in that neither proves to be an adequate instrument for the interpretation of the novel as a whole. For though Beckett has introduced into the opening pages of the work two "myths" — the pilgrimage into hell and the Stations of the Cross — either of which is capable of being expanded or developed so that it could support the whole of *Watt*, neither is sustained, and both disappear from the novel almost immediately.

Other meager and implausible interpretations of particular incidents could be added. We are apparently to make the inference from Watt's posture and behavior on his way back to the railroad station (w, 220, 223) that Watt is a spent phallus and that his tenure at Knott's house is to be understood as a fruitless sexual adventure; that "Nackybal" is an anagram on "Caliban" of Shakespeare's *Tempest* (or of Browning's "Caliban upon Setebos"); that Mr. Knott is God; and so on. Every major character, every major scene and incident, invites interpretation based on esoteric intelligence.

For example, we may take a paragraph to gloss the name of the servant whom Watt is replacing. Arsene (Arsenius) was an anchorite and saint who died ca. 450 at the age of ninety-five. He was called out of a secular and voluntary seclusion by the Emperor Theodosius to be the tutor of Arcadius and Honorius, the emperor's sons. Disliking the public life he was forced to lead, Arsenius contrived to put himself in disfavor with Arcadius by using the rod on him; which stratagem worked so well that the tutor's life was endangered. To discover the will of God in the matter, Arsenius prayed, and heard a voice saying (the French is Claude Fleury's, from whom I am taking this information), "Arsene fui les hommes, & tu te sauveras." [3] He promptly sailed to Alexandria and thence proceeded to the desert of Scetis where he became a resolute eremite. Seeking instruction in the way of salvation, he prayed again, and again heard a voice, which said to him, "Arsene fui, garde le silence & le repos; ce sont les moyens d'éviter le péché." [4] In time, Arcadius relented, and offered Arsenius all the tribute of Egypt to distribute to monasteries and the poor, but Arsenius replied, "Dieu veüille nous pardonner à tous nos péchez: pour la distribution de l'argent, je n'en suis point capable, puisque je suis déja mort." As a trade he made palm mats, all the time keeping "un mouchoir" (handkerchief; sudarium?) in his bosom "pour essuier les larmes qui tomboient continuellement de ses yeux: ce qui dura pendant toute sa vie." [5] He was left an estate in the will of a relative, but refused it saying, in language similar to that which he had used to Arcadius, "Je suis mort devant lui; & ne voulut rien recevoir du Testament." [6] In his old age his hair was completely white and his beard hung down to his waist; moreover, the tears he had shed his whole life had caused him to lose his eyelashes. Arsene will reappear, unnamed, in *The Unnamable*, to be recognized only by his tears, his beard (see TN, 404), and perhaps by the fact that he is "already dead."

We can take another paragraph to contribute to the controversy over the ladder mentioned by Arsene in his "short statement." Describing the course of thought and feeling, followed by a new servant in Mr. Knott's house, he says that one is first content, but after a time this sense of well-being slips or changes. "What was changed was existence off the ladder. Do not come down the ladder, Ifor, I haf taken it away" (w, 44). The image of the ladder is common in texts exhorting spiritual or intellectual development: as we have seen (Ch. I), it occurs in Descartes and Augustine and Yeats and the author of the *Scala Paradisi*, Johannes Climacus. Hegel used the image in the Preface to his *Phenomenology of Spirit*, and Kierkegaard, who knew both Hegel and Climacus, derided the philosopher (and himself) in the ascetic's terms.[7] In his *Johannes Climacus or De Omnibus Dubitandum Est* he tells the story of a young man, J.C. (Johannes Climacus), who sets out to follow the advice of sceptical and dialectical philosophy.

It was his delight to begin with a simple thought, and from that to mount up step by step along the path of logical inference to a higher thought, for Inference formed his *Scala Paradisi*, and his bliss in mounting this ladder was to him more glorious than that of Jacob's angels. . . . Things did not, however, always go as he wished. If in his descent he did not receive precisely the same number of bumps as there were links in the inference, he would be distressed. . . . He paid no heed to other people, and never imagined they might pay heed to him. He was always alien to the world.[8]

J.C.'s way of thinking reminds us of Watt's efforts in the same line:

Thinking was and remained his passion. But as yet he lacked the collectedness of mind necessary for acquiring any profound coherence of thought. Results were not of great consequence to him. Only the movements of thought as such interested him. Sometimes I suppose he would notice that he reached one and the same conclusion from quite different starting-points. But this did not in any deep sense engage his attention. His only delight was to be always pressing on. Especially when he suspected a labyrinth did he set himself to find a way through it. Once he had started, nothing could bring him to a halt. If he found the going difficult and became tired of it before he ought, he would adopt a very simple plan. He would shut himself into his room, make everything as solemn as possible, and then say in a loud voice, "I *will* do it." [9]

In writing the story of J.C., Kierkegaard took little from the desert saint but his name and the title of his book, but between Climacus' *Scala* and Beckett's *Watt* there are some interesting substantive parallels. Some common themes are withdrawal from the world, the mortification of the senses, and the relation between the novice (Watt) and his spiritual director (Arsene, and in some ways, Mr. Knott). Perhaps the most important matter for our purposes is Climacus' description of the goal of the monastic life. It is described in the twenty-ninth Step (there are thirty Steps altogether, corresponding to the age of Christ at his baptism). The heading reads, "Concerning heaven on earth, or godlike dispassion and perfection. . . ." The text follows:

1. Here are we who lie in the deepest pit of ignorance, in the dark passions of this body and in the shadow of death, having the temerity to begin to philosophize about heaven on earth.

2. The firmament has the stars for its beauty, and dispassion [*apatheia*] has the virtues for its adornments; for by dispassion I mean no other than the interior heaven of the mind, which regards the tricks of the demons as mere toys.

· ·

11. He who has been granted such a state, while still in the flesh, always has God dwelling within him as his Guide in all his words, deeds, and thoughts. Therefore, through illumination he apprehends the Lord's will as a sort of inner voice.[10]

Climacus uses two terms to refer to the ideal state of the soul: *hesychia*, meaning stillness or peace or holy quiet, the result of interior prayer; and *apatheia*, meaning the dispassion or quietude of soul which is its condition when "a burning love for God and men leaves no room for selfish and animal passions."[11] The monastic virtue of "apathy" is therefore considerably different from the Stoic virtue of "apathy" or "ataraxy," for the latter is simple indifference, whereas the former is a fervid but spiritual passion for God to the exclusion of all temporal or sensual pleasure. The two sets of values are similar, however, in that they both reject the definition of man's good in terms of material or earthly values in favor of intellectual or spiritual values. Spiritual peace is indeed celebrated by Arsene in his "statement": "The sensations, the premonitions of harmony are irrefragable, of imminent harmony, when all outside him will be he, the flowers the flowers that he is among him, the sky the sky that he is above him, the earth trodden the earth treading, and all sound his echo. When in a word he will be in his midst at last, after so many tedious years spent clinging to the perimeter" (w, 40–41). Are we to suppose, then, when Watt's speaking is described as "soliloquy, under dictation" (w, 237), that he has achieved monastic perfection and that he "apprehends the Lord's will as an inner voice"? No, for "they" have taken away the ladders by which saints once ascended to spiritual perfection and philosophers climbed from simple, clear, and distinct ideas to universal truth. The voice that speaks in Watt is the voice that spoke in Mr. Endon — the voice which, half-straightened, half-audible, murmurs in the mud in *How It Is.*

Neither spiritual nor philosophical perfection is of Watt's world; but these are heady goals, and Watt is not really that ambitious. He would like to be able to deal on a simpler level with his environment, however, and to do so he needs to use language — to name things, for example. He is therefore greatly vexed when he discovers that he can no longer connect a name with a thing.

Paraphrase being out of the question, I quote at length from the celebrated passage describing Watt's muddied intellectual transaction with a piece of Mr. Knott's kitchen equipment.

Not that Watt desired information, for he did not. But he desired words to be applied to his situation, to Mr. Knott, to the house, to the grounds. . . . For Watt now found himself in the midst of things which, if they consented to be named, did so as it were with reluctance. . . . Looking at a pot, for example, or thinking of a pot, at one of Mr. Knott's pots, of one of Mr. Knott's pots, it was in vain that Watt said, Pot, pot. Well, perhaps not quite in vain, but very nearly. For it was not a pot, the more he looked, the more he reflected, the more he felt sure of that, that it was not a pot at all. It resembled a pot, it was almost a pot, but it was not a pot of which one could say, Pot, pot, and be comforted. It was in vain that it answered, with unexceptionable adequacy, all the purposes, and performed all the offices, of a pot, it was not a pot. And it was just this hair-breadth departure from the nature of a true pot that so excruciated Watt. For if the approximation had been less close, then Watt would have been less anguished. For then he would not have said, This is a pot, and yet not a pot, no, but then he would have said, This is something of which I do not know the name. And Watt preferred on the whole having to do with things of which he did not know the name, though this too was painful to Watt, to having to do with things of which the known name, the proven name, was not the name, any more, for him. (w, 81)

The intransigent refusal of the pot to be named and hence to be brought within the ken or grasp or power of Watt is a paradigm of the semantic impasse and epistemic dead end which defines his condition in Knott's employ.

The picture hanging in Erskine's room threatens to become still another such unnamable entity. The picture is very simple. "A circle, obviously described by a compass, and broken at its lowest point, occupied the middle foreground. . . . In the eastern background appeared a point, or dot. The circumference was black. The point was blue, but blue! The rest was white" (w, 128). Watt undertakes his usual analysis of the possible relationships between the two parts of the painting ("And he wondered what the artist had intended to represent . . . a circle and its centre in search of each other, or a circle and its centre in search of a centre and a circle respectively, or . . ."); and having come to at least a tentative conclusion ("it was perhaps this, a circle and a centre not its centre in search of a centre and its circle respectively, in boundless space, in endless time, . . ." [w, 129]), Watt wonders whether the picture is part and parcel of Mr. Knott's establishment or whether it belongs to Erskine. Watt concludes, by absolutely invalid reasoning, that the picture was merely one in a series, "like the series of Mr. Knott's dogs, or the series of Mr. Knott's men, or like the centuries that fall, from the pod of eternity" (w, 131). And having thus plugged another potential leak in his dike against reality, Watt can continue about his master's business.

Which brings up the problem of the identity of Watt's master, Mr. Knott. A considerable amount of information is available concerning this remarkable gentleman. He seems to be incapable of looking after himself, and therefore employs two — but only two — retainers (w, 61). He dines at noon and at seven in the evening, on a "poss" containing ". . . fish, eggs, game, poultry, meat, cheese, fruit, . . . absinthe, mineral water, tea, . . . stout, beer, whiskey, . . . insulin, digitalin, calomel, . . . salt and mustard, pepper, . . . and of course a little salicylic acid, to delay fermentation" (w, 87). He both speaks and sings in Watt's hearing, but not to Watt's edification. His appearance is subject to extreme and diurnal alteration. "For one day Mr. Knott would be tall, fat, pale and dark, and the next thin, small, flushed and fair, and the next sturdy, middlesized, yellow and ginger, and the next" etc. (w, 209–11) In spite of this chameleonic behavior, Knott's establishment is permanent (w, 131); and, though apart from Mr. Knott there is only languor and fever, yet "to Mr. Knott, and with Mr. Knott, and from Mr. Knott, were a coming and a being and a going exempt from languor, exempt from fever, for Mr. Knott was harbour, Mr. Knott was haven" (w, 135). Or, to alter the metaphor, Mr. Knott is very like the sun, for "the earlier Mr. Knott rose the later he retired, and . . . the later he rose, the earlier he retired" (w, 86). And the few glimpses that Watt had of Mr. Knott, during the first half of Watt's tenure, "were not clearly caught, but as it were in a glass, not a looking-glass, a plain glass, an eastern window at morning, a western window at evening" (w, 147).

In spite of this sizable amount of interesting and important information, or rather, precisely because of it, Watt must admit to himself, toward the end of his service on the ground floor of Mr. Knott's house, that no conception is to be had of Mr. Knott, that concerning Mr. Knott nothing is known. Watt's ignorance is only compounded by the more immediate experience of his employer entailed by Watt's graduation to service on the first floor of the establishment; and when he finally leaves his master, Watt knows even less than when he first arrived.

He confesses as much to Sam, the narrator of the novel, and fellow inmate of an unnamed mental institution. In consequence of thinking too much upon the event, Watt's mind has sustained serious injury, and his attempt to communicate to Sam the meaning of the relationship between himself and Mr. Knott is much impaired by the fact that Watt must invert the letters in the words he speaks, the words in the sentence, the sentences in the period, or one or more combinations of these inversions. (There is another reason why Watt should communicate in such a peculiar fashion. His speeches indicate that he is a sensitive, lonely, and abysmally unhappy man, and the tone of the novel is in danger of becoming unqualifiedly pathetic. This, however, would quite upset the careful balance thus far maintained between pathos and comedy in the work, and the novelist cannot permit this to happen. Hence, he "distances" the reader from Watt's plight by requiring the reader to untangle Watt's speeches.)

Watt's speeches correspond to the several stages of "the second or closing period of Watt's stay in Mr. Knott's house" — that is, of Watt's service on the first floor, in close proximity to Mr. Knott. The first of these speeches is reproduced unmodified. The rest but one are given unscrambled, though the spelling is unchanged.

Day of most, night of part, Knott with now. Now till up, little seen so oh, little heard so oh. Night till morning from. Heard I this, saw I this then what. Thing quiet, dim. Ears, eyes, failing now also. Hush in, mist in, moved I so.

To orb, pal[e] blur, dark bulk. To [ear] drum, low puf, low puf. To skin, gros mas, gros mas. To smel, stal smel, stal smel. To tung, tart swets, tart swets.

Abandoned my little to find him. My little to learn him forgot. My little rejected to have him. To love him my little reviled. This body homeless. This mind ignoring. These emptied hands. This emptied heart. To him I brought. To the temple. To the teacher. To the source. Of nought.

Wat did need? Knot. Wat ad got? Knot. Was kup ful? Pah! But did need? Praps not. But ad got? Know not.

[The fifth is omitted.]

So livd, for tim. Not sad, not gay. Not awak, not aslep. Not aliv, not aded. Not bod[y], not sprit. Not wat, not knot. Til day cam, to go.

Sid by sid, to men. Al day, part of nit. Dum, num, blin. Knot look at Wat?

No. Wat look at Knot? No. Wat talk to Knot? No. Knot talk to Wat? No. Wat den did us do? Niks, niks, niks. Part of nit, al day. Two men, sid by sid. (w, 164, 165, 166, 167, 168)

Of the eighth or final stage of the closing period of Watt's stay in Knott's house, which Watt described by inverting "in the brief course of the same period, now that of the words in the sentence, now that of the letters in the word, now that of the sentences in the period, now simultaneously that of the words in the sentence and . . ." Sam records nothing.

These speeches tell more about Watt than they do about Mr. Knott. They tell us that Watt is pathetically alone, though in search of companionship; that he has exerted himself in order to establish some kind of human relationship between himself and his master; that he has failed, and is deeply disappointed; and that, though his sense perception has begun seriously to degenerate, he is not insensitive to the irony which attends the fact that two men can be so close to each other and yet so unspeakably distant.

Watt fails in his effort to get to know Mr. Knott, just as Murphy had failed in his effort to make contact with Mr. Endon. The reasons for the failure are very different, however. Murphy is prevented from coming to know Mr. Endon because the latter has retreated behind the walls of his pathological condition, but Watt is frustrated by the fact that Mr. Knott is a fluid and continuously changing Self. The former is a medical and psychological illness that can be "cured." The latter is an existential fact, a condition of being-in-the-world to which there is no alternative, for which there is no "cure."

II

◀ ▶ The retreat from reality which necessitates Watt's being committed to a mental institution is the consequence of the epistemological defeat he suffers while working for Mr. Knott. Watt should have been put on his guard against this eventuality by Arsene's short statement, however; for the gist of it is that, whereas Mr. Knott's establishment holds out the promise of being a paradise where a man's desires are fulfilled, where existence is not estranged from essence, and where life has meaning, it in fact is none of these. Arsene himself apparently suffered the same delusion, but his period of service on Mr. Knott's premises cured him of hope and made him into a cynic. His statement is a prediction that Watt too will in the course of time become disenchanted and disillusioned: he too will have to exist "off the ladder." The difference between the two men is that Arsene can take refuge in cynicism, but Watt, being of a more sanguine, romantic, and idealistic temperament, will be all but totally destroyed by the disparity between what he had hoped to find and what in fact he does find.

Watt's collapse is all the more surprising in view of the fact that he really did not demand all that much of Mr. Knott's domain. Neither his past training nor present values require him to desist from thought only after having attained to a knowledge of the essence of things. Watt had always been content with much less than that, for he "had lived, miserably it is true, among face values all his adult life" (w, 73). Nor did Watt demand a great deal of the incident of the Galls: although he could not accept such an incident as one of "the simple games that time plays with space," and was obliged, because of his peculiar character, to inquire into what such incidents meant, yet he was obliged to inquire "oh not into what they really meant, his character was not so peculiar as all that, but into what they might be induced to mean, with the help of a little patience, a little ingenuity" (w, 75).

Watt's attitude toward reality can hardly be termed pugnacious. He wants simply to get on in the world, he wants simply not to be inconvenienced. He longs for peace. He longs to hear the voice of Erskine, a senior retainer, "wrapping up safe in words the kitchen space, the extraordinary newel-lamp, the stairs . . . and the bushes" (w, 83). Watt seeks a "pillow of old words" for his head, for it is this pillow which intervenes between Watt and reality. Words, for Watt, make up the shield wherewith to fend off the assaults of reality on his "mind, whatever that might mean." For Watt considered that he was successful in foisting a meaning where no meaning appeared, as in the incident of the Galls, "when he could evolve, from the meticulous phantoms that beset him, a hypothesis proper to disperse them. . . . For to explain had always been to exorcize, for Watt" (w, 77–78).

Beckett's earlier hero, Murphy, sought not to achieve a pact of coexistence with reality, with the "big world," but was full of purpose to abdicate entirely from the colossal fiasco. Watt, on the other hand, is prepared to endure the big blooming buzzing confusion, but only on terms which will permit him to domesticate reality, to lead it about on a leash of words, to keep himself unspotted by the splash of things. Hence, of things for which he had never known the name, Watt could hope that someday he would learn it, "and so be tranquilized." But the peculiar kind of purgatory constituted by Mr. Knott's house and grounds requires that Watt be afflicted with things and incidents whose *esse* is incapable of being exhausted or tamed by the application of names and words.

Watt is not always defeated, however. He is tormented not by any and every entity which comes his way, for as long as Watt is capable of locating a thing or event in a sequence or series of events or things, or as long as he is capable of constructing one or more hypotheses capable of accounting for the entity, he can remain reasonably at his mental ease. He is busy, of course, for it takes no small amount of cerebration to discover, for example, twelve possible combinations in regard to the arrangements for Mr. Knott's meals. Here is the first: "1. Mr. Knott was responsible for the arrangement, and knew that he was responsible for the arrangement, and knew that such an arrangement existed, and was content" (w, 89). By a judicious distribution of negatives, Watt is able to vary this formula in eleven different ways: Knott was not responsible but was content; was responsible but not content; etc. This is the sort of problem which Watt can take in stride, since it involves a situation whose possibilities are susceptible of being exhausted by a finite number of hypotheses. One of the twelve is a true account of the arrangements for Knott's meals — or perhaps the true account is one of those which occurred to Watt but which he put aside as unworthy of consideration. Just which one of these is the true hypothesis is not a question of serious importance; what is important is that the true hypothesis is available, and with this Watt can rest in tranquillity. For Watt's character, let us recall, was not so peculiar as to require him to inquire into what an event *really* meant.

And when Watt details the movements of Mr. Knott about his room, one senses that Watt's eye is clear, his hand steady, his brain untroubled, as he records that here Mr. Knott stood, "Here he sat. Here he knelt. Here he lay. Here he moved, to and fro, from the door to the window, from the window to the door; from the window to the door, from the door to the window; from the fire to the bed, from the bed to the fire; . . ." And so on, for thirty-five lines. Or again, he expends eighty lines as he records the alterations both in location and posture of the furniture in Knott's room: ". . . the tallboy on its feet by the fire, and the dressing-table on its head by the bed, and the night-stool on its face by the door, and the washhand-stand on its back by the window; . . ." (w, 205). Or he can retell, with an apparently exquisite accuracy, a twenty-eight–page story which has no discernible relation to the main story. Or, finally, there is a lengthy analysis of the manner in which a dog is procured to consume the remains of Mr. Knott's meal; and when this analysis has been completed, we are told that Watt had not for a moment supposed that he had penetrated the forces at play, or obtained "the least useful information concerning himself, or Mr. Knott, for he did not. But he had turned, little by little, a disturbance into words, he had made a pillow of old words, for a head" (w, 117). And this is all that Watt asks of his hypotheses and descriptions: that they shield him from reality, that they insulate him from the particularity of things.

When, however, this semantic dike springs a leak, Watt is in trouble. The incident of the Galls is one such occasion, and the naming of the pot is another. In both cases, words fail not only to deliver up the essence of the situation — and this of course is more than Watt has ever asked of his terms and hypotheses; but they fail even in their minimal task of interposing between Watt and the thing or event in question. And in the case of the unnamable pot, there are alarming ramifications. For Watt finds that, just as he cannot give a name to the pot, so he can no longer give a name to himself. Watt, when he turned for reassurance to himself,

made the distressing discovery that of himself too he could no longer affirm anything that did not seem as false as if he had affirmed it of a stone. . . . And Watt was greatly troubled by this tiny little thing, more troubled perhaps than he had ever been by anything, and Watt had been frequently and exceedingly troubled, in his time. (w, 82)

Watt's sojourn in the land of Knott is clearly meant to be a parody of some of the major philosophical methods and problems that have occupied the attention of serious men since the beginning of self-consciousness. The principal theme is, of course, the problem of knowledge, but epistemological inquiries cannot be separated from such other questions as the nature of reality, the being of God, and the criteria of value. All of these problems enter into the novel, and it is important to look at them, if only briefly.

We may begin by looking at an idea which receives hardly any development in the novel. It occurs in the part of Arsene's statement where he is trying to describe what it is like to serve Mr. Knott. To facilitate his explanation, Arsene constructs an analogy: the coming and going of Mr. Knott's retainers is like the coming and going of parlormaids. Let the name of the former maid be Ann, and that of the latter, Mary, explains Arsene,

and let there exist a third person, the mistress, or the master, for without some such superior existence the existence of the house and parlour maid, . . . is hardly conceivable. Then this third person, on whose existence the existences of

Ann and Mary depend, *and whose existence also in a sense if you like depends on the existence of Ann and Mary,* says to [the former maid] . . . (w, 50–51; italics added.)

Mr. Knott retains servants, it would appear, so as to guarantee his own existence by requiring others to depend for their existence upon him. The point is made more explicit later, as Watt summarizes the content of his understanding of the nature of Mr. Knott. As far as Watt could see, Mr. Knott needed only two things — not to need, and a witness to his not needing. "And Mr. Knott, needing nothing if not, one, not to need, and, two, a witness to his not needing, of himself knew nothing. And so he needed to be witnessed. Not that he might know, no, but that he might not cease" (w, 202–3).

The idea that Mr. Knott needed to be witnessed so that he might not cease to exist will remind the reader who remembers his history of philosophy that, in the opinion of George Berkeley, the being of an idea consists in its being perceived. His argument runs as follows. The objects of human knowledge are three: ideas actually imprinted on the senses; ideas which are perceived by attending to the passions and operations of the mind; or ideas formed by help of memory and imagination.[12] But besides these ideas, there is "something which knows or perceives them," and this is what he calls mind, spirit, soul, or myself. By these words he does not mean any one of his ideas, but "a thing entirely different from them, wherein they exist, or, which is the same thing, whereby they are perceived — for the existence of an idea consists in being perceived." [13] Therefore, whatever exists does so as an idea in a mind or spirit, either as an object of human knowledge or as an object of Divine Knowledge.

The table I write on I say exists, that is, I see and feel it; and if I were out of my study I should say it existed—meaning thereby that if I was in my study I might perceive it, or that some other spirit actually does perceive it. There was an odor, that is, it was smelled, there was a sound, that is to say, it was heard; a color or figure, and it was perceived by sight or touch. This is all that I can understand by these and the like impressions. For as to what is said of the absolute existence of unthinking things without any relation to their being perceived, that seems perfectly unintelligible. Their *esse* is *percipi*, nor is it possible they should have any existence out of the minds or thinking things which perceive them.[14]

We shall have occasion to refer to Berkeley later on, but let us for the moment simply notice that the being of Mr. Knott is governed by the principles of the Bishop of Cloyne's *Principles*.

An allusion to a second philosopher occurs in a passage already quoted from Arsene's introductory discourse to Watt, wherein the elder servant describes the "premonitions of harmony" which the younger probably feels as he is about to enter the service of Mr. Knott. He then goes on to say that, although a new servant may have regrets, these are soon dissipated. "Why is this?" asks Arsene. It is, he replies to himself,

because of the nature of the work to be performed, because of its exceptional fruitfulness, because he comes to understand that he is working not merely for Mr. Knott in person, and for Mr. Knott's establishment, but also, and indeed chiefly, for himself, that he may abide, as he is, where he is, and that where he is may abide about him, as it is. Unable to resist these intenerating considerations, his regrets, lively at first, melt at last, melt quite away and pass over, softly, into the celebrated conviction that all is well, or at least for the best. (w, 41)

The last three words (and two pages later the allusion to Lisbon) announce the presence of Gottfried Wilhelm Leibniz. Our world, says Leibniz in the *Monadology*, is the best of all possible worlds, for God's infinite wisdom tells him what is best, his infinite goodness makes him choose the best, and his infinite power enables him to produce it.[15] The world is a composite of "monads" created by God, which monads "have no windows through which anything could enter or depart," each of which is different from all others (§9) and cannot be altered or changed internally by any other (§7), although each is the source of its own internal actions (§18). A monad is both soul and body, both active and passive; soul does not affect body, nor does body affect soul; nonetheless, ultimate order prevails.

Therefore souls or vital principles . . . change nothing in the ordinary course of bodies and do not even give God the occasion for doing so. The souls follow their laws, which consist in a definite development of perceptions according to goods and evils, and the bodies follow theirs, which consist in the laws of motion; nevertheless, these two beings of entirely different kind meet together and correspond to each other like two clocks perfectly regulated to the same time. It is this that I call the theory of *pre-established harmony*.[16]

It is this celebrated theory which regulates, or gives the appearance of regulating, the comings-in and goings-out of Mr. Knott's servants: "For the service to be considered was not the service of one servant, but of two servants, and even of three servants, and even of an infinity of servants, of whom the first could not out till the second up, nor the second up till the third in . . . And in this long chain of consistence, a chain stretching from the long dead to the far unborn, the notion of the arbitrary could only survive as the notion of a pre-established arbitrary" (w, 133–34) It may be doubted, however, that a pre-established arbitrary is any arbitrary at all.

And immediately following this analysis of the entrances and exits of servants, there comes the description of the trio of frogs, the first of which croaks Krak! the second Krek! and the third Krik! Beginning together at beat one, the first then croaks at intervals of eight, emitting his Krak! at beats one, nine, seventeen, etc.; the second croaks at intervals of five, going Krek! on beats one, six, eleven, etc.; and the third frog Kriks in waltz time. Each monad-frog pursues its own rhythm, preserving its being in striving for the perfection of itself, and in the pursuit of its own good; and after fifteen croaks of Krak! twenty-two of Krek! and thirty-two of Krik! on the one hundred and twenty-first beat their voices are reunited in a glorious *tutti*:

```
_____  _____  _____  _____  _____  _____  _____ Krak!
_____  _____ Krek! _____  _____  _____  _____ Krek!
_____ Krik! _____  _____ Krik! _____  _____ Krik!
```

("And they say there is no God," laughed Mr. Case at the end of the novel.) [17]

Leibniz may also be responsible for some other elements in the novel. We have noticed how everything connected with Mr. Knott — his appearance, his furniture, his movements — are subject to continuous change. At the same time, this change and variety are always kept in a strict order. This, for Leibniz, is the definition of perfection. The mutual accommodation of each monad to every other, effected by the pre-established harmony, causes each monad to have relations which express all the others and consequently "to be a perpetual living mirror of the universe" (*The Monadology*, §56); and infinite relations among the infinite monads is the means of obtaining "the greatest variety possible, but with the greatest possible order; that is to say, this is the means of attaining as much perfection as possible" (*ibid.*, §58). Moreover, spirits or rational souls are capable of knowing the system of the universe (*ibid.*, §83), and this is why spirits can enter into a society with God. This society Leibniz calls "the city of God," and here God's relationship is not just that of inventor to machine but also that of a prince to his subjects and even a father to his children (*ibid.*, §84). We want to add, and perhaps as employer to employee.

Finally, let us consider two passages from the writings of Benedict Spinoza. Beckett thought enough of the first to use a parody of it as the epigraph to the chapter in *Murphy* which describes Murphy's mind. It is the famous thirty-sixth Proposition in Part V of the *Ethics*: "The intellectual love of the mind towards God is that very love of God whereby God loves himself, not in so far as he is infinite, but in so far as he can be explained through the essence of the human mind regarded under the form of eternity; in other words, the intellectual love of the mind towards God is part of the infinite love wherewith God loves himself."[18]

In Spinoza's system, the term "God" is interchangeable with the term "nature" (*Deus sive natura*), and substance is one (*Ethics*, I, Props. XII, XIII), as contrasted with the multeity of substance because of the infinity of monads in Leibniz. Spinoza's God does not transcend nature and is impersonal, and so where Leibniz could speak of God as a prince or father, Spinoza cannot indulge such anthropomorphic fancies. God is wholly impersonal; and he who loves God "cannot endeavor that God should love him in return" (*Ethics*, V, Prop. XIX). This is not to say that God does not love man, for, substance being one, God, insofar as he loves himself, loves man; and the love of God toward man and the intellectual love of the mind toward God are identical. This intellectual love of God is free of every taint of emotion, for emotion, treated in Part IV under the title "Of Human Bondage," is what prevents man from becoming free — i.e., intellectually active, i.e., rational.

There are three kinds of knowledge. The first is that drawn either from "particular things represented to our intellect fragmentarily, confusedly, and without order through our senses," or from symbols — that is, from having heard or read certain words from which we form ideas. This kind of knowledge is called opinion or imagination. The second kind is called reason, in virtue of which we have notions common to all men and adequate ideas of the properties of things. The third is intuition. "This kind of knowledge proceeds from an adequate idea of the absolute essence of certain attributes of God to the adequate knowledge of the essence of things" (*Ethics*, II, Prop. XL, Note II).

It is evident that Watt is barely able to lay claim to the first kind of knowledge. The reason is not that he is driven by passions such as envy or hate, but that he has only a mediocre sensory apparatus and hardly any ability to conceive a clear and distinct idea. Thus, when confronted with Mr. Knott and his incredible variety, Watt is stumped. ("Spiritual unhealthiness and misfortunes," says Spinoza [*Ethics*, V, Prop. XX, Note], "can generally be traced to excessive love for something which is subject to many variations, and which we can never become masters of.") Not being blessed with the gift of clear conceptions, he must inevitably be confused by things — pots, for example; and as the activity of his mind decreases, so does the activity of his body (and this is particularly true of his later avatars Molloy, Malone, et al.); all of which is in keeping with the formula laid down by Spinoza: "He, who possesses a body capable of the greatest number of activities, possesses a mind whereof the greatest part is eternal" (*Ethics*, V, Prop. XXXIX). The Proof of this assertion is also relevant.

Proof. — He, who possesses a body capable of the greatest number of activities, is least agitated by those emotions which are evil (IV. xxxviii.) — that is (IV. xxx.), by those emotions which are contrary to our nature; therefore (V. x.), he possesses the power of arranging and associating the modifications of the body according to the intellectual order, and, consequently, of bringing it about, that all the modifications of the body should be referred to the idea of God; whence it will come to pass that (V. xv.) he will be affected with love towards God, which (V. xvi.) must occupy or constitute the chief part of the mind; therefore (V. xxxiii.), such a man will possess a mind whereof the chief part is eternal. *Q.E.D.*

At the end of his calamitous journey, Malone will write, "There are men and there are things, to hell with animals. And with God" (TN, 225). It is not to be supposed that the chief part of Malone's mind is eternal.

The second passage from Spinoza to be mentioned (all the preceding having been commentary on the intellectual love of God), and the last in this short excursion into rationalist philosophy, is from a letter to Jarig Jelles. Spinoza is discussing the idea of figure as related to determinate bodies:

Qui enim se figuram percipere ait, nil aliud eo indicat quam, se rem determinatam, et quo pacto ea sit determinata, concipere. Haec ergo determinatio ad rem juxta suum esse non pertinet: sed econtra est ejus non esse. Quia ergo figura non aliud quam determinatio, et determinatio negatio est; non poterit, ut dictum, aliud quid quam negatio esse.

For he who says that he perceives a figure, merely indicates thereby, that he conceives a determinate thing, and how it is determinate. This determination, therefore, does not appertain to the thing according to its being, but, on the contrary, is its non-being. As then figure is nothing else than determination, and determination is negation, figure, as has been said, can be nothing but negation.[19]

Determinatio negatio est: Determination is negation. To be is not to be. To be Something is not to be Something Else. To be Watt is not to be

Knott; to be Knott is not to be Watt. Not that not-Knott is therefore Watt, for it is not, nor is not-Watt Knott. For it is possible to be not-Watt and be Arsene, for example, or Erskine, for that matter. But it is impossible to be both Watt and Knott, at the same place, at the same time.

III

◄ ► René Descartes bequeathed to his successors a methodological principle and a substantive problem. The principle is stated in his *Discourse*, where it is the first of the four general rules he devised for governing philosophical inquiry: I resolved, he said, "to accept nothing as true which I did not clearly recognize to be so: that is to say, carefully to avoid precipitation and prejudice in judgments, and to accept in them nothing more than what was presented to my mind so clearly and distinctly that I could have no occasion to doubt it." [20] The substantive problem was the bifurcation of substance into mind and body.

The methodological principle was received generally, and used with various modifications by Geulincx, Malebranche, Spinoza, and Berkeley. The substantive problem was also faced by the succeeding philosophers, but Descartes' attempt to solve it by using the pineal gland as a mediator between the kinds of substance was universally rejected. In place of the theory of the pineal gland, Geulincx and Malebranche substituted the doctrine of Occasionalism, and Leibniz developed the theory of the pre-established harmony. Spinoza avoided the problem by denying that there was more than one kind of substance, which he called God or Nature. Berkeley, too, obviated the problem by doing away with a material and self-subsisting substance; he maintained that real things exist, but only as ideas in the mind of a perceiver. What is common to Descartes' successors is that each one solved the problem by recourse to God. For the Occasionalists God is the worker of miracles; for Leibniz he is the supreme architect, the clockmaker who built such a perfect mechanism that the spiritual and hyletic dimensions of the monads are always in perfect synchronization; for Spinoza he is the one substance, whose intellectual love for himself is identical with the intellectual love wherewith he loves man and wherewith man loves God; and for Berkeley, God is the Mind in which the ideas of things subsist.

Beckett's novel is an assault by way of parody upon both the methodological principle and the theistic answer to the problem posed by the antithesis of mind and body. Watt is, of course, the Cartesian hero, ready and willing to form clear and distinct ideas of whatever there is to have such ideas of. His cross is that he is not able. He tries manfully, and actually tries to carry out Descartes' program. The process is illustrated in Watt's attempt to reconstruct the solution to the problem of disposing of Mr. Knott's table scraps (w, 93–117, but esp. 93–98). He divides up the problem into its parts (this is the second of Descartes' rules), setting them in order (the third), and sets out hypotheses and the objections to the hypotheses. But before doing this, as avoiding precipitation in judgment (the first), he ponders certain questions of a prolegomenal nature, as, by whom the problem of disposing of the scraps had been solved, when it had been solved? Finally — and this is Watt's forte; here he is unsurpassed — he makes "enumerations so complete and reviews so general" that he will be certain of having omitted nothing (the fourth rule). In the end, it avails him nothing: "Not that for a moment Watt supposed that he had penetrated the forces at play, in this particular instance, or even perceived the forms that they upheaved, or obtained the least useful information concerning himself, or Mr. Knott, for he did not" (w, 117). So all his careful observance of the rules leads him nowhere.

The result of following the rules laid down in Descartes' *Discourse* (or in Spinoza's *On the Improvement of Human Understanding*, or Malebranche's *De la Recherche de la vérité*, or Berkeley's *Principles*) was not supposed to be intellectual confusion or mere words, however, but a clear and distinct idea, which in turn would give rise to other ideas equally distinct and clear, the whole process culminating in a perfect and unloosable grasp upon the nature of things. So when, after a careful analysis of the factors involved in the preparation of Mr. Knott's meals, or the possible relations between the center and circumference of the circle in Erskine's picture, or the means of disposing of the remnants of Mr. Knott's meals, or the possible rationale of the comings and goings of his servants, Watt must confess that he has no better understanding of the event than he did before he thought about it, his confession amounts to a declaration of the bankruptcy of the deductive method and the principles of rationalist philosophy.

This is not the end of the attack on philosophy, however, for in his effort to come to know Mr. Knott, Watt is inductive and empirical. As he weighs, counts, and measures the ingredients in Mr. Knott's meals, so Watt describes, lists, reports, and compiles all the data he can, with the result that "Of the nature of Mr. Knott himself Watt remained in particular ignorance" (w, 199). Such massive ignorance is easily explained: "Of the many excellent reasons for this, two seemed to Watt to merit mention: on the one hand the exiguity of the material propounded to his senses, and on the other the decay of these. What little there was to see, to hear, to smell, to taste, to touch, like a man in a stupor he saw it, heard it, smelt it, tasted it, touched it" (w, 199).

Empirical knowledge is to be had, however, only where the data are copious and the sensorium delicate. Where one is lacking, improvisation is still possible. Where both are lacking there is nothing for it but to quit. Being aware of his condition and an honest man to boot, Watt does what he must do: he gets a ticket for the further end of the line. Neither the from-leadings of rationalism nor the to-leadings of empiricism can get Watt anywhere in his quest for knowledge.

The second result of our survey of philosophical themes is that we are able to define more precisely the nature of Mr. Knott and of his house and grounds. Watt entered Mr. Knott's service with "premonitions of harmony," if we can believe Arsene. The reason for his sense of well being, as we may now say, is that Watt believed he was entering Leibniz's City of God, "the most perfect state, formed and governed by the greatest and best of monarchs. Here there is no crime without punishment, no good action without a proportionate reward, and, finally, as much virtue and happiness as is possible." [21] In Leibniz' harmonious city all is coherence, happiness, and peace. But of course the novel is a parody of this and its sibling theory, Occasionalism. The rude fact is that in Mr. Knott's house a pot is not a pot and events do not make sense. More: it is not the case that no crime is without its punishment, for when Watt, in direct violation of express orders, refuses to assist at the eating, by the dog, of the remains of Mr. Knott's meal, "no punishment fell on Watt, no thunderbolt" (w, 115). Nor is his punishment postponed to a later date; his disobedience never has any consequence at all.

If Mr. Knott's estate is the City of God, it follows as the thunderbolt the crime in the best of all possible worlds that Mr. Knott is God. The trouble is that the knowledge of God is of that order of knowledge which, in Arsene's words, "partakes in no small measure of the nature of what has so happily been called the unutterable or ineffable, so that any attempt to utter or eff it is doomed to fail, doomed, doomed to fail" (w, 62). Just so. And yet it is Watt's peculiar penalty to have to contravene Wittgenstein's dictum, and talk about things he cannot talk about.[22] At times, indeed, at the moments of his extremest epistemological passion, he is forced to talk about nothing. To talk about God, then, is a task of no ordinary sort, but Watt (or perhaps Sam) emerges with a solution: we must assert that "the only way one can speak of nothing is to speak of it as though it were something, just as the only way one can speak of God is to speak of him as though he were a man, which to be sure he was, in a sense, for a time, and as the only way one can speak of man, even our anthropologists have realized that, is to speak of him as though he were a termite" (w, 77).

So the fact that Mr. Knott is described in such prolific and anthropomorphic detail is no evidence against the interpretation of him as an ikon of the divine. If God is to be talked about, he must be talked about as if he were a man. As a man he bears the qualities of the God both of the theologians and philosophers. In the first vein, Watt desires to see Mr. Knott "face to face," and the few glimpses he has of his master are as if he were looking into the sun. The verbal echoes here are of I Cor. 13, II Cor. 3:18, and the first chapter of Revelation. As the god of the philosophers he appears otherwise, in a "gesture" (uniquely allowed by the novel to be "characteristic") which consists in "the simultaneous obturation of the facial cavities, the thumbs in the mouth, the forefingers in the ears, the little fingers in the nostrils, the third fingers in the eyes and the second fingers, free in a crisis to promote intellection, laid along the temples" (w, 212). This is about as close as you can get to an adequate anthropomorphic image of Nous nousing nous. The unmoved mover, writes Aristotle in Book Lambda of the *Metaphysics*, exists by necessity and is in this sense a first principle.

On such a principle, then, depend the heavens and the world of nature. And it is a life such as the best which we enjoy, and enjoy for but a short time (for it is ever in this state, which we cannot be), since its actuality is also pleasure. . . . And thought thinks on itself because it shares the nature of the object of thought; for it becomes an object of thought in coming into contact with and thinking its objects, so that thought and object of thought are the same.[23]

Not, alas, in Watt's experience are thought and the object of thought the same. The difference between the idea of a pot and the pot itself is exactly what excruciates Watt. Aristotle continues:

If, then, God is always in that good state in which we sometimes are, this compels our wonder; and if in a better this compels it yet more. And God *is* in a better state. And life also belongs to God; for the actuality of thought is life, and God is that actuality; and God's self-dependent actuality is life most good

and eternal. We say therefore that God is a living being, eternal, most good, so
that life and duration continuous and eternal belong to God; for this *is* God.[24]

And we nest awhile in his branches; we ride at peace in the harbor which
he is.

Haw! laughs the cynical Arsene.

The bitter laugh laughs at that which is not good, it is the ethical laugh. The
hollow laugh laughs at that which is not true, it is the intellectual laugh. Not
good! Not true! Well well. But the mirthless laugh is the dianoetic laugh, down
the snout — Haw! — so. It is the laugh of laughs, the *risus purus*. (w, 48)

Thus Arsene mocks one of the most venerable passages in the entire history of Western thought. *Actus* becomes *risus*, act becomes laughter. It is
perhaps the only strategy for dealing with meaninglessness. But in the pathos of the moment, let us not forget to note that Mr. Knott's needing not
to need is the novel's equivalent for the aseity of the Deity which Aristotle calls his "self-dependent actuality." Nor should we forget to suggest
that the reader who does not like to see Mr. Knott's characteristic gesture
read as an allusion to the God of Aristotle may, if he likes, read it as an allusion to the God of Spinoza, who loves himself with an intellectual love.

The novel will not permit us simply to evaporate the person of Mr. Knott
into a symbol of God, however, for in spite of the enormous weight of al-
lusiveness he bears, he is still, in some sense, a human being. Still operating
on the symbolic level, however, we may suggest that he is The Rationalist
Philosopher, DeMalespinley. His wickedly misleading senses anesthetized,
he is Descartes in his poêle. Or he is Malebranche's Theodore inducting the
novice Aristes into the mysteries of pure thought, for which there is wanted
the proper setting: "Draw the curtain. This bright light will inconvenience
us a little and perhaps give too much lustre to certain objects. That is all
right. Be seated. Reject, Aristes, all that has come into your mind by the
means of the senses. Silence your imagination. Let all things in you be in
perfect silence. Forget also, if you can, that you have a body."[25]

He seems also to be a Berkeleyan atheist. There is no other way of accounting for the odd passages in the novel concerning his need to be witnessed. For if he is a Berkeleyan, and still does not believe that his being is
maintained as an idea in the divine mind, then it would be necessary for
him to hire two servants to witness him, and thereby guarantee that he will
continue to exist in *somebody's* percipere.

We have dressed Mr. Knott pretty heavily in the robes of symbolism,

though not, I hope, without justification. As a symbol of the God of the philosophers, or as the philosopher himself, he is an object of parody; but as an
image of the God of religion he is not. Instead, he is the object of yearning
and love: "Abandoned my little to find him. My little to learn him forgot.
My little rejected to have him. To love him my little reviled."

If we now divest him of his symbolic accretions to consider his "veritable
aspect" (a trick Watt never did turn [w, 211]), he stands before us as nothing more than a man. This is not to suggest that as such he is available and
intelligible either to Watt or to us, for even as a man, and perhaps especially
so, he is an enigma. He is enigmatic because he is unique; and if we look
back over Watt's history we find that those occasions which leave Watt
comfortless are precisely those in which he has to do with an incomparable
ejaculation of being, as for example a particular historical event (the Galls),
this concrete Thing that is present here and now (the pot), a new artistic
creation (Erskine's picture), or that unlikely conspissation of fluxions, a
person (Mr. Knott). Unable to be inferred from an hypothesis, unable to
be constructed out of sense data, Mr. Knott is not to be located as a term in
a series (the notion that he can is relegated to the "Addenda" [w, 253]),
nor can he be domesticated by the bridles, whips, and leashes of language,
but abides in his ineffability, at an infinite distance from Watt's need.

For Watt lives under Spinoza's dictum — curse, rather — *determinatio
negatio est*. This phrase is the formulation of the fact that in my being I am
alienated from every other being. Between myself and the other there lies
the abyss impassable even to intuition. Leibniz was unperturbed by the consequence of his theory of monads, that one monad or spiritual being could
have no effect upon the interiority of any other monad; and Berkeley was
not distressed by his assertion that we cannot know other spirits except by
their operations or effects. But for Watt, the distance between man and
man is what finally breaks his mind and his heart. "Sid by sid, two men. Al
day, part of nit. Dum, num, blin. Knot look at Wat? No. Wat look at
Knot? No. Wat talk to Knot? No. Knot talk to Wat? No. Wat den did us
do? Niks, niks, niks. Part of nit, all day. Two men, sid by sid" (w, 168).

The significance of *Watt* in the career of the man who, four years after
its completion and four years before its publication, told George Duthuit
that there is nothing to paint and nothing to paint with, should by now be
coming clear. The novel is Samuel Beckett's version of the human experience which Jean-Paul Sartre in *La Nausée* (1938) and Albert Camus in *Le
Mythe de Sisyphe* (1942) defined as the sense of the absurd. Existence off

the ladder is Beckett's phrase for what Sartre calls "contingency" and for what Camus describes as life after the "stage sets collapse." "Things are divorced from their names," wrote Sartre, as Watt found out to his terrible consternation.[26] Camus said, "Men, too, secrete the inhuman. At certain moments of lucidity, the mechanical aspect of their gestures, their meaningless pantomime makes silly everything that surrounds them."[27] In Mr. Knott as well as in Watt himself, Beckett exhibited the truth of the assertion. But from his novel and the fact of contingency, Sartre went on to construct an elaborate philosophical system, and from his essay and the fact of rebellion Camus developed a program for living the human life. Both in some sense manage to transcend the condition of the absurd, the one by understanding it, the other by rebelling against it.

Neither of these strategies is available to Beckett. Having entered the domain of Knott, the domain of the absurd, Beckett will not leave it, even though it seems that Watt does. From this time forward, Beckett must and will conduct the art of narrative fiction on premises which will not permit him to escape from the ascesis imposed by the irrationality of existence. These premises are two. The first is that, if God is not dead, he is at any rate unavailable to man and has abdicated from responsibility for the universe. He can no longer be counted on to work the appropriate miracle on the occasion of my unextended etc. wanting to impart a motion to my extended etc.; nor does the empirical evidence prove or even suggest that there is a pre-established harmony within the monad which I am (or Watt is) or among the infinite number of monads which constitute the world. The second premise is actually a corollary of the first: in the absence of the absolute (and in the presence of Spinoza's principle of negation), knowledge is impossible. Neither rational inferences from clear and distinct ideas (supposing for the moment that Watt was ever in possession of an idea with those attributes), nor empirical accumulations of data, nor — for that matter — historicism's recitation of all there is to be known concerning the precedent events (the history of the Lynch family), is capable of disclosing to Watt the thing itself; and before the pot, as before Knott, as indeed before Watt himself, Watt is reduced to a stupefied aphasia.

In a world such as Knott's, and with senses such as Watt's, the only possible statement is "perhaps," the only possible human style that of the sceptic — not the methodological doubt of Descartes, whose first operation is to prove the existence of the self and of God and thereafter the coherence of the universe, but the unqualified, uncontrollable Pyrrhonism that calls all things into question and is incapable of calling them back into the answer. Henceforward, the hero of Beckett's art is the Zetetic, whose nature is aporetic, and whose method is ephectic. He is the late-born scion of the intellectual family which counts among its ancestors Empedocles of Acragas, Democritus of Abdera, Pyrrho of Elis, and Sextus Empiricus. From this tradition come the two words which define the method and goal of the later fictional heroes: *epoché*, or suspension of judgment, and *ataraxia*, or peace. The first of the fictional characters to appear will be Molloy. He will be simply dressed, as befits a true Zetetic, and will carry with him the symbol of his vocation, a staff, which will in time be hypostatized as club, stick, gaff, and even a very short Venus pencil, sharpened at both ends.

IV

WHICH I
IS I?
THE TRILOGY

In speech the self-existent singleness of self-consciousness comes as such into existence, so that its particular individuality is something for others. Ego *qua* this particular pure ego is non-existent otherwise. . . . The I, that expresses itself, is apprehended as an ego; it is a kind of infection in virtue of which it establishes at once a unity with those who are aware of it, a spark that kindles a universal consciousness of self. That it is apprehended as a fact by others means *eo ipso* that its existence is itself dying away: this its otherness is taken back into itself; and its existence lies just in this, that, *qua* self-conscious Now, as it exists, it has no subsistence and that it subsists just through its disappearance. This disappearance is, therefore, itself *ipso facto* its continuance; it is its own cognition of itself, and its knowing itself as something that has passed into another self that has been apprehended and is universal.

Hegel

But who then am I? Let nobody ask. If it has not occurred to anybody to ask, I am relieved, for then I am over the worst of it. Besides, I am not worth asking about, for I am the most insignificant of all things. . . . I am "pure being" and therefore almost less than nothing. I am the pure being which is the accompaniment of everything yet never observable, because I am constantly *aufgehoben.*

Kierkegaard

The Self of everyday Dasein is the *they-self*, which we distinguish from the *authentic Self* — that is, from the Self which has been taken hold of in its own way. As they-self, the particular Dasein has been *dispersed* into the "they," and must first find itself. . . . If Dasein discovers the world in its own way and brings it close, if it discloses to itself its own authentic Being, then this discovery of the 'world' and this disclosure of Dasein are always accomplished as a clearing-away of concealments and obscurities, as a breaking up of the disguises with which Dasein bars its own way.

Heidegger

But what I am at this time, at the very moment of making my confessions, divers people desire to know, both who knew me and who knew me not — who have heard of or from me — but their ear is not at my heart, where I am whatsoever I am. They are desirous then of hearing me confess what I am within, where they can neither stretch eye, nor ear, nor mind; they desire it as those willing to believe — but will they understand? . . . I would therefore

86

confess what I know concerning myself; I will confess also what I know not concerning myself.
Augustine

Knock, and it shall be opened unto you.[1]
Matt. 7:7

I

◄ ► Consider the novelist at his work: a man, for preference, writing perhaps with a five- or six-faced wooden pencil, very short, perhaps not, on a piece of ordinary paper that is, who knows, unlined. He puts the pencil to the paper, moves the point over the paper by an immensely complicated process involving nerves, bones, muscles, the physics of friction, etc., and on the paper there appears

or

       Call me Ishmael

or

       Strether's first question, when he reached the hotel,

or even

       riverrun, past Eve and Adam's, from swerve of shore

       The sun shone, having no alternative, on the
       nothing new.

And as page piles upon manuscript page, lo! a world emerges, landscapes take shape, cities rise, characters — people — spring to life. The artist has sent forth his spirit to move upon the waters of the primal and unformed Being, and where there was formlessness now there is Form, where Potency, now Act: the mystery of creation, as old as the universe, is renewed, for man has created man. See Hamlet there, and Lear, and Huck and Lucifer and Nana, the company of Dickens and the tribe of Hawthorne; and we know them, each one, better than we know our neighbors — better even, perhaps, than we know ourselves. Or so the Introductions to Literature would have it.

But the Introductions have been composed by those, the gloss of whose surface evidences no collision with "the mess," no fracture of the principles of the science of drama or the craft of the novel. For them it is enough that the artist does a little better the same old thing, goes a little farther down the old (but never dreary) road; and they are satisfied if he disturbs only a certain order of the feasible: "records" a character's stream of consciousness; reports in detail upon phases of human life which hitherto, and for excellent reasons, were thought to be irrelevant or unimportant; or employs x number of languages and x^y number of dialects to hold the mirror up to nature sleeping.

Not so in the case of Samuel Beckett, of course; for as we have seen, by the time of his conversation with Duthuit, Beckett had given up the contemporaneous validation of art—"expressionism," as it happened to be then. Self and world, the two terms which establish the axioms of expressionism, are, said Beckett, either absent for the modern artist, or they are present but not available to him. In such a situation the problems of art cannot be defined in terms of the artist's efforts to articulate some sort of Crocean self, nor can they be defined in terms of the artist's effort to clarify or edify his—or some other—world. And though Beckett was not, in 1949, so far gone into nihilism that he could in fact subscribe to the utter absence of self and world, yet his formulation of the program of modern art neatly excludes the artist, or conceives of the artist as simply the instrument of technique. Let us hear him again. "Two things are established, however precariously: the aliment, from fruits on plates to low mathematics and self-commiseration, and its manner of dispatch. All that should concern us is the acute and increasing anxiety of the relation itself" (PTD, 124). The world—fruit, mathematics, self-commiseration—is still with the artist, but only as aliment, as nutrition for artistic assimilation. But the artist himself, as a self, is absent; and in his place we have only the "manner of dispatch"—technique disencumbered of the weight of its humanness.

Moreover, we must not make the error of thinking that Beckett would have this absent artist take "the aliment" for his concern. The aliment, and the manner in which the artist dispatches it, together compose a relationship, and it is this relationship to which the modern artist must attend. "All that should concern us is the acute and increasing anxiety of the relation itself," for this relation seems to be "shadowed more and more darkly by a sense of invalidity, of inadequacy." The questions which modern art must attempt to answer are not questions about the artist's capabilities, functions, or responsibilities, nor about the kind of world which is to be imitated, represented, or expressed in art. The questions for modern art are questions which threaten to repeal or invalidate the whole artistic enterprise. Not only are the world and the self unavailable as occasions for artistic expression: the relation between the two, which is the only valid concern, is increasingly suspect of being invalid, inadequate. Beckett is not asking whether modern art is or can be successful, for he is convinced that it cannot be. He praises Bram van Velde, let us remember, for being "the first to admit that to be an artist is to fail as no other dare fail, that failure is his world." Rather, Beckett is asking How, in the modern world, in the time of our great confusion — How is art possible at all?

Even *Watt* had not carried the matter to such a length. *Watt*, as Miss Hoefer and other critics have remarked, sets itself a problem in epistemology — How does one know the Other (things, God perhaps, man certainly)? The answer is that one cannot. One can know only the obvious, the superficial, the irrelevant. But if man cannot know man, what is the writer to write about? Indeed, the epistemological dead end to which *Watt* brought Beckett, we may surmise, was precisely what raised the issues debated (the word is perhaps too strong) in the "Three Dialogues." For surely what the expressionists mean by "the world" is the world *of man*, the world *for man*; else writers ought all become botanists or physicists or such. And if man and his world are unknowable, or, if knowable, once known, ineffable, the artist has indeed "nothing to paint." But we cannot stop here. For if one cannot know the Other, then it is surely ignorance which presumes to claim knowledge of the Self. Hence the incontrovertible fact that there is nothing to paint with. And there goes the other half of the aesthetics of expressionism.

The problem of knowledge raised in *Watt* left Beckett (this is of course speculation) with a world and a self both of which are unintelligible — absent; or present, but not available to the needs of the artist. Since this is the case, and since the artist is still, inexplicably, under an obligation to paint (or write), the artist has no choice but to give up the world and self as occasions for expression and turn to what is yet left him: the world as "aliment" and art as the manner of the aliment's "dispatch." That is to say, the artist is to concern himself with the relation between the world and art. Painting ought to be "about" the technique of painting. Writing, presumably, ought to concern itself with the process of writing — with the investigation of the writer writing.

Two years after the dialogue with Duthuit, Beckett published *Molloy* (1951), the first of the novels in the trilogy. *Molloy* is about a writer writing. "I am in my mother's room. . . . There's this man who comes every week. . . . He gives me money and takes away the pages. So many pages, so much money. Yes, I work now, a little like I used to, except that I don't know how to work any more." [2] In the second half of the novel a different character takes over, but he too is a writer writing: "My report will be long. Perhaps I shall not finish it. My name is Moran, Jacques. That is the name I am known by. I am done for" (TN, 122). A writer writing is also the hero of the second part of the trilogy, *Malone Dies*: "I write about myself with the same pencil and in the same exercise-book. . . . I hear the noise of my little finger as it glides over the paper and then that so different of the pencil following after" (TN, 283, 284). And the Unnamable, for whom the third division of the trilogy is named, is only slightly disturbed because he cannot give an adequate account of how he is able to report or record what he is saying.

Looked at from this point of view, the trilogy is the execution of the program which Beckett projected for modern art in his discussion with Duthuit. For in the trilogy, Beckett's art is concerned with "the acute and increasing anxiety of the relation" between the aliment and its dispatch, between all that is left to the artist of "the world" — that is, whatever it is that is "not-artist" and, by reason of its nutritive character, keeps the artist going (the obligation?) — and all that is left to the artist of the "self" — that is, artistic technique, the craft of writing, "form." Or, to put it another way, the trilogy is not, like *Watt*, about "nothing." (Even granting the imperance of Malone's italics, "*Nothing is more real than nothing*" [TN, 262], one still wants to know whether it is possible for a novelist who has written one book about "nothing" to write a second about the same thing.) Rather, the trilogy is "about" the writing of a novel when the author's sense of the nature of the human self and of human existence has invalidated the novelist's traditional material. Or, the trilogy is what a writer writes when, horrified and desperate, he realizes that for him there is nothing about which to write and nothing from which to write, the felt obligation to write continuing, however, to persist.

II

◄ ► We should not be surprised, then, to come upon a transposition and variation of this same theme of helplessness in Molloy's autobiography, for Molloy, like his creator, is a writer, and suffers under a similar condemnation to failure and a similar obligation: "Not to want to say, not to know what you want to say, not to be able to say what you think you want to say, and never to stop saying, or hardly ever, that is the thing to keep in mind, even in the heat of composition" (TN, 32). Moreover, like any other writer

Molloy worries about what he has written. The thirsty man who comes every Sunday to pick up the week's work has told him that he had begun all wrong. "He must be right. I began at the beginning, like an old ballocks. . . . Here's my beginning. . . . I took a lot of trouble with it. . . . Is what I do now any better?" (TN, 4). The question goes unanswered, but Molloy finally gets into his account, which proceeds along the following lines.

Having awakened at his usual hour, sometime between eleven o'clock and noon, Molloy looked out from his perch on an elevation, where he lay like Belacqua (or Sordello), and saw below him two men, A and C, approach each other, meet, and separate. He then resolved to go and see his mother . . .; and the rest of his story tells of the adventures and misadventures which befall him on his odyssey. His resolution is apparently effected, for his first words are "I am in my mother's room" (TN, 3). He does not know how he got there, however; for the last thing he remembers about his journey, and therefore the last thing he is able to recount, is that he collapsed into a ditch, where, unable to go any farther, he heard a voice telling him not to fret, that help was on the way.

Molloy's destination — his mother's room — is as reasonable a goal for the Questing Hero as most others — the soft arms of a Penelope, for example. And Molloy's journey does in fact resemble that of Homer's wanderer: Molloy encounters a shepherd, as Odysseus had encountered the pastoral Cyclops (TN, 33); he is the cause of the death, not of the Oxen of the Sun, but of a venerable animal, Teddy, a dog "uniformly yellow" (TN, 39ff.); he is detained by Sophia Lousse (or Loy), a Circe whose "miserable molys" were insufficient to hold him there permanently (TN, 60); there is an episode which could perhaps be called "The Wandering Rocks" (Molloy's sucking stones [TN, 90–98]); another involving a kind of Nausicaa (TN, 98); and so on.

Molloy, however, prefers to understand his travels — his life as a whole, in fact — in terms of a pattern which we have already come across in *Watt*. He has, after all, descended from a high place or mount, made a more or less triumphal entry into the city seated upon his bicycle (Molloy too is a Cartesian hero, and an ass, or a colt, the foal of an ass, will not do for him), was arrested, forced to walk through the streets ("Was there one among them," Molloy mused at the time, "to put himself in my place . . .?") He has been arraigned before "a very strange official" (Caiaphas) who threatened him and asked after his identity, to which Molloy replied nothing; was remanded to a guardroom with other "malefactors"; attended by a kind of Magdalen, who offered him a sop of green tea and dry bread which he rejected; etc. And in contemplating this period of his life, Molloy says:

And of that life too I shall tell you perhaps one day, the day I know that when I thought I knew I was merely existing and that passion without form or stations will have devoured me down to the rotting flesh itself and that when I know that I know nothing, am only crying out, . . . more or less piercingly, more or less openly. Let me cry out then. (TN, 29)

And he cries out, but not Eli, Eli. Later in the work, Molloy makes much the same evaluation in much the same language: "But I am human, I fancy, and my progress [through the woods] suffered, . . . was changed, saving your presence, to a veritable calvary, with no limit to its stations and no hope of crucifixion, though I say it myself, and no Simon" (TN, 103).

Such cryings out, and such self-commiserations, though not uncommon, are yet by no means the rule in Molloy's discourse. He is more often occupied by the telling of his story, a telling which evidences a lively sense of humor. He attempts to explain (he has just mentioned Watt, and the shadow of the solipsist falls over Molloy's explanation) the difficulties which beset him once his good leg starts to go bad:

For when the two legs shorten at the same time, and at the same speed, then all is not lost, no. But when one shortens, and the other not, then you begin to be worried. . . . For I didn't know which foot to land on, when I came down. . . . Follow me carefully. The stiff leg hurt me, admittedly, I mean the old stiff leg, and it was the other which I normally used as a pivot, or prop. But now this latter, as a result of its stiffening I suppose, and the ensuing commotion among nerves and sinews, was beginning to hurt me even more than the other. What a story, God send I don't make a balls of it. For the old pain, do you follow me, . . . (TN, 101)

Or he describes how, immediately after he left the seashore, on his way, of course, to his mother, his "weak points," previously unimportant, began to "gallop"; and it is at this period that he fixes "the dastardly desertion of my toes, so to speak in the thick of the fray" (TN, 106).

It is his sense of humor which makes Molloy supportable, even agreeable to the reader. For physically, Molloy is repulsive, and grows more so as he continues on his journey. He is also obscene and blasphemous, cruel, arbitrary. There is even the suspicion of murder (his victim is the "charcoal-burner," whom he knocked down with a blow of his crutch and then kicked vigorously). He is, as we have already noticed, deeply infected by the Weltschmerz — and, if one may say so, by a Dingschmerz as well —

common to Beckett's heroes; and he is indignified and embarrassed by the possession of a mind ("I was not purely physical, I lacked something" [TN, 114]).

None of these facts enlightens Molloy's peculiar mystery, however. That mystery, of course, has to do with his quest: Why must he see his mother? Who is she? What does he expect to accomplish by seeing her again? Molloy himself has no answer to these difficult and important questions. If he had not attempted to see her, if, for example, he had remained in the forest instead of pressing on, he would have had, he says, the feeling of "going against an imperative," or of "committing a fault, almost a sin" (TN, 114). He does his best to explain, but in the process obfuscates as much as he clarifies.

And of myself, all my life, I think I had been going to my mother, with the purpose of establishing our relations on a less precarious footing. And when I was with her, and I often succeeded, I left her without having done anything. And when I was no longer with her I was again on my way to her, hoping to do better the next time. And when I appeared to give up and to busy myself with something else, or with nothing at all any more, in reality I was hatching my plans and seeking the way to her house. (TN, 115–116)

Molloy half realizes his aim; for upon waking from the coma which befell him in the ditch at the edge of the forest, he discovers that he is in fact in his mother's room. "I have her room. I sleep in her bed. I piss and shit in her pot. I have taken her place. I must resemble her more and more. All I need now is a son" (TN, 4). But nowhere in the room is there to be discovered the "poor old uniparous whore" — as Molloy, with a lamentable lack of delicacy, refers to her — who is responsible for his filiation, who "brought me into the world, through the hole in her arse if my memory is correct. First taste of the shit" (TN, 16). Molloy's sense of humor utterly fails him when he contemplates the human being who was responsible for setting him forth on the Via Dolorosa which is his existence.

The second half of the novel is the "report" written by Jacques Moran dealing with his attempt to find the lost Molloy. Moran is an "agent" in the employ of a potent and mysterious personage named Youdi; and on a certain August morning, at about eleven o'clock, there appears in Moran's garden a messenger from Youdi, Gaber by name, who gives Moran his instructions and thereby initiates the quest for Molloy.

In the course of the search the Seeker is progressively assimilated to the Sought, but before this the two men are very dissimilar. Molloy is oriented to his mother, Moran to his son, "thirteen or fourteen at the time. He was big and strong for his age. His intelligence seemed at times little short of average" (TN, 124). Where Molloy is homeless and isolated, Moran lives in solid bourgeois comfort: the house is tended by an old woman, Martha; he keeps bees and a small flock of chickens; is only slightly chafed by a minimal catholic Christianity. His bunch of keys weighs over a pound, and not a "door, not a drawer in my house but the key to it goes with me, wherever I go." Symptomatic of his obsession with order, efficiency, precision, the keys are attached to Moran's braces by a very long chain; and it is a black day for Moran when he loses them. He attempts to indoctrinate his son with an ethic which hinges creakily on Goethe's dictum, *Sollst entbehren*, and on a "horror of the body and its functions." Tyrannical and overbearing, self-centered but dependent on others (his son, his housekeeper, Youdi), Moran is a humorless, punctilious, offensive individual. Jacques Jr. has complained of a stomach-ache:

A stomach-ache! Have you a temperature I said. I don't know, he said. Find out, I said. He was looking more and more stupefied. Fortunately I rather enjoyed dotting my i's. Go and get the minute-thermometer, I said, out of the second right-hand drawer of my desk, counting from the top, take your temperature and bring me the thermometer. I let a few minutes go by and then, without being asked, repeated slowly, word for word, this rather long and difficult sentence. . . . As he went out, . . . I added jocosely, You know which mouth to put it in? I was not averse, in conversation with my son, to jests of doubtful taste, in the interests of his education. (TN, 157–58)

After some fifty pages of preparations and meditations, Moran and his son set out "to see about Molloy." On the way Moran encounters a variety of shadowy and semimythical beings (there is for him, as for Theseus, a Corynetes or Club-bearer); and one of these, a man whose face momentarily resembles his own, Moran is obliged to kill. Before the trip is over Moran loses the use of a leg; buys a bicycle which he must patch up and which is stolen by his son when he deserts; loses and then finds his precious keys; and exhausts his provisions. He never does reach Molloy, but collapses within the sight of the lights of Bally, the town where, according to his information, Molloy resides. There Gaber finds him again and reads him Youdi's new instructions: "Moran, Jacques, home, instanter." So home he goes, mission unaccomplished, and after a winter-long trek arrives in a condition of incredible and almost complete ruin at the place he had set out from. There he finds that his keys no longer work, Martha the housekeeper is gone (Jacques Jr. returns eventually), and the hens and bees are dead. He decides to "clear out," but before he does, and just a year from the time he had set out to find Molloy, he writes his report.

No doubt of it, the stories of Molloy and Moran are obscure, and leave the reader darkling. What men or gods are these? What mad pursuit? What gongs and voices? What wild despair? Hugh Kenner, bemused, ponders the possibility that perhaps "a Molloy is what a Moran turns into when he goes looking for a Molloy." [3] Edith Kern argues the same, though with more assurance. Molloy is Moran's subconscious, antithetical self, she says, and, as Moran seeks his quarry, he slowly changes into that other self and comes to resemble Molloy. Moran-Molloy is an example of what Joseph Campbell has named the "one hero in two aspects"; and it is the task of this hero to discover and assimilate his opposite and unsuspected self. [4] The hypothesis is worth examining.

Even before he begins his search, Moran knows a surprising amount about Molloy, and even "Mother Molloy, or Mollose, was not foreign" to him. However, he is ignorant of the circumstances through which he had acquired this knowledge, and goes so far as to suggest that perhaps he had invented Molloy (TN, 150). Moran knows that Molloy "had very little room," and this would be the case if Molloy is that very small portion of the subconscious which finds expression in the daylight world which is Moran's environment. Molloy's "time too was limited." So also is Moran's, for he complains that his life is running out through some unknown breach; and one of his favorite parables for human life is that of the dayfly. Moreover, Moran ponders his "natural end" and asks if his own would not be at the same time as Molloy's. What follows in Moran's recitation (he is lying in bed, where he can "best pierce the outer turmoil's veil, discern my quarry") of what he knows about Molloy seems to be a deliberate attempt to personify or caricature the popular conception of the Id:

[Molloy] hastened incessantly on, as if in despair, towards extremely close objectives. Now, a prisoner, he hurled himself at I know not what narrow confines, and now, hunted, he sought refuge near the centre.
He panted. He had only to rise up within me for me to be filled with panting.
Even in open country he seemed to be crashing through jungle. He did not so much walk as charge. In spite of this he advanced but slowly. He swayed, to and fro, like a bear.
He rolled his head, uttering incomprehensible words.

He was massive and hulking, to the point of misshapenness. And, without being black, of a dark colour.

He was forever on the move. I had never seen him rest. Occasionally he stopped and glared furiously about him. (TN, 151–52).

The hypothesis propounded by Miss Kern appears to be entirely plausible. Molloy, the subconscious, antithetical, or Dionysian self, is sought out and assimilated by Moran, the conscious, thetic, or Apollonian self; the novel as a whole is cyclical, and Moran's quest is continued in Molloy's. "Thus Moran-become-Molloy, the antithetical self of his subconscious, proceeds even further on the road towards the core of his artistic existence: his mother's room." [5]

Now all this would be very well, except for one thing: Moran's quest is a failure. He never encounters Molloy. Rather, he never encounters the Molloy whose image he presented, the Molloy who panted and who had only to rise up in Moran for him (Moran) to be filled with panting. Moran himself is aware of the fact that he may be in error as to the identity of Molloy, for he recognizes that "Between the Molloy I stalked within me thus and the true Molloy, . . . the resemblance cannot have been great." Indeed, Moran realizes that there is not just one Molloy: "The fact was there were three, no, four Molloys. He that inhabited me, my caricature of same, Gaber's and the man of flesh and blood somewhere awaiting me. To these I would add Youdi's. . . ." (TN, 154).

At least five Molloys, then ("For there was this about Youdi, that he changed his mind with great facility"; and with every change of mind there appears a new Molloy); and if Moran encounters and assimilates Molloy, it is not the Molloy whom Moran "caricatures" as he lies in bed and tells over what he knows about his quarry. Finally, Moran, in the last stages of his journey home, remarks, "And with regard to the Obidil [an obvious anagram on "Libido"], of whim [sic] I have refrained from speaking, until now, and whom I so longed to see face to face, all I can say with regard to him is this, that I never saw him, either face to face or darkly, perhaps there is no such person, that would not greatly surprise me" (TN, 220).[6]

Although the interpretation of Molloy as Moran's subconscious or antiself is not wholly accurate, a part of it still must be retained. Moran's "caricature" of his quarry seems to indicate that Moran himself believed, at least before he set out on his search, that he was seeking a person so unlike himself as to be reasonably described as an "antiself." Further, if "Obidil" means "Libido," and if the caricature is meant as a description of the Id, then Moran believes — still wrongly — that the object of his quest is himself, his truer, larger, complete Self.

He is mistaken, then, in the nature of his quarry and in the nature of his quest. This, however, does not necessarily mean that he fails to encounter Molloy. It means only that the Molloy he seeks is quite different from the Molloy he finds. I suggest that in fact Moran does find Molloy, but fails to recognize him; and I suggest further that the story of their encounter is told twice, once in Molloy's version and once in Moran's. But just as the Found is so different from what the Finder had expected as to be unrecognizable, so the two versions of the finding are so different that they can hardly be recognized as being the same incident. Here is Molloy's version.

I had a certain number of encounters in this forest, naturally, where does one not, but nothing to signify. I notably encountered a charcoal-burner. I might have loved him, I think, if I had been seventy years younger. But it's not certain. . . . He was all over me, begging me to share his hut, believe it or not. A total stranger. Sick with solitude probably. I say charcoal-burner, but I really don't know. I see smoke somewhere. . . . A long dialogue ensued, interspersed with groans. I could not ask him the way to my town, the name of which escaped me still. I asked him the way to the nearest town. . . . He did not know. He was born in the forest probably and had spent his whole life there. I asked him to show me the nearest way out of the forest. I grew eloquent. His reply was exceedingly confused. Either I didn't understand a word he said, or he didn't understand a word I said, or he knew nothing, or he wanted to keep me near him. . . . [When] I made to go, he held me back by the sleeve. So I smartly freed a crutch and dealt him a good dint on the skull. (TN, 110–11)

Here is Moran's version of the same incident:

It was evening. I had lit my fire [Moran the charcoal-burner] and was watching it take when I heard myself hailed. . . . There I was face to face with a dim man, dim of face and dim of body, because of the dark. Put it there, he said. . . . And indeed there reigned between his various parts great harmony and concord, and it could be truly said that his face was worthy of his body, and vice versa. . . . What are you doing in this God-forsaken place, he said, you unexpected pleasure. . . . [He] was precisely the kind of pest I had thought he was, . . . Can you tell me [presumably, "the way to the nearest town"], he said. I shall have to describe him briefly. . . . He was on the small side, but thick-set. He wore a thick navy-blue suit (double-breasted) of hideous cut and a pair of outrageously wide black shoes, with the toe-caps higher than the uppers. . . . Do you happen to know [presumably, "the nearest way out of the forest"], he said. The fringed extremities of a dark muffler, seven feet long at least, wound several times round his neck, hung down his back. He had a narrow-brimmed dark blue felt hat on his head, with a fish-hook and an artificial fly stuck in the band. . . . Do you hear me? he said. But all this was nothing compared to the face which I regret to say vaguely resembled my own. . . . He thrust his hand at me. . . . I can still see the hand coming towards me, pallid, opening and closing. . . . I do not know what happened then. But a little later, perhaps a long time later, I found him stretched on the ground, his head in a pulp. . . . I bent over him. As I did so I realized my leg was bending normally. He no longer resembled me. . . . His legs too were on the stiff side, but there was still some play in the hip joints, fortunately. (TN, 203–6)

Moran is identifiable only by his proximity to a fire; Molloy by his "dim-ness," perhaps his questions, and his two stiff legs. But in a novel by Beckett this is enough, it is more than enough. And only in a novel by Beckett can the two major characters slay one another and then retire each to his room to write each his own version of the inconsequential, insignificant episode.

That Moran is a writer and that his search for Molloy is a parabolic pres-entation of a certain facet of the task or art of writing seems a reasonable conclusion to be drawn from the second half of the novel. But Moran is not just any writer, not just any of Youdi's "agents"; for he counts among the "clients" or "patients" of his previous assignments persons whose acquaint-ance we have made in other settings.

I lost interest in my patients, once I had finished with them. I may even truth-fully say I never saw one of them again. . . . Oh the stories I could tell you, if I were easy. What rabble in my head, what a gallery of moribunds. Murphy, Watt, Yerk, Mercier and all the others. . . . Stories, stories. I have not been able to tell them. I shall not be able to tell this one. (TN, 185–86)

Moran has just mentioned Yerk; Mercier is a character in one of Beckett's unpublished works, *Mercier et Camier*; Murphy and Watt we know, if only to nod to. Although we shall not grasp at the proffered conclusion, shall continue to refer to the author-hero of the second half of *Molloy* as Moran, we shall have occasion to take advantage of it and account for some of Moran's statements by referring to Beckett's ideas.

As Author, Moran is a pseudo creator, a demiurge, who through the power of his craft brings into existence what was not: in the terms of quest, he is a deliverer or a hunter. Moran in bed meditates upon the nature and importance of his mission and on the problems posed by the Molloy affair:

Far from the world, its clamours, frenzies, bitterness and dingy light, I pass judgment on it and on those, like me, who are plunged in it beyond recall, and on him who has need of me to be delivered, who cannot deliver myself. . . . There somewhere man is too, vast conglomerate of all of nature's kingdoms, as lonely and as bound. And in that block the prey is lodged and thinks himself a being apart. Anyone would serve. But I am paid to seek. I arrive, he comes away. His life has been nothing but a waiting for this, to see himself preferred, to fancy himself damned, blessed, to fancy himself everyman, above all others. (TN, 148)

The prey who thinks himself a being apart is for Author Moran a character who can be tracked down, caught, and brought back alive to be exhibited in the *Tiergarten* of his art: in this specific case, the prey is Molloy. But being a man, or a kind of man, Molloy can also aspire to the prerogatives of humanity — blessedness, damnation. To find, liberate, very nearly create Molloy is the high vocation which is Moran's.

The passage is of course ironic, and the irony results from the discrepancy between Moran's inflated conception of himself and of his powers, and his actual ineptness and miserable failure in his assigned task. Moran continues his bed-thoughts: "For it was only by transferring it to this atmosphere, how shall I say, of finality without end, why not, that I could venture to consider the work I had on hand. For where Molloy could not be, nor Moran either for that matter, there Moran could bend over Molloy" (TN, 149).[7] In bed, yes, in the imagination, the author sees himself victorious; but in the quest itself, in the very act of writing, of trying to capture the prey, the artist is doomed to failure. And the irony is renewed and reenforced when, in Moran's version of the encounter, he remarks that he "bent over" the body of his victim — not Molloy delivered but Molloy dead.

Agent Moran is employed by one Youdi, whose instructions are transmitted to Moran by the messenger Gaber. Youdi's name seems to be an inversion of the phonemes in "Dieu"; and Gaber's name is perhaps a contraction of "Gabriel," "man of God," he who made the Annunciation to Mary. Such a speculative interpretation of these names is, if not correct, at least appropriate; for if Youdi is God, then Author Moran as well as Agent Moran comes under the special blessing and direction of the Divine. Moran is not explicit in this matter, but he believes that his task is of a rare and enduring significance. "For what I was doing I was doing neither for Molloy, who mattered nothing to me, nor for myself, of whom I despaired, but on behalf of a cause which, while having need of us to be accomplished, was in its essence anonymous, and would subsist, haunting the minds of men, when its miserable artisans should be no more. It will not be said, I think, that I did not take my work to heart" (TN, 154). This moving passage, it should be noted, is the work of a man who also takes the job of writing to heart, for in describing the period of his life before the Molloy affair, Moran is once more the man who suffered it. It is, he says, one of the features of the "penance," as he calls his report, that he may not come straight to the heart of the matter; but "that must again be unknown to me which is no longer so and that again fondly believed which then I fondly believed, at my setting out. . . . [And I observe this rule] with such zeal that I am far more he who finds than he who tells what he has found" (TN, 179).

If Moran believed, fondly or not, that before his setting out his work was conducted under the auspices of the Numinous, that belief ends in as ruinous a condition as Moran himself at the end of his quest. The passage in celebration of the anonymous cause is probably the zenith of Moran's religiosity; thereafter he declines into scepticism. Moran is describing the "vast organization" of which he, as agent, is a member.

But to me at least, who knew how to listen to the falsetto of reason, it was obvious that we [Gaber and himself] were perhaps alone in doing what we did. Yes, in my moments of lucidity I thought it possible. And, to keep nothing from you, this lucidity was so acute at times that I came even to doubt the existence of Gaber himself. And if I had not hastily sunk back into my darkness I might have gone to the extreme of conjuring away the chief [Youdi] too and regarding myself as solely responsible for my wretched existence. (TN, 144)

From scepticism he sinks into despair (the parable of the dayfly [TN, 201] and the dance of the bees [TN, 231]); and to theological pruriency ("Did Mary conceive through the ear, as Augustine and Adobard assert?" [TN, 227]). As he writes about his experiences he expresses his disenchantment with the Divine in stronger language, and declines from pruriency to revulsion ("I don't like men and I don't like animals. As for God, he is beginning to disgust me" [TN, 141]); and collapses ultimately and inevitably into a sullen blasphemy: "There are men and there are things, to hell with animals. And with God" (TN, 225).

The record of Moran's progress to godlessness is a concise history of that portion of Western art which begins with the nameless monks who illuminated missals and books of hours in devotion to an ultimate Cause, and ends with nineteenth-century naturalism and twentieth-century "absurdism." We should notice, however, that it is in keeping with Beckett's assertion that for the modern artist there is no principle, no cause, which provides an ultimate validation for his work: there is nothing to paint, and nothing to paint with.

Even for Beckett, however, there is a kind of motive energy, which he called, for the benefit and in the language of Duthuit, the "obligation to express." This obligation appears in *Molloy* as "the voice"; and it is this voice which takes over the seat of authority after Moran has evicted Youdi-Dieu. Moran is explaining why he must write a report.

I am still obeying orders, if you like, but no longer out of fear. No, I am still afraid, but simply from force of habit. And the voice I listen to needs no Gaber to make it heard. For it is within me and exhorts me to continue to the end the faithful servant I have always been, of a cause that is not mine, and patiently fulfil in all its bitterness my calamitous part. . . . Yes, it is rather an ambiguous voice and not always easy to follow, in its reasonings and decrees. But I follow it . . . in this sense, that I know what it means, and in this sense, that I do what it tells me. (TN, 178)

Youdi ultimately asks Moran for a report, but it is out of obedience to the voice and not to the "chief" that Moran writes (TN, 239, 240).

Moran thinks of his writing as a kind of "pensum" — a task imposed by a schoolmaster; but when he has completed his task, undergone his punishment, the erring schoolboy is permitted a recess. "It also tells me, this voice I am only just beginning to know, that the memory of this work brought scrupulously to a close will help me to endure the long anguish of vagrancy and freedom" (TN, 178). To write, for Moran, is both penance and a means of grace, as it were; for through it he expiates some unknown sin, and, at the same time, he is in some mysterious way renewed. At the conclusion of his report, Moran says that the voice told him to write it. Then he asks, "Does this mean I am freer now than I was? I do not know. I shall learn" (TN, 240). Moran's report is only superficially his account of his effort to "deliver" Molloy. At bottom it is the means which he has taken to deliver himself.

So ends, but for four sentences, the report which Moran had begun with these words: "It is midnight. The rain is beating on the windows. I am calm." But with the last four sentences Moran demolishes the whole structure which he had so carefully erected. For these last sentences read: "Then I went back into the house and wrote, It is midnight. The rain is beating on the windows. It was not midnight. It was not raining" (TN, 240). For nearly one hundred and twenty pages the reader has given himself in that act of acquiescence which is demanded by the novel as a narrative, and in the last two sentences he finds that he has been gulled, seduced, betrayed. It either was or was not raining, and one way or another Moran is lying. We must refuse to credit his report, for it appears to be nothing but a mere fiction.

But no sooner do we start to make these objections, to complain about a violation of trust, and to invoke the inviolability of the principle of the suspension of disbelief, than the strategy of the novel begins to come clear. Of course Moran's report is a fiction: no claim has been entered to the contrary. Beckett has given us a narrator who tells us a story and then tells us that he has told a story. And something like this should have been expected from the man who insisted that it is no longer possible to "express." Until the last eight words, the second half of *Molloy* stood in danger of being art. From so dreadful a fate the author has rescued it by calling attention to the fact that the novel is a deception and a lie. He has, indeed, underlined the absurdity of the novel's implicit claim to our serious attention; and in so doing he seems to be suggesting that the novel's value (if that is the right word) is to be discerned in some other dimension than that of its capacity for "expressing" a world or the author's self. Indeed, in any expressionistic sense, *Molloy* is not a novel at all. Rather, it is an account of the way in which an "author" (Moran) failed again in his effort to write.

But we have neglected him for whom the novel is named. Who is Molloy? The answer, I believe, is that Molloy is a character. That is, just as Moran is a writer in search of a character to put in a story, so Molloy is a character in search of an author who has a story capable of accommodating him. The little episode which is the prologue to the novel, the episode of the encounter between A and C, announces the theme of the rest of the work, for it is the story of the brief meeting of A (Author) and C (Character).[8] So when Molloy speaks — in vulgar detail — of having taken his mother's place, he means that he, a character, has usurped the place of his "mother," the person who brought him into the world — that, for him, being an author. And Molloy is of course the author of his own story.

Molloy has no mother because he has no author. And why has he no Mother-Author? Because he killed him. Inadvertently, of course: Molloy took him for a charcoal-burner.

We may complicate further. Where did Molloy get that little silver thing which consisted of "two crosses, joined, at their points of intersection, by a bar," which resembled a tiny sawing horse? He got it at Sophia Lousse's (Loy's) house (TN, 82). And what is this little silver thing? It is a knife rest. Whose? Moran's (TN, 155). But who could have stolen it? Jacques Jr. Then who is Jacques Jr.? Molloy: unless Moran himself took it, in which case Moran is Molloy.

However we adjust the intricate mergings and separations of the major figures in *Molloy*, the main theme abides: A character (Molloy) seeks an author who will put him in a story, find him a home, and so bring to an end his ceaseless wandering. Unable to find one, he himself turns author and takes the author's (mother's) place. An author (Moran), driven by a kind of divine compulsion, seeks a character who will show the author his true self and so set him free. And just as the character finds no story and no one able to write, and must finally save himself by turning author, so the author, finding no one to write about but still obliged to write, must turn character and suffer himself to be written about.

III

◄ ► Let us return for a moment to the scene of the writer at his work: a man, writing something, on something, with something. No fruit on plates needed here, no draped or undraped human companion to clutter the room with talk, no pile of stone, no mound of clay, no piano to test a modulation: nothing at all really to look at or hear or taste or smell or touch. Just someone to write, something to write on, something to write with.

Something to write on: a clay tablet, parchment, paper, an empty notebook, an exercise book — a child's exercise book will do. And something to write with: typewriter, pen, quill and ink, anything; even a very short five-sided Venus pencil, hard lead, sharpened at both ends. And of course someone to write: reasonably alive, at least from the waist up (he has no need of feet, could just as well be lying in bed); with the use of his hands, or of one hand; and possessed of a sum of experience not so ample as to confuse overmuch a minimal mnemonic apparatus nor so meager as to incapacitate an occasional fanciful juxtaposition or extension of events.

The picture is of course that of Malone, the writer reduced to the Least Possible. The hero of *Malone Dies*, the second novel in the trilogy, is lying, dying, in bed, in a "plain private room apparently, in what appears to be a plain ordinary house" (TN, 248). He is not, he feels, in a hospital or a madhouse. There is a cupboard in the room which Malone has never looked into, and in a corner in a little heap are his "possessions." He has a long stick with which he can rummage in the heap, draw out certain items to himself, and send them back. Out of a window in the room he can see roofs and sky, can catch a glimpse of street; he can even see into a room of the house across the way. His needs and wants are cared for: an old woman brings him regularly a bowl of soup (he is toothless); and his chamber pot is emptied from time to time. "What matters is to eat and excrete. Dish and pot, dish and pot, these are the poles" (TN, 251). His body is nearly impotent: there is virtually nothing that he can do. He seems to be paralyzed from the waist down; his arms, once they are in position, can exert a little force, but he finds it very difficult to guide them. His head he can move, but his sight and hearing are very bad. He lies on his back under some blankets.

Malone's is the condition of almost complete privation. Both his world and his own body are lost and absent, or — if present — unavailable for his use. There remains to him nothing but the minimal requirements for doing what he has done in the past and continues to do now. He has left a mind, an arm together with its attached hand and fingers, a child's exercise book, and a short — a very short — Venus lead pencil, sharpened at both ends. It is not much, but for a writer as committed to his work as is Malone, it is enough, it is a great plenty.

So having nothing else to do, and knowing nothing else, Malone writes. He thinks about the timetable of his death, proposes a tentative schedule, amends it, and finally decides on a five-part program. He will discuss his present state; he will tell himself three stories — one about a man and woman ("there is not matter there for two"), then one about an animal, and finally one about a thing, "a stone probably"; and he will conclude the whole with an inventory of his possessions. (An occasional "interlude," he adds is also to be feared.) In such a state of superb order does Malone prepare to leave the world.

The description of his present condition raises no problem, but Malone recognizes a certain hazard in connection with the stories. He is resolved to let himself die quietly, "without rushing things"; and in his delicate condition this means that he must not become excited, lest he hasten the inevitable. He will not "weigh upon the balance any more, one way or the other," whether to will his own death or to struggle to preserve the modicum of life which yet remains to him.

I shall be neutral and inert. No difficulty there. Throes are the only trouble, I must be on my guard against throes. . . . Of course I still have my little fits of impatience, from time to time, I must be on my guard against them. . . . Without exaggeration to be sure, quietly crying and laughing, without working myself up into a state. Yes, I shall be natural at last, I shall suffer more, then less, without drawing any conclusions, I shall pay less heed to myself, I shall be neither hot nor cold any more, I shall be tepid, I shall die tepid, without enthusiasm. (TN, 243–44)

The new stories he is going to tell himself are not to be like the old ones. The new stories are to be neither beautiful nor ugly: "they will be calm, there will be no ugliness or beauty or fever in them any more, they will be almost lifeless, like the teller." Having thus willed the amputation of his will, Malone embarks upon his program. He gets handsomely through the description of his present state and begins his first story. It is the story of Saposcat, or Sapo for short. It is a dull story ("What tedium," interjects Malone, "This is awful"); and he frequently interrupts himself to engage in one of the "interludes" he had feared would be necessary. After an especially long digression (TN, 297–310), Malone returns to the narrative, but is so displeased with his hero's name that he changes it to Macmann (TN, 314). Shortly thereafter he suffers the first death-spasm, later a second. Alarmed, he quickly makes inventory of his possessions, then continues the story of Macmann, which now takes place in a mental institution called the House of St. John of God. He interrupts the story again to report that he has had a visitor, and, finally, in a series of narrative gasps, falls into silence and expires.

Malone's relation to the two protagonists of the first part of the trilogy is as complex and obscure as Moran's relation to Molloy. Like Molloy, Malone does not know how he got to where he finds himself, but speculates that it was in an ambulance, a vehicle of some kind certainly (TN, 248–49; cf. 3). He vaguely recollects fragments of his antesupinated life: that he had walked for the greater part of it; that he had lived in a coma; that while in a forest he had been stunned by a blow on the head and had lost consciousness ("never any great loss"). From these hints the reader is likely — let us get it over with — to see in Malone the next personification of the hypostatic "I" whose previous names had been given as "Molloy" and "Moran." That is, Malone appears to be the "charcoal-burner" whom Molloy met and beat in the forest (cf. TN, 111); and while the charcoal-burner is Moran, Moran seems to disintegrate into Molloy; and Malone, in turn, seems to be merely Molloy at his last gasp. In the inventory of his "possessions" Malone mentions a club, stained with blood ("but insufficiently, insufficiently. I have defended myself, ill, but I have defended myself" [TN, 342]), and one is reminded of the man with a club whom Moran met (TN, 198), and of the "dim man" — presumably Molloy — whom Moran found "stretched on the ground, his head in a pulp" (TN, 205). Among his possessions Malone also notes the cap of his bicycle bell and half a crutch, both of which are reminiscent of Molloy's story; but he also notes the absence of an item he mistakenly believed he retained — a needle stuck at each end into a cork; and this, perhaps, is what Moran's little silver knife rest has degenerated into. Finally, Malone's story of the visit made to him sounds suspiciously like that of Molloy's visit to his mother (TN, 17–20), with this difference, that it is told from Mother's point of view.

I felt a violent blow on the head. He had perhaps been there for some time. . . . His mouth opened, his lips worked, but I heard nothing. He might just as well have said nothing. . . . I had a clear view of him. Black suit of antiquated cut, or perhaps come back into the fashion, black tie, snow-white shirt, heavily starched clown's cuffs almost entirely covering the hands, oily black hair. . . . A folding-rule, together with a fin of white handkerchief, emerged from the breast pocket. . . . He went a first time, came back some hours later, then left for good. (TN, 370–71) [9]

This description of Molloy, if it is of Molloy, is about as accurate as Molloy's of Moran as charcoal-burner, or as Moran's of Molloy as the dim man. If the description is meant to be of Molloy, however, then Malone is Molloy's mother. And in the sense that, as his "agent," Moran is responsible for rescuing Molloy and is therefore his author or creator and therefore his "mother," then Malone is also Moran.[10]

And yet it would be very wrong to insist that Malone be identified with one or the other of the two earlier figures, or even with them both; for Malone also transcends them both. He implies that their existence is dependent on his — and not only theirs, but the existences of others as well.

And if I ever stop talking it will be because there is nothing more to be said, even though all has not been said, even though nothing has been said. But let us leave these morbid matters and get on with that of my demise, in two or three days if I remember rightly. Then it will be all over with the Murphys, Merciers, Molloys, Morans and Malones, unless it goes on beyond the grave. (TN, 323)

How many, he asks himself, has he killed by hitting them on the head or setting fire to them? "Off-hand I can only think of four, all unknowns, I never knew anyone." Murphy is of course the one to whom he set fire; Molloy and Moran each did away with one (with one another); for the fourth, Malone thinks perhaps of himself. There is also a fifth, Malone realizes — the butler in London who cut his throat with a razor (cf. M, 132–36).

In some sense, then, perhaps the same as that in which they were the "clients" or "patients" of Moran, all the characters of the earlier works are the creatures of Malone. Malone thinks of them as his playmates and of writing as "playing."

I never knew how to play, till now. I longed to, but I knew it was impossible. And yet I often tried. I turned on all the lights, I took a good look all round, I began to play with what I saw. People and things ask nothing better than to play, certain animals too. All went well at first, they all came to me, pleased that someone should want to play with them. . . . But it was not long before I found myself alone, in the dark. That is why I gave up trying to play and took to myself for ever shapelessness and speechlessness, incurious wondering, darkness, long stumbling with outstretched arms, hiding. (TN, 245)

Malone's career as a writer has been, in his own estimation, a general failure. But he is also astute enough to recognize the reason for his lack of success. The reason is that he has been too grave, too serious, too earnest in his work; he has not been able to "play."

Live and invent. I have tried. I must have tried. Invent. It is not the word. Neither is live. No matter. I have tried. While within me the wild beast of earnestness padded up and down, roaring, ravening, rending. I have done that. And all alone, well hidden, played the clown, all alone, hour after hour, motionless, often standing, spellbound, groaning. That's right, groan. I couldn't play. (TN, 265) [11]

Because of this inability to be less than earnest, he could not permit either himself or his creatures to continue in their happy, pointless play.

I turned till I was dizzy, clapped my hands, ran, shouted, saw myself winning, saw myself losing, rejoicing, lamenting [Malone the child on the "playground"]. Then suddenly I threw myself on the playthings, if there were any, or on a child, to change his joy to howling, or I fled, to hiding. The grown-ups pursued me, the just, caught me, beat me, hounded me back into the round, the game, the jollity. For I was already in the toils of earnestness. That has been my disease. I was born grave as others syphilitic. (TN, 265–66)

It was impossible for him to escape this disease. Even when he struggled to be grave no more, he struggled gravely not to be grave. "Such is the earnestness," he says, "from which, for nearly a century now, I have never been able to depart." And even now there hangs over him the dreadful possibility that he will be unable to evade earnestness, that he will find himself abandoned, in the dark, "without anything to play with."

He has, however, hope, even high hopes, that this time will be different. He resolves never to do anything henceforth but play. Well, a great part of the time he will play, the greater part, if possible. And such a resolution is eminently appropriate for someone in such delicate condition that he must be on the lookout for throes: one ought to be able to remain tepid when involved in a mere game. So after a particularly successful passage in the story about Sapo, Malone stops to congratulate himself: "we are getting on." For he is convinced that this time he has cured himself of his disease, that he will not be abandoned in the thick of the fray. "Yes, now my mind is easy, I know the game is won, I lost them all till now, but it's the last that counts" (TN, 264).

He is wrong, of course.

Unfortunately or not, Malone is unable to stick to frivolity. His first death-spasm, for example, interrupts a passage which could almost be taken for an excerpt from that gravely Cartesian and mortally serious book, *Watt*. Macmann has replaced Sapo in the narrative, and his eyes are the subject of Malone's earnest prose.

Bluer scarcely than white of egg the eyes stare into the space before them, namely the fulness of the great deep and its unchanging calm. But at long intervals they close, with the gentle suddenness of flesh that tightens. . . . Then you see the old lids all red and worn that seem hard set to meet, for there are four, two for each lachrymal. And perhaps it is then he sees . . . the heaven of the sea and of the earth too, and the spasms of the waves . . . and the so different motion of men for example, who are not tied together, but free to come and go as they please. And they make full use of it and come and go, their great balls and sockets rattling and clacking like knackers, each on his way. And when one dies the others go on, as if nothing had happened.

I feel

I feel it's coming. (TN, 319–20)

And the second death spasm is preceded by a passage no less guilty of gravity. Macmann's degeneration has advanced to the stage where his sole mode of locomotion is that of rolling across the countryside.

And without reducing his speed he [Macmann] began to dream of a flat land where he would never have to rise again and hold himself erect in equilibrium, first on the right foot for example, then on the left, and where he might come and go and so survive after the fashion of a great cylinder endowed with the faculties of cognition and volition. And without exactly building castles in Spain, for that

Quick quick my possessions. Quiet, quiet . . . (TN, 338)

Malone should have realized that he could not so closely approximate, both in the tenor of despair and the actions of the characters, the stories of Molloy and Moran, both of whom also rolled, without treading on the ground of the earnest.

Malone's fatal disease should have been recognized earlier in the work, however. The first thing on his program is a discussion of his present state. He knows that to remind himself of himself is a mistake, a weakness, but he indulges it anyway, in the assurance that he will play with all the more ardor afterward. He also realizes that in order to speak of his possessions (the "inventory") he will have to become earnest again. In the description of his present state, Malone gets on well enough so long as he sticks to the dish and pot, the old woman, the prospect from his room. But when he volunteers a few words on himself, we hear in his voice the unmistakable quality of the earnest.

My sight and hearing are very bad, on the vast main no light but reflected gleams. All my senses are trained full on me, me. Dark and silent and stale, I am no prey for them. I am far from the sounds of blood and breath, immured. I shall not speak of my sufferings. Cowering deep down among them I feel nothing. It is there I die, unbeknown to my stupid flesh. That which is seen, that which cries and writhes, my witless remains. Somewhere in this turmoil thought struggles on, it too wide of the mark. It too seeks me, as it always has, where I am not to be found. It too cannot be quiet. On others let it wreak its dying rage, and leave me in peace. (TN, 253)

Now while this is just the thing that Malone had hoped to avoid, it is nonetheless the pattern of the rest of the novel. Immediately he begins his story about Saposcat. He struggles through fifteen lines on Sapo's childhood—

He was a precocious boy. He was not good at his lessons, neither could he see the use of them. He attended his classes with his mind elsewhere, or blank. . . . He made a practice, alone and in company, of mental arithmetic. And the figures then marshalling in his mind thronged it with colours and with forms. (TN, 254)

—and then, "What tedium," he sighs. He resumes the narrative, "playing" with Sapo, but subsides easily and quickly into the forbidden vein. Sapo has seized his teacher's cane and flung it out the window, "which was closed, for it was winter."

This was enough to justify his expulsion. But Sapo was not expelled, either then or later. I must try and discover, when I have time to think about it quietly, why Sapo was not expelled when he so richly deserved to be. For I want as little as possible of darkness in his story. A little darkness, in itself, at the time, is nothing. You think no more about it and you go on. But I know what darkness is, it accumulates, thickens, then suddenly bursts and drowns everything. (TN, 258–59) [12]

By the time he is well into the story about Macmann (he never does get to the story about the animal or the one about the thing), Malone seems to have forgotten entirely his promise to remain tepid and to "play" casually with his creatures. We have already noticed that Macmann, in the best tradition of the earlier and earnest heroes Molloy and Moran, gets around only by rolling on the ground like a great cylinder. His clothing (TN, 310–13) is strikingly like Watt's, as is one of his postures — spread-eagled on the ground. He is as incompetent in the affairs of the world as Murphy at his worst, as homeless as Molloy, as unsuccessful as Moran. It is inevitable that his mind should engage the same problems and deal with them in much the same manner as the rest of Malone's playthings. When Malone really played, it had been with the child Sapo; when he gets earnest, he makes of Macmann and his nurse Moll ancients of the incalculable age of the charcoal-burner or of Molloy's mother. Only thirteen pages from the end of the story, Malone uses exactly the same language ("When it rained, when it snowed . . ." [TN, 386]) he had used in telling the story of Moran (cf. TN, 233).

So it is to be expected, really, when, after recounting with tenderness the love affair between Macmann and Moll, Malone declares, "Moll. I'm going to kill her"; and expeditiously effects his threat. By the time he gets to the story of the excursion of the inmates of St. John of God, Malone is simply wallowing in seriousness. The patients are in the charge of Moll's replacement, one Lemuel (? Le Mulet, the dead mule buried by the Lamberts [TN, 289–91], the photographed ass [TN, 345], Malone himself), and included in the group are Murphy (or Geulincx) ("a young man, dead young"), Watt (the "saxon"), Moran (a small thin man), and Molloy or Nackybal (the "misshapen giant"). The excursion ends in dire earnestness when, after Lemuel splits with an axe the skulls of two sailors and leaves Lady Pedal to die of a broken hip, he gets his patients back into the boat and they all drift far out into the bay.

Macmann, my last, my possessions. . . . [Malone, delirious, gasping his last]
  Lemuel is in charge, he raises his hatchet on which the blood will never dry, but not to hit anyone, he will not hit anyone, he will not hit anyone any more, he will not touch anyone any more, either with it or with it or with it or with or
    or with it or with his hammer or with his stick . . .
    or with his pencil or with his stick or
. . . .
anymore. (TN, 397–98)

In the confusion of his death throes, Malone identifies himself with Lemuel, and Lemuel's death-dealing axe with his own life-and-death-dealing pencil. "All I ask," said Malone early in his narrative, "is that the last [story] of mine, as long as it lasts, should have living for its theme" (TN, 270). His request, like his resolution to play, falls victim to the disease of earnestness, and his story ends with a scene of death, abandonment, "absurd lights," and a hopeless crew of insane men, lying together in a heap, adrift in a vacant bay. Ironically, Malone is not abandoned by his playthings: he abandons them.

IV

◀ ▶ The third novel in the trilogy is *The Unnamable*. It begins: "Where now? Who now? When now? Unquestioning. I, say I. Unbelieving. Questions, hypotheses, call them that. Keep going, going on, call that going, call that on. . . . I seem to speak, it is not I, about me, it is not about me. These few general remarks to begin with" (TN, 401). The three questions, and especially the first two, are to be taken very seriously. In fact, they define the concern of the novel and the problems to be untangled in order to understand it. Where is this "I" who is speaking now? Who is he? At what point in the development of the trilogy as a whole does he speak? We may add one of our own: What relation does this "I" have to the narrators of the previous parts of the trilogy?

These are the usual questions, the necessary questions, which a reader asks of any character who appears in a fiction.

"What is his name?"
"Bingley."
"Is he married or single?"
"Oh! single, my dear, to be sure! A single man of large fortune; four or five thousand a year. What a fine thing for our girls."

Very good. So, when Bingley does appear in *Pride and Prejudice*, he appears not as a stranger, but as one concerning whom there is a certain amount of public information: a name; a marital status; and, in the judgment of Mrs. Bennet, most important, a fortune of no ordinary sort. Bingley is located in time, in space, in society, in relation to others. He is or can be the cause of this one's hope, of that other's dismay. He has a revealable and intelligible past, an available present, and a various future. Most concretely, most stolidly, Bingley exists.

Molloy and Moran exist too — more tenuously, to be sure, and in the case of Malone, most precariously indeed. But each exists, after his fashion. Each has a space — his mother's room, his own house, a town called Bally in a province (or something) called Ballyba, or a bed in a room in a house. Each has also a time, vaguely modern: the time of a bicycle, an autocycle, a Venus lead pencil. And, though none of them has much in the future to look forward to, and has a present almost wholly occupied with writing, each of them has a past, a history, which he narrates and analyzes at length. It is by reference to such coordinates as these that the reader is able to take hold of the character who demands his attention. One upon a time there was a man named Molloy and he went to a certain place and said this, did that, encountered such a one, went on to another place, at another time, and there, . . . and then, . . .

Now obliterate these coordinates, or confuse them by drawing other, conflicting axes, and the reader is deprived of those principles in terms of which he is able to orient himself in the world inhabited by the character with whom he is concerned. Gone are the specifications of time, place, past, present, future, causality, and relationship. And since it is these categories which establish the existence and identity of characters, gone too are their existences and their identities. And this of course is just what Beckett has done in the case of *The Unnamable*.

Everything we know about the narrator we know because he tells us. But the narrator himself is ignorant, or mostly ignorant, of himself, of his retrospects, of his prospects. "What am I to do," he asks himself, "what shall I do, what should I do, in my situation, how proceed?" Ought he to proceed in the tradition of the Academics and of Descartes, "By aporia pure and simple?" Or ought he to proceed in the manner of a sceptical Socrates, "By affirmations and negations invalidated as uttered, or sooner or later?" His answer: "Generally speaking" (TN, 401). The first paragraph of his narration confirms this answer. He asks three questions and immediately denies that he questions. "I," he says, apparently in the belief that it is indeed himself ("I") who says "I"; and then denies that he believes it. By affirmations and negations invalidated as uttered, indeed. Or by aporia pure and simple: "Can it be . . .? Perhaps . . . Perhaps . . . I seem . . . Can one . . .? I don't know. . . . The fact would seem to be, . . . if . . . if . . ."; all in the same first paragraph. So by the time we come to the last lines of his narration, seventeen paragraphs, one hundred and seventy-seven pages, and some fifty-five thousand words later, neither he nor we are any more knowledgeable with regard to his spatial situation: ". . . where I am, I don't know, I'll never know, in the silence you don't know."

There have of course been hypotheses: he is inside a skull (TN, 418) or a head (TN, 486); or, since it is difficult to separate the question of location from the question of identity, he is a "sperm dying, of cold, in the sheets, feebly wagging its little tail, perhaps I'm a drying sperm, in the sheets of an innocent boy, . . . no stone must be left unturned, one mustn't be afraid of making a howler" (TN, 527). Early in the story he says that he likes to think that he occupies the center (of what?), but that nothing — aporia pure and simple — is less certain. For in a sense he would be better off at the circumference (of what?); but he is certainly not — negated as soon as affirmed — at the circumference, for Malone wheels about him (TN, 406–7).

In fact, in the first pages of his monologue, the Unnamable tentatively proposes a considerable number of facts and statements concerning himself and his situation. Malone, wearing a brimless hat, wheels around him; dim intermittent lights suggest a kind of distance; he believes that not only Malone is present, but that "they are all here, at least from Murphy on." Malone has a beard; he (the Unnamable) himself sits with his hands on his knees, tears streaming down his face from unblinking eyes (St. Arsenius bewailing his sins). He is not deaf, for he can hear sounds. During his stay there an incident occurred: two shapes, oblong like man, entered into collision before him, fell down, and disappeared: he thought of the "pseudo-couple Mercier-Camier." He has a certain amount of knowledge, though he does not know how he acquired it. He knows about his mother, about God, about fellow creatures; he was given courses on love and intelligence; he was taught to count and reason. There surrounds him a kind of air, a grey, "first murky, then frankly opaque," but nonetheless luminous; it is shot with rose (TN, 414–15). He sits (as Macmann sat on his bench [cf. TN, 311]) with his spine in the vertical, his thighs at right angles to the spine, the shins at right angles again to the thighs; he feels an unknown pressure against his rump and against the soles of his feet. (For these events see TN, 403–20.) And so on and so on.

But none of this information about his location, posture, sensory apparatus, or environment is credible, for, true to his stated method, he either contradicts himself sooner or later, or so qualifies an assertion with sceptical amendments that one is permitted to adopt only an ephectic stance with regard to the assertion. "I shall not be alone, in the beginning," he says, and immediately follows this with "I am of course alone" (TN, 402). He is not at all seated, in an angular posture; he is a "big talking ball, . . . round and hard" (TN, 422). There are no sounds and no lights, and he is surrounded not by grey but by black (TN, 419); but not by black either (TN, 422).

"The thing to avoid," says the Unnamable, "I don't know why, is the spirit of system" (TN, 402; cf. 418, 498). But though it is inundated by words, words, words, by proposition and contradiction, assertion and refutation, there is a definite method at work in the narrative. The method is itself, we may speculate, the corollary of a rule or resolution which the Unnamable once adopted for the governance of his thinking: He resolved to accept nothing as true which he did not clearly recognize to be so. That is to say, he decided carefully to avoid precipitation and prejudice in judgments, and to accept in them nothing more than what was presented to his mind so clearly and distinctly that he could have no occasion to doubt it. This "rule" is of course the first of those set out by Descartes in his *Discourse on Method* (Pt. II); and using this rule, Descartes could come to much the same understanding of his existence as does the Unnamable: "And then, examining attentively that which I was, I saw that I could conceive that I had no body, and that there was no world nor place where I might be." Nonetheless, there is a point beyond which Descartes could not go: "But yet . . . I could not for all that conceive that I was not." [13] This conception is not so impossible, however, for the Unnamable.

In spite of his mistrust of the "spirit of method," the Unnamable does in fact employ the Cartesian rule advocating the aporetic attitude. The dialectic of doubt, however, requires for its exercise the positing of a somewhat — a proposition, a "thing" — which is capable of being doubted. Scepticism cannot endure a vacuum. Hence the Unnamable must affirm something of himself or of his situation before he can deny or question it. His narrative then becomes a sequence of affirmation and denial, assertion and negation: and since the negative term invariably succeeds the positive, the dialectic acts as a chisel on stone, and eventually the narrative approximates the point where there is nothing left but nothing. This is how Vivian Mercier reads the novel. "The Unnamable's interior monologue may go on to infinity, for all we know. If it were to, we might describe this novel as a curve having one of its axes as an asymptote. In other words, as y (the length of the novel) approached infinity, x (the content of the novel) would approach nearer and nearer to zero. Content zero, length infinity — these are the mathematical limits of the novel." [14]

This, however, is not the only way of looking at the process which is the novel. We may also see it as the reverse of the method employed in the earlier work, *Watt*. There the author piled detail upon irrelevant detail in the effort to show who and what Mr. Knott was by showing what he was not. In *The Unnamable*, Beckett has stripped away every conceivable Aristotelian "accident," every detail of particularity, every trace of local existence, and has preserved only the single element which is finally important — the Unnamable's talk.

The novel has a remarkable impetus to it. It drives — and one has the sense that it is driving to some particular place, but it is difficult to say where. If we accept Mercier's hypothesis concerning the work, the answer is evident. Its destination is Zero, nothingness. Even to get to Zero, though, one must start somewhere; and if one is to carry others — readers — along with him, it is necessary to provide a course, a pathway. And it is necessary as well to provide signposts which must be of such a nature as to let one know when one has arrived at the place where he is going. And what is the adequate signification of the fact that one has arrived at Nothing? One does not go directly from Limbo to the Giudecca, because in order fully to comprehend what the Giudecca is and means, it is necessary to have witnessed and understood what lesser orders of evil are and mean. So, too, one does not arrive at Nothing, and know and appreciate it for the Nothing which it is, unless one has come by way of Something, and known and appreciated it as well. Mercier may be right: the novel goes through Something in order to arrive at Nothing. But there is also another possibility. Perhaps the novel goes through Something and demolishes it on the way in order to get to Something, or Someplace, unapproachable by any way other than this version of the *Via Negativa*.

For all of its obscurity and difficulty, the narrative does in fact tell us something about the narrator. He is — but let us leave it at that, and not attempt to inquire into the mode in which he is. Also, he talks. Why does he talk? Here are some of his reasons, and some of his comments on his talk.

The search for the means to put an end to things, an end to speech, is what enables the discourse to continue. . . .

I who am here, who cannot speak, cannot think, and who must speak, and therefore perhaps think a little, cannot [speak and think] in relation only to me who am here, to here where I am, but can [speak and think] a little, sufficiently, I don't know how, unimportant, in relation to me who was elsewhere, who shall be elsewhere, and to those places where I was, where I shall be. . . . And indeed I greatly fear, since my speech can only be of me and here, that I am once more engaged in putting an end to both. Which would not matter, . . . but for the obligation, once rid of them ["me" and "here"], to begin again, . . . from no one and from nothing and win to me again, to me here again. . . .

All these Murphys, Molloys and Malones do not fool me. They have made me waste my time, suffer for nothing, speak of them when, in order to stop speaking, I should have spoken of me and of me alone. . . .

And yet I do not despair of one day sparing me, without going silent. And that day, I don't know why, I shall be able to go silent, and make an end. . . . Yes, it is to be wished, to end would be wonderful. . . .

Yes, I have a pensum to discharge, before I can be free, free to dribble, free to speak no more, listen no more, and I've forgotten what it is. . . . I was given a pensum, at birth perhaps, as a punishment for having been born perhaps. . . .

For all I need say is this, that if I have a pensum to perform it is because I could not say my lesson, and that when I have finished my pensum I shall still have my lesson to say, before I have the right to stay quiet in my corner, . . . my tongue at rest, far from all disturbance, all sound, my mind at peace, that is to say empty. . . .

Strange notion . . . that of a task to be performed, before one can be at rest. Strange task, which consists in speaking of oneself. Strange hope, turned towards silence and peace. (For these quotations, see TN, 413, 416–17, 419, 417, 428, 429)

It is this theme of the pensum, together with its concomitants of the condemnation to speech, inability to speak, and the goal of speechlessness, which runs through the entire work; and with brief exceptions (TN, 433–34), the theme is exempt from the attrition of the Unnamable's scepticism and the destruction of his negations.

It's of me now I must speak, even if I have to do it with their language [Murphy's, Molloy's], it will be a start, a step towards silence and the end of madness, the madness of having to speak and not being able to, except of things that don't concern me, that don't count, that I don't believe, that they have crammed me full of to prevent me from saying who I am, where I am, and from doing what I have to do in the only way that can put an end to it, from doing what I have to do. (TN, 449)

The Unnamable speaks, then, because he is under an obligation to do so. At times he personifies the obligation as a "master," and berates him for not being of more assistance. The master says to him that he wants all to be well with him.

To which I reply, in a respectful attitude, I too, your Lordship. I say that to cheer him up. . . . A little more explicitness on his part, since the initiative belongs to him, might be a help. . . . Let the man explain himself. . . . Let him inform me once and for all what exactly it is he wants from me, for me. . . . If he wants me to say something, for my good naturally, he has only to tell me what it is and I'll let it out with a roar straight away. (TN, 432–33) [15]

The master may not be one, however; he may be a group, each member of which is equally good, equally concerned with the Unnamable's welfare, but "differing as to its nature." Or perhaps the affair is being handled by a committee of deputies. Or the whole business of the pensum is false: there is no labor, no master; there is only the absurd fact that having nothing to say and having no words but the words of others, he must speak (TN, 434). This last hypothesis will not do, however, for the Unnamable recognizes that he is in fact under an obligation of some kind, and the obligation is simply that he must speak.

The subject of the Unnamable's speech is to be — ought to be — himself. "It's of me now I must speak, even if I have to do it with their language, it will be a start, a step towards silence." He has spoken before, but of the wrong things. "All these Murphys, Molloys and Malones do not fool me. They have made me waste my time, suffer for nothing, speak of them when, in order to stop speaking, I should have spoken of me and of me alone" (TN, 419). To the prompt performance of his task the Unnamable perceives two obvious hindrances. First, he has no language but the language of others in which to speak of himself; and perhaps their language is not adequate to the task of speaking of himself. Second, and even more embarrassing, he really has no information about himself. Well into the last quarter of the text the narrator reminds us and himself that "it has not yet been our good fortune to establish with any degree of accuracy what I am, where I am" (TN, 540).

These are no doubt considerable obstacles; yet, if they are not overcome, they are circumvented, for the Unnamable does in fact manage to talk, even if it is in the language of others, and there is some suspicion that he succeeds in saying something about himself. If he manages to do so, it is by the strategy of circumlocution and parable.

For consider the problem which is the Unnamable's; and for the purposes of clarity, consider it from the point of view which is really very important to him — the point of view of grammar. The Unnamable's task is to speak of himself. That is, the "I" who is the Unnamable, or which the Unnamable is, is to speak of the "me," who is not the Unnamable or which the Unnamable is not. Concisely put, the Unnamable is not the same person or being in the objective case as he is in the nominative. It is impossible, that is to say, at least from the grammatical point of view, that I should speak of "I"; for I can speak only of "me." And whatever name we give to the place which the Unnamable occupies, it is a place where "I" is not identical with "me."

Hence, in order properly to speak of that of which he must speak, the Unnamable invents surrogates for himself. The first of these is Mahood (né Basil). It was Mahood, says the Unnamable, who "told me stories about me, lived in my stead, issued forth from me, came back to me, entered back into me, heaped stories on my head" (TN, 427). It is Mahood's voice which has mingled with the Unnamable's and "sometimes drowned it completely." The Mahood-voice, speaking through the Unnamable, is apparently responsible for telling stories about what is sometimes called "the without." In a Mahood-story, there is a world, there are people, and the people have appendages and parts, they live in places and go to other places. The Unnamable has confessed to speaking of Murphy, etc., but we may surmise that when he did so it was in the Mahood-voice. In the present narrative there are two Mahood-stories, with Mahood as the hero, and told in the Mahood-voice (speaking of course through the Unnamable and, presumably, completely drowning the Unnamable's own proper voice). The first is the story of Mahood's helicoidal, one-legged trip back home, into the yard, to the bosom of his family. The second is the story of Mahood stuck in a jar. Both of these stories are parabolic renderings of some aspect of the Unnamable. The first is a metaphor of the Unnamable's method for arriving at the place where he can in fact attempt to speak of himself. The second is a metaphor of the existence to which the Unnamable has been reduced: he is little more than a thing, an object, ignored by the world, barely alive.[16]

The trouble, of course, is that these are metaphors; they speak of the Unnamable at one remove, as it were, but even one remove is not close enough to the true, the necessary topic of speech, which is "I." Even more grave than this, however, is that "I" or the Unnamable in himself is in danger of believing these stories about Mahood, or in danger of believing that these stories are about himself. This in fact is precisely the favorite ruse of "those" who heretofore have attempted to prevent the Unnamable from speaking of himself. By "those," the Unnamable means those other characters — Murphy, Watt, Molloy — who have been his previous surrogates. No sooner does the Unnamable begin to believe one of these stories, to "adhere" to, say,

Molloy (or in this case, to Mahood stuck in the jar), than the character leaves him high and dry (at the end of the novel), "with nothing for my renewal but the life they have imputed to me. And it is only when they see me stranded that they take up again the thread of my misfortunes" (TN, 457).

So to avoid being taken in by Mahood and his stories, the Unnamable jettisons him and births a new surrogate, whom he baptizes Worm. (The name, as Frederick J. Hoffman has pointed out, comprises in itself significant elements of the names of all the other major Beckett characters.[17]) Now the Unnamable, in his Mahood-voice, continues the narrative of the man in the jar, but this time it is Worm who is the hero, and not the Unnamable himself. Apparently the Unnamable's defensive plan is a success, for the story soon flags, dies. "The stories of Mahood are ended," reports the Unnamable, and in fact there are in the rest of the narrative no more such stories. Mahood, or the Mahood-voice, has given up, because he has realized that the stories could not be about "I" (TN, 478–79). The Unnamable has parried yet another attempt on the part of "them" to get him to deny his own proper identity and "adhere" to some other.

This complicated maneuvering on the part of the Unnamable to get himself into the right place in order to talk about himself has really got him no nearer to the goal, however, for no sooner is the Mahood-voice ended, than he seems to hear Worm's voice beginning. So the danger is there yet, that he will never speak of himself, or, perhaps worse, that he will begin to adhere to Worm and will lose himself entirely. The Unnamable has, as it were, outsmarted himself, and this he recognizes with chagrin. "To think I thought he [Worm] was against what they [Murphy, Malone, Mahood] were trying to do with me!" (TN, 480). That is, the Unnamable had hoped that by naming himself Worm, and then telling himself (in Mahood's voice) a story about Worm (the second half of the "jar story"), he could finally achieve his ultimate purpose—to speak of himself. But Worm upsets the careful plan by refusing to stay a character, as it were, in the story told by Mahood, but becomes himself, on Mahood's decease, the teller of a story. This in turn means that the Unnamable becomes himself the told, the narrated, the talked about: that is, he becomes an object in Worm's purview. But being an object means that he is a "me" and not an "I," and so the whole problem of talking about himself in the nominative case is raised once again.

Finally, the Unnamable presents both Mahood and Worm to be looked at one last time (TN, 527–28); and though it is not, of course, the last time, it is very nearly so, for their names appear only fleetingly, or as poorly re-membered. After dismissing the two surrogates, the Unnamable under-takes in his own person the narrating of — something, not a story so much as babble, talk which moves now closer to and now more distant from the person of the narrator. There are about forty pages of talk —

I don't know who it's all about, that's all I know, no, I must know something else, they must have taught me something, it's about him who knows nothing, wants nothing, can do nothing, if it's possible you can do nothing when you want nothing, who cannot hear, cannot speak, who is I, who cannot be I, of whom I can't speak, of whom I must speak, that's all hypotheses, I said nothing, someone said nothing, it's not a question of hypotheses, it's a question of going on, it goes on. . . . (TN, 562–63)

— and then the talk ends:

. . . where I am, I don't know, I'll never know, in the silence you don't know, you must go on, I can't go on, I'll go on. (TN, 577)

But go on to where? Where does the Unnamable go as he goes on? We have already heard the answer suggested by Vivian Mercier: he just goes on and on and on, to infinity; and as he goes, the content of what he says declines proportionally toward Zero, Nothing. But Professor Mercier has overlooked a quality of the penultimate lines which seems to indicate that the end of the story is not simply a termination, more or less arbitrary, but the finishing of a whole. The Unnamable realizes that he is coming to the end, that the words which are being issued through him are coming to an end: ". . . quick now and try again, with the words that remain, try what, I don't know, I've forgotten, it doesn't matter, I never knew, to have them carry me into my story, the words that remain, my old story, which I've for-gotten, far from here, through the noise, through the door, . . . perhaps it's the door, perhaps I'm at the door, . . . I can depart, all this time I've journeyed without knowing it, it's I now at the door. . . ." (TN, 576) This does not sound so much like the talk of a person who can go on forever in the same vein, but more like the talk of one who is about to finish one chap-ter or period of his existence and go on to another. But again, where does he go to? What door is this, and what does it open to?

There are, no doubt, as many doors as there are ladders. But only slightly daunted by this consideration I am going to suggest two possible interpre-tations of the end of *The Unnamable* in addition to Professor Mercier's (and in Ch. VI, I shall offer what amounts to still another). The two have very different implications for the final assessment (if there can be such a thing) of the meaning of the work: for if Professor Mercier's reading implies an infinite progression of talk, my first suggestion implies a definite conclusion, and the second implies a cyclical form to the trilogy as a whole.

Two of the more important themes running through *The Unnamable* are the pensum or task to be performed, and the goal of peace. In the discussion of *Watt* I mentioned the fact that the same goal was important to both the Greek sceptical tradition and to the anxiety-ridden eremetic tradition as exemplified by St. Arsenius and especially by St. John Climacus. We can now return to the *Scala Paradisi* for a clue as to what the author intended, as Watt might say, by the concluding lines of the trilogy.

In "Step Five" of the *Ladder*, Climacus describes the "prison" where the abbot sent those of the brotherhood who had fallen into sin after being admitted to the monastery. It is a scene of religious hysteria.

From the number of their prostrations their knees seemed to have become wooden, their eyes dim and sunk deep within their sockets. They had no hair. Their cheeks were bruised and burnt by the scalding tears. Their faces were pale and wasted. They were quite indistinguishable from corpses. Their breasts were livid from blows; and from their frequent beating of the chest, they spat blood. Where was to be found in this place any rest on beds, or clean starched clothes? They were all torn, dirty and covered with lice.[18]

When in the course of time, one of these ascetics was ready to "precede" the others "by finishing his course," the rest would gather about him "while his mind was still active," and begin to question him.

"How are you, brother and fellow criminal? What will you say? What do you hope? What do you expect? Have you accomplished what you sought with such labor or not? Has the door been opened to you, or are you still under judgment? Have you attained your object, or not yet? Have you received any sort of assurance, or is your hope still uncertain? Have you obtained freedom, or is your thought clouded with doubt?"[19]

To this we may add two *dicta* from the thirtieth and concluding "Step":

Hope is a wealth of hidden riches. Hope is a treasure of assurance of the treasure in store for us.
It is a rest from labours; it is the door of love. . . .[20]

Is there enough here to justify the assertion that the *Ladder* is one of the documents that lies behind the conception of the trilogy? It is of course translated into secular and even existential terms, but the structure is all there: the whole of the trilogy, but especially the last volume, is an exercise in hesychasm, contemplative prayer, performed by an ascetic as a penance for the sin of being born. If at the end the Unnamable has in fact propitiated his task-master, then the door of hope is opening to him and admitting him to the *apatheia*, the peace, for which he sought so strenuously. And though the connotations of the term are very different in the Sceptical tradition and in the Ascetic, still the same word is used to define the goal (or one of the two goals) pursued by the Zetetic: "According to some authorities the end proposed by the Sceptics is insensibility [*apatheia*]; according to others, gentleness." [21] On this interpretation of the end of the trilogy, the Unnamable has won through to some kind of victory, and the whole work must be thought of as coming to a conclusion of at least a penultimate nature.

The second way of reading the last pages carries with it the thesis that the trilogy, like *Finnegans Wake* or perhaps *A la recherche du temps perdu*, is cyclical. This interpretation will in turn require us to identify the Unnamable as the last *persona* of the one Being who has been talking from the beginning.

Suppose that after the Unnamable's last words, "I'll go on," the words he goes on to say are, "I am in my mother's room. It's I who live there now. I don't know how I got there. . . ." These are of course the opening words of *Molloy*, the first novel in the trilogy; and by suggesting that these are the next words of the Unnamable, I mean to say that the Unnamable is Molloy. I would also suggest that this tells us not only who the Unnamable is, but also where he is. For in point of time, Molloy's words are later than the actions he recounts. He has attained his mother's room only after a long wandering—a wandering which began after he had observed the meeting of A and C. His observation post, let us recall, is a perch on some eminence, behind a rock "in the shadow of which I [Molloy speaking] crouched like Belacqua [sic], or Sordello" (TN, 8). If this hypothesis is correct, we ought to understand the answer to the Unnamable's question, "Where now?" to be, "In the Ante-Purgatory." For the Unnamable's long, dream-like, nightmare-like monologue seems to be conducted in circumstances similar to those in which the procrastinating Belacqua must wait because "l'angel di Dio che siede in su la porta" will not open the door to him. [22] The difference between the Unnamable and Belacqua, however, is that whereas for the latter the door is shut against him, for the Unnamable it is about to open. It is about to open not onto the purgatorial way to Paradise, however, but onto

another round of the pensum which is human existence. Molloy reports
that he waked between eleven o'clock and midday, and heard the angelus,
recalling the incarnation. In this case it is not the incarnation of Christ
which is signified by the bells, but the incarnation of the Unnamable in the
form of Molloy.

I have suggested that Molloy is to be understood as a character in search
of an author with a story capable of accommodating Molloy, of giving him
a home; but that failing to find him, or rather, finding him and then killing
him, Molloy must himself turn author and write his own story. Alone
among the four major figures in the trilogy, Molloy has no knowledge of
previous Beckett characters (though there is the mention of a Watt [TN,
100]). Like the Unnamable, however, he sometimes thinks of himself as
existing in a sealed jar, and reports that when in the jar you have to be careful, "ask yourself questions, as for example whether you still are, and if no
when it stopped, and if yes how long it will still go on" (TN, 62); and these
are just the questions which the Unnamable asked of himself. Molloy also
uses as an image of his existence another of the Unnamable's images, that
of the galley slave aboard Ulysses' ship.[23] But even if the Unnamable is in-
carnated in Molloy, it is in such a fashion that Molloy's story is not adequate
to define the mysterious identity of the "I" of the Unnamable. Molloy apparently knows this, for though he says that his "dwelling" is "deep down,"
still it is not the "deepest down," but is only somewhere between the mud
and the scum. The "deepest down" dwelling is reserved for the Unnamable
himself.

The Unnamable is rather less in evidence in the second part of *Molloy*
than in the first. Moran is so concerned with the business of his mission and
the impediments thereto, and is so misled as to the nature of his quarry by
his own preconception of Molloy, that he has little time or inclination to inquire deeply within himself. Only toward the end of his unsuccessful quest
does he begin seriously to question the nature of his own being. Nonetheless, the "voice" which begins to supersede the authority of Youdi is either
that of the Unnamable himself, or—and it makes little difference—that
which is transmitted through the Unnamable from an unknown source. If
the Unnamable does in fact appear in a bodily manifestation to Moran, it is
as the "Corynetes," or club-bearer (TN, 198). In any case, the club-bearer is
an Author, perhaps The Author, for, in the trilogy, the club or any variation on the club is the sign of the writer. The club appears first in the hands
of "C" (TN, 7). That is, it is carried by the Character-as-author, Molloy.

When it next appears, however, it is held by the Author-as-author, the man who visits Moran and asks him for a piece of bread. When Moran hefts the visitor's club, its lightness astounds him (TN, 198–99).[24] Later, Moran is interrupted at his fire building by the "dim man," Molloy, the Character-as-character; and as Character, Molloy asks Moran if he has seen an old man with a stick pass by; for Molloy-as-character is in search of his Author. What happens next is confused, but Moran later finds Molloy's head in a pulp (TN, 205). The weapon is not identified, but it is presumably Moran's umbrella, a surrogate for the author's club. In *Malone Dies*, the club becomes Malone's stick, the implement with which Malone dips among his "possessions," brings them to him and sends them back. In the same novel, the dying Malone quite obviously relates Lemuel's axe with a stick and then with a pencil; and perhaps we are to understand even the knives belonging to Louis (Big) Lambert as the sign of the author, for it is Louis who buries the mule; and perhaps this too accounts for the intermittent appearances of the little silver knife-rest, carried never by an author (Moran, Malone), but only by characters (Molloy, Macmann), in token of the fact that the lethal weapon is in the hands of the murdering author.

In his condition of privation and corporeal impotence and decay, Malone is more sensitive than the other author in the trilogy, Moran, to the fact that his labors are foolish, vain, unsuccessful. He is aware as well that the apparent subjects of his stories — Sapo and the Lamberts and even Macmann — are not in fact the real ones, and that all his previous efforts at telling stories have been wretched failures. In the "live and invent" passage, he tries to explain what has been his history as an author. At each fresh attempt at telling his stories, he says, he lost his head and fled "to my shadows as to sanctuary, to his lap who can neither live nor suffer the sight of others living." The allusion seems to be to the kind of person — or place — which the Unnamable is — or occupies. Malone goes on. "After the fiasco, the solace, the repose, I began again, to try and live, cause to live, be another, in myself, in another. . . . But little by little with a different aim, no longer in order to succeed, but in order to fail. Nuance" (TN, 266). We catch here the echo of the words of the author as Art Critic, who noted that Bram van Velde was the first artist "to admit that to be an artist is to fail as no other dare fail, that failure is his world. . . ." But we interrupt Malone: he is launched into his apologia: "What I sought, when I struggled out of my hole, then aloft through the stinging air towards an inaccessible boon [Malone as Icarus-Dedalus], was the rapture of vertigo, the letting go, the fall, the gulf, the relapse . . . to home, to him waiting for me always, who needed me and whom I needed, who took me in his arms and told me to stay with him always, who gave me his place and watched over me, who suffered every time I left him, whom I have often made suffer and seldom contented, whom I have never seen" (TN, 266).

Malone refers to none other, surely, than the Unnamable himself. And the Unnamable, for his part, would seem to agree. He knows Malone by the name of Basil, but rechristens him Mahood. It was Mahood, says the Unnamable, who "told me stories about me, lived in my stead, issued forth from me, came back to me, entered back into me, heaped stories on my head" (TN, 427).

v

◄ ► Let us return for a last time to the writer at work. He sits, perhaps, at a desk, it may be, and writes. He writes with something; he writes on something. He writes about something. What does he write about?

There was a time — and a very good time it was — when the writer wrote about people, other people: about knights and nuns and millers; about people who ruled and loved and avenged evil; about people in high and low stations of life, and their respective "manners"; about people in the grip of political, economic, or social forces stronger than themselves; and so on. And in those days, it was not uncommon for the writer to be himself of the people: he was a diplomat, an actor, a politician, a clergyman, a sailor, an adventurer. He travelled, he was known by many, and knew many.

Things have changed, since then. For perhaps a century — Professor Hoffman suggests Dostoevsky's *Notes from the Underground*, published in 1864, as an early example [25] — the writer, some writers, have tended to look away from people, other people, and the world they live in, and they have looked rather at themselves, and the world which is in them. Dostoevsky, Kafka, Joyce, Virginia Woolf, Yeats, Eliot — even Lawrence and Hemingway — have taken as the object of serious concern the structure of the self. The old stories, the old questions, asked, What is society? or What is man? But increasingly we have heard, rather, Augustine's and Soren Kierkegaard's question, What is the self? or Who am I?

Beckett's trilogy is a sustained effort to give an answer to this question. For by now it should be clear that the only adequate answer to the Unnamable's question, "Who now?" is "Samuel Beckett." Early in his story of Sapo, Malone breaks off to ask, "I wonder if I am not talking yet again about myself. Shall I be incapable, to the end, of lying on any other subject?" (TN, 257). His "lies," his stories, are in fact about himself; and so, too, are the stories told by all the other persons of the trilogy. There are all about "the Unnamable"; they simply come at him from different angles. At least since *Murphy*, Beckett has written about nothing other than Samuel Beckett. He is the teller and he is also the subject of what is told. Hence, he is to himself both author and character. As Molloy, he is the character in search of an author; as Moran, he is the author in quest of a character — mistakenly believed to be his Self. As Malone he is the author who has given up the search for himself, and finds that in spite of himself he seeks himself still. And as the Unnamable, he is that for which, as Malone, as Moran, as Molloy, he sought. But as the Unnamable, he cannot be described, as Molloy-as-writer described Molloy-as-character; as Moran described Molloy; as Malone described Macmann and Lemuel — and, in the very process of talking about them, described himself.[26]

The reason for the Unnamable's ineffability is, at this point in the history of modern thought, very nearly a commonplace. It can be found in Kierkegaard, Nietzsche, Sartre, Buber, Tillich. It can be found, that is, in any system of thought which asserts that a man cannot be reduced to or treated as an object merely, but must be understood also as a subject, a Thou. If I take for my proof-text a passage from Martin Heidegger, it is not because I believe that Beckett is more indebted to him than to any other modern thinker, but because the passage is such a remarkably apt and accurate answer to the Unnamable's question "Who now?" To this question Heidegger, with his own emphasis, replies:

If the "I" is an Essential characteristic of Dasein [loosely, Man], *then it is one which must be Interpreted existentially.* In that case the "Who?" is to be answered only by exhibiting phenomenally a definite kind of Being which Dasein possesses. . . .

But if the Self is conceived 'only' as a way of Being of this entity, this seems tantamount to volatilizing the real 'core' of Dasein. Any apprehensiveness however which one may have about this gets its nourishment from the perverse assumption that the entity in question has at bottom the kind of Being which belongs to something present-at-hand, even if one is far from attributing to it the solidity of an occurrent corporeal Thing. Yet man's *'substance'* is not spirit as a synthesis of soul and body; it is rather *existence*.[27]

In answer to the question "Who now?" Heidegger neatly turns us around and points us back to the trilogy, particularly to the last novel, where in fact there is exhibited phenomenally the definite kind of Being which the Unnamable possesses: for the Unnamable's existence is his talk. He *is* only in his speech; his being is his speaking.

His goal, as we have seen, is that of silence, and to achieve his goal he must stop speaking of Murphy and Molloy and Malone, and speak only of himself (TN, 419). But the only words he has are "their" words: "It's of me now I must speak, even if I have to do it with their language, it will be a start, a step towards silence." "I have no language but theirs, no, perhaps I'll say it, even with their language, for me alone" (TN, 450). But since in the trilogy speaking is identical with being, the fact that the Unnamable has no words of his own but only "their" words means that he has no being of his own but only "their" being. In Heidegger's terms, this kind of being is called "Being-with-one-another," and in "Being-with" one loses one's own being to "the Others."

Dasein, as everyday Being-with-one-another, stands in *subjection* to Others. It itself *is* not; its Being has been taken away by the Others. Dasein's everyday possibilities of Being are for the Others to dispose of as they please. These Others, moreover, are not *definite* Others. On the contrary, any Other can represent them. . . . One belongs to the Others oneself and enhances their power. 'The Others' whom one thus designates in order to cover up the fact of one's belonging to them essentially oneself, are those who proximally and for the most part *'are there'* in everyday Being-with-one-another. The "who" is not this one, not that one, not oneself, not some people, and not the sum of them all. The 'who' is the neuter, *the "they"* [*das Man*].[28]

The Others who "are there" for the Unnamable and to whom he belongs are Murphy, Molloy, and all the rest about whom the Unnamable has told stories in the only language he knows, the language that belongs to "them." Now, in order to find his own language, he tells a story about Mahood, hoping in the process to tell a story about himself and thereby speak in his own words and be himself. This fails, as it has to, and he shifts to Worm: "Perhaps it's by trying to be Worm that I'll finally succeed in being Mahood, I hadn't thought of that. Then all I'll have to do is be Worm. Which no doubt I shall achieve by trying to be Jones. Then all I'll have to do is be Jones. Stop, perhaps he'll spare me that . . ." (TN, 470). But all of these Worms and Mahoods are merely the Unnamable's "vice-existers," mere impersonations, masks, disguises for the Unnamable's own proper being. What he seeks is his "authentic" self, not a "they-self." Dispersed as he is into the

"they," he must find his authentic being. But if Dasein is to disclose to itself its own authentic Being, says Heidegger, this disclosure is always accomplished by "a clearing-away of concealments and obscurities," by "a
breaking up of the disguises with which Dasein bars its own way." This
means that he must stop using language to tell stories; he must stop inventing characters, for they are "disguises" of his own authentic being. He must
stop being an artist, for to be an artist is to fail. Rather, he must use whatever words he knows in whatever ways he knows how:

. . . you have only to wait, without doing anything, it's no good doing anything, and without understanding, there's no help in understanding, and all
comes right, nothing comes right, nothing, nothing, this will never end, this
voice will never stop, I'm alone here, the first and the last, I never made anyone
suffer, I never stopped anyone's sufferings, no one will ever stop mine, they'll
never depart, I'll never stir, I'll never know peace, neither will they, but with
this difference, that they don't want it, they say they don't want it, they say I
don't want it either, don't want peace . . . (TN, 529)

The writer can give us many things, but he cannot give us "existence." If
he is to give us "the Self," he must do so, as it were, at one remove. But as
soon as he attempts to talk about the Self, he volatilizes its core, for he attributes to it (I skirt Heidegger's careful distinction) "the solidity of an occurrent corporeal thing" and sticks him in a jar, perhaps. Hence the method
of the trilogy. It presents the Self in its several aspects or manifestations, in
one disguise after another, but presents it finally in a fashion as close to its
true existence as possible. It presents the Self, that undenominatable I, in its
being as speaking: speaking and complaining and remembering and thinking and confessing. Above all confessing—confessing its failures, its
doubts; confessing its weaknesses, its alienation from itself, its homeless-
ness, its fear and hope of death; confessing its obligation to confess, its inability to confess. And then, after nearly six hundred pages, perhaps the Self,
exhibited phenomenally in its confessional Being, does just begin to emerge.

V   TIME, GROUND, AND THE END: THE DRAMA

We sail within a vast sphere, ever drifting in uncertainty, driven from end to end. When we think to attach ourselves to any point and to fasten to it, it wavers and leaves us; and if we follow it, it eludes our grasp, slips past us, and vanishes for ever. Nothing stays for us. This is our natural condition, and yet most contrary to our inclination; we burn with desire to find solid ground and an ultimate sure foundation whereon to build a tower reaching to the Infinite. But our whole groundwork cracks, and the earth opens to abysses.

Pascal

Dasein comports itself towards something possible in its possibility by *expecting* it. . . . To expect something possible is always to understand it and to 'have' it with regard to whether and when and how it will be actually present-at-hand. Expecting is not just an occasional looking-away from the possible to its possible actualization, but is essentially a *waiting for that actualization.* . . .
The "they" has always kept Dasein from taking hold of these possibilities of Being. . . . So Dasein makes no choices, gets carried along by the nobody, and thus ensnares itself in inauthenticity. This process can be reversed only if Dasein specifically brings itself back to itself from its lostness in the "they."
. . . When Dasein thus brings itself back from the "they," the they-self is modified in an existentiell manner so that it becomes *authentic* Being-one's-Self. . . . But because Dasein is *lost* in the "they," it must first *find* itself. In order to find *itself* at all, it must be 'shown' to itself in its possible authenticity. In terms of its *possibility*, Dasein is already a potentiality-for-Being-its-Self, but it needs to have this potentiality attested.

Heidegger

To every Action there is always opposed an equal Reaction; or the mutual actions of two bodies upon each other are always equal, and directed to contrary parts.
    Newton

Heat cannot, of itself, pass from a colder to a hotter body.
        Clausius

Then shall the kingdom of heaven be likened unto ten virgins, which took their lamps, and went forth to meet the bridegroom. And five of them were wise, and five were foolish. . . .[1]
    Matt. 25:1–2

I

◄ ► It is a matter of time.

In the novel time is manipulable: three spaced periods catapult the reader over hours, days, years, as easily to land him in the future as to land him in the past. It is the novelist's privilege to catch in midflight the Present Moment, to freeze it, to hold it, to look at it and exploit it until he is satisfied that he has done with it. Then, in his own good time, he will let it resume its flight. Nor is the Moment, once out of his hands, wholly irretrievable. The novelist can recall it, re-establish it as Present, review it, reuse it, and then once more send it back to its place in the Past. In the hands of the novelist, time is plastic.

The dramatist, however, has no such command over time. He may make time skip a bit between scenes and acts: a ten-minute intermission may represent a day, a year or more. But Lear's line, "What! Fifty of my followers at a clap? / Within a fortnight?" does not sit well, for time has been impossibly telescoped here within a single scene.

Moreover, the "direction" of time in the theater tends to be unidirectional and irreversible. It is very difficult for the playwright to "stop" time and present on stage an event which both chronologically and causally precedes "Stage Present." It would seem, indeed, to be almost axiomatic that in the theater, the place is "here," the time "now." And this Now is not the elastic present available to the novelist. The content of a moment in one of James's novels may be enormous or it may be slight; it may take pages to describe, or it may take a line or two. But the content of a moment on stage is roughly equivalent to any other given moment. Time on stage is regular, rigid. Its tempo for any whole scene is sixty seconds to the minute.

The moments of stage time are, then, like compartments of equal size, and these compartments must be "filled" with the sort of goings-on whose character it is to be so lively, interesting, distracting, that the audience is unaware that time is passing. The careful playwright will do all he can to make "stage time" so significant that the audience will forget its own, "natural," time. The successful play is the one which manages to make the audience forget itself, lose itself in the play, lose its time in "stage time."

Comments upon time and the stage such as the foregoing presuppose that time itself is not an appropriate matter to deal with in the theater. Time is thought of rather as a play's environment or framework; it is a structural element, not a thematic one. The theater may deal with events that happen in time, but the theater is not the vehicle for dealing directly with time. At least, it was not until quite recently.

"Have you not done tormenting me with your accursed time!" The line is Pozzo's, but it could as well be spoken by any of the other three characters in Beckett's *Waiting for Godot*. Time is the common enemy. To Pozzo it brings only privation and decay: he loses in its course his pipe, his vaporizer, his watch, his sight, his dignity, and his pride. To Lucky it brings no relief from his slavery, except that in the second act he seems to have lost the power to speak. To Didi and Gogo it brings only frustration and, occasionally, a brief interlude in their otherwise tedious waiting for the promised one. "That passed the time," says Didi after the departure of Pozzo and Lucky in the first act. Characteristically, Gogo attempts to restrain Didi's modest effort to see life as more than unrelievedly burdensome: "It would have passed in any case." Didi weakly replies, "Yes, but not so rapidly." Passing the time is the chief occupation of the two men-in-waiting. Hence the advent of Pozzo and Lucky provides a welcome diversion. But when master and slave leave, Didi and Gogo are returned to their plight.

ESTRAGON. What do we do now?
VLADIMIR. I don't know.
ESTRAGON. Let's go.
VLADIMIR. We can't.
ESTRAGON. Why not?
VLADIMIR. We're waiting for Godot.
ESTRAGON. (*despairingly*). Ah!
              (WFG, 31a–32)

The two propose various stratagems for passing time. They try to converse calmly, but the conversation declines into an intolerable silence — intolerable, because it leaves each alone with his thoughts, and to think is "misery." But even here time is against them, for, as Vladimir observes, "What is terrible is to *have* thought." The present is strewn with the corpses of dead ideas; it is a "charnel-house" where the fleshless bones of past thoughts are immured. And to make matters worse, "You can't help looking" at these skeletons.

Or they play at being Pozzo and Lucky; or they "abuse each other"; or they do their "exercises":

ESTRAGON. Our movements.
VLADIMIR. Our elevations.
ESTRAGON. Our relaxations.

VLADIMIR. Our elongations.
ESTRAGON. Our relaxations.
VLADIMIR. To warm us up.
ESTRAGON. To calm us down.
VLADIMIR. Off we go.
                            (WFG, 49)

They hop from one foot to another, but quickly cease. "That's enough," says Gogo. "I'm tired." Not merely fatigued, either, but bored — bored with a life that is as senseless as if it were a mere hopping from foot to foot. "I'm tired breathing."

The business of living, for Didi and Gogo, is a matter of filling up the gaping holes in time. It does not matter with what one fills or passes time, so long as it is filled, so long as it is got rid of, so long as it is passed into the Past, where it can be ignored and forgotten.

ESTRAGON. I tell you we weren't here yesterday. . . .
VLADIMIR. And where were we yesterday evening according to you?
ESTRAGON. How would I know? In another compartment. There's
    no lack of void.
                            (WFG, 42a)

Time and space are void, and any particular time ("yesterday evening") or particular space ("here") is just one of several compartments in the void. The Now is empty, though it is exactly the emptiness of the Now which the two men cannot abide and which, therefore, they do their best to fill with whatever comes to hand.

Consequently, when one has beguiled the time successfully, one may be permitted to boast a bit. "That wasn't such a bad little canter," says Estragon after a brisk exchange with Didi. Or, later, "We don't manage too badly, eh Didi, between the two of us? . . . We always find something, eh Didi, to give us the impression we exist?" But more frequently it is the other way round. In the midst of one of their little canters, Gogo or Didi will suddenly realize the futility and meaninglessness of it all. Gogo, doing the last of the "exercises," abruptly stops, brandishes his fists, and at the top of his voice roars, "God have pity on me!" More pitiful, because more terrifying in its implications, is Didi's announcement, "Time has stopped." Didi is moved to this judgment by a wholly inconsequential exchange between Gogo and Pozzo. For them, time may be passing, but for Didi, who is outside this dialogue, who is, as it were, a witness to its absurdity, time has quit moving. The Present in the fullness of its nothingness has encompassed him. Shortly thereafter, he, not the more restless Gogo, suggests that they leave the place. It would seem to be an effort to escape time by changing place.

It is a foolish and impossible idea, of course, and both Didi and Gogo seem to realize it; although each proposes to the other that they go away, they never act on the proposal. They seem to realize that to exist is to exist in time. And to exist in time, one must be able to tolerate the guilt of the past, the meaninglessness of the present, and the death which lies in the future.

Mercifully, Didi and Gogo are largely spared the burden of the past, for their memories are so defective that little of earlier time remains to them. There is something about picking grapes and Gogo's attempted suicide which they both remember, but very vaguely. Otherwise, Gogo can hardly remember what happened the preceding day. Since time is void, it is difficult to distinguish between one absence and another. Didi points to the tree as palpable evidence of the fact that the "here" where they find themselves today is identical with the "here" where they found themselves yesterday. But Gogo, who has spent all his life "crawling about in the mud," is unimpressed with the argument. It is as difficult to tell the mud of here from the mud of not-here as it is to distinguish kinds of void.

It is rather the present and the future which present the serious threats to the pair. It is, indeed, the character of the future which determines the character of the present, and makes existence in the now of time so difficult to sustain. For the future is ambiguous, vague. It holds both threat and promise. It is, as it were, the home of Godot, for whom they wait, and upon whose decision their very lives depend. They have made Godot "a kind of prayer," "a vague supplication," and they wait now for his answer. Until it comes, they can plan nothing, do nothing — nothing, that is, but pass or fill time, improvise, ad lib. Like their speech, their existence is extemporaneous, out of time, where time is conceived as the ambiance of purposive, teleological action. For they have no goal, and can have none, until Godot appears to tell them of his decision. Their existence is absolutely contingent upon the event "the arrival of Godot." Until that event occurs, Didi and Gogo can do nothing but wait.

But this, of course, is what the play is all about. *Waiting for Godot* presents to us the image of that kind of existence which is radically, absolutely dependent for its significance upon time future, upon that-which-is-about-to-be: which is to say, it is a play about existence. For existence, human being in time, has its value or worthwhileness corroborated only by events which are yet to appear. The significance of the present can be apprehended only when present events are translated into the past. Only then can one say, Ah yes, now it is clear that such a decision was right (or wrong), for these later events have shown it to be so.

If it is necessary, then, to identify Godot in some special way, we may begin by saying that Godot is simply Time Future. He is arriving at every instant of time, of course, but as soon as he passes the barrier between Time Future and Time Present, he is no longer Godot but someone or something else: Pozzo and Lucky, for example, or the Boy. And the Boy speaks truly, in his account of Godot.

> BOY. (*in a rush*). Mr. Godot told me to tell you he won't come this evening but surely to-morrow.

Godot will not come this evening, because "this evening" is Now. He will come "to-morrow" and will come all future tomorrows because tomorrow is Time Future. Spinoza's saying, *Determinatio negatio est*, applies to *Zeit* as well as to *Sein*: to be tomorrow is not to be today; to be Future is not to be Present. Since Godot is Time Future, he cannot be Time Present, so while he is always on the way he can never arrive.

He is more than Time Future, however. He is the Answer to which the being of man is the Question. What he is *materialiter*, then, depends on the terms in which the Question is asked. If it is asked in terms of the bifurcation of man into body and mind, he is the pre-established harmony or the God of the Occasionalists — that is, the principle of unity and cooperation. If it is asked in terms of the class conflict, as exhibited in the relationship of Pozzo and Lucky, he is the Classless Society. If it is asked in terms of the classical Christian tradition, he is "a personal God . . . outside time without extension who . . . loves us dearly" and will forgive man his sin. If, however, the Question is put in its ancient gnostic form or modern existentialist form — the form that holds that the sin man must repent is, in Gogo's words, "Our being born," — then Godot is simply Death or nonbeing.

All of which is to say that Godot is the Absolute — or, more precisely, he is thought by Didi possibly to be the Absolute. He and Gogo are waiting to "see what he says," "hear what he has to offer," and then they will take it or leave it. The point, however, is that the initiative lies with Godot, not with Didi and Gogo. Their being is contingent upon his being; he is, in Murphy's words, "the prior system."

Godot can then be summed up in phrases such as "the Future Ground" or "Possible Absolute." But as either Future or Possible, he is not and cannot be Present and Actual; and if he cannot be Present and Actual, then he who waits for him can never have that sure and certain Ground which he is waiting and longing for as the authorization of his being and the validation of his Time. Hence, Godot and his decision is an event which will forever dangle before the two men, like the carrot before the donkey (Estragon: "I'll never forget this carrot"), leading them, that is, to the "place" which is the border between time present and time future, between what is and what may be.

Because they understand themselves as contingent upon Godot, the two men do not understand themselves as free. The first words spoken in the play are Gogo's: "Nothing to be done." And though the immediate reference is to the task of pulling off his boots, the larger meaning is that he and Didi are not free to decide for themselves who and what they shall be and do. The phrase appears again in its larger significance a little later.

> VLADIMIR. Nothing you can do about it.
> ESTRAGON. No use struggling.
> VLADIMIR. One is what one is.
> ESTRAGON. No use wriggling.
> VLADIMIR. The essential doesn't change.
> ESTRAGON. Nothing to be done.
>   (WFG, 14a)

Tossed off like this, the phrases are mere clichés, the rationalizations of the resigned. Taken seriously, however, they are the expression of the Essentialist doctrine of man as set out, for example, by Hegel. Spirit and Nature unite, he says, in something called "human nature."

> In speaking of human nature we mean something permanent. The concept of human nature must fit all men and all ages, past and present. This universal concept may suffer infinite modifications; but actually the universal is one and the same essence in its most various modifications. . . . The universal type appears even in what seems to deviate from it most strongly; in the most distorted figure we can still discern the human.[2]

The characteristics of the Spirit in man are self-consciousness and freedom. These are also the characteristics of God, and to the extent that man actualizes them in himself he is the image of God. Didi and Gogo are no doubt "distorted figures" who deviate from the "universal type," but they do not fool Pozzo. He recognizes them instantly: "You are human beings

. . . As far as one can see . . . Of the same species as myself . . . Of the same species as Pozzo! Made in God's image!"

Essence then precedes existence. The essence of human nature is universal and must fit all men at all times in all places. The task of the particular man, the individual existence, is to actualize in himself that essence which he has in common with all other men. But what if one does not know what Hegel knew? What if one does not know what one's essence is? One could actualize for all one is worth, but it would all be futile, for one wouldn't know one's essence even if by chance one actualized it. Without a knowledge of the essence which one is to become or actualize, all existence is vanity, history is without orientation or direction and is therefore pointless, meaningless, void. All one can do in such a situation is pass the time until someone comes along who knows what the essence is and will explain it. Then one will know where he stands, and will be in a position to accept or reject the explanation and all it entails.

What we have in *Waiting for Godot* is Eschatology without Incarnation, the teleological suspension of the ethical effected by or accounted for not by faith (as Kierkegaard accounted for Abraham's willingness to sacrifice Isaac), but by the utter absence of any present, actual event which can provide a reason for initiating ethically determined action. Godot's offer is what is wanted, but that is constantly being put off until tomorrow, so it can never enter the present; and even if it did enter the present, it would only be of the order of the possible (the tramps can take it or leave it) and not the necessary. What the two men need and want is an Absolute on which to base their own contingent existence.

The duo no doubt represents once again Cartesian man, Didi tending toward mind, Gogo toward body. Didi stinks from his mouth, Gogo from his feet. At the very opening of the play, Gogo is seen trying to remove a boot. He finally succeeds, and the stage directions report that he peers inside the boot, "feels about inside it, turns it upside down, shakes it, looks on the ground to see if anything has fallen out." Didi has gone through much the same operation with his hat: "He takes off his hat again, peers inside it, feels about inside it, knocks on the crown, blows into it, puts it on again." On Gogo's vain attempt to eliminate the pain in his foot by repairing his boot, Didi scornfully comments, "There's man all over for you, blaming on his boots the faults of his feet." But Didi's own action with regard to his hat indicates that he himself is blaming on his hat the faults of his head.

The irritant which vexes Didi's head at the moment is an historical and theological question. One of the thieves who was crucified with our Saviour was saved. But of the four Gospel accounts of the crucifixion, only one of them includes this incident, though all four evangelists were there, "or thereabouts."

ESTRAGON. Well? They don't agree and that's all there is to it.
VLADIMIR. But all four were there. And only one speaks of a thief being saved. Why believe him rather than the others?
ESTRAGON. Who believes him?
VLADIMIR. Everybody. It's the only version they know.
ESTRAGON. People are bloody ignorant apes.

(WFG, 9a)

Estragon's contemptuous reply clearly indicates that he means to exclude himself—and possibly Didi—from the class "people." A little later, however, and immediately following Didi's assertion that they have got rid of their "rights," the two take up a posture ("arms dangling, heads sunk, sagging at the knees") which is remarkably simian. People may be bloody ignorant apes, but the fact remains that they believe. People commit themselves to causes and principles which entail decisions and actions. Didi's question, "Why believe him rather than the others?" is in fact an inquiry into those conditions in which a reasonable man, having no recourse to unquestionable proof, may make a decision, commit himself to a course of action. How much and what kind of evidence does a man need in order to assent to a proposition or give himself to an act? Didi in fact is asking, "What are we doing here? Why believe Godot?"

That they are where they are is evidence enough that they give credence to Godot's promise that he will come. But why should they believe this? Why, that is, should man stand in expectation of the future? Why should he conduct his life in such a way that he is oriented to the things which are yet to come? And yet more preposterous, why should he expect to find in the yet-to-be grounds more relevant and urgent for establishing his life than those which he finds in the what-now-is?

To this question there seems to be no answer that is much better than Gogo's: "People are bloody ignorant apes." Man believes because it is the nature of man to believe. Man waits because it is his nature to wait. Because he believes, because he lives in continual expectation, he cannot bring himself to cut short the time of waiting, and Didi and Gogo do not hang themselves. And as it is in the nature of man to wait, so it is the nature of existence that his waiting shall be purposeless. Man waits for his existence to be grounded on something other than what he himself is and does, but there is nothing else than man here, man now.

The only nourishment they provide for themselves consists of certain vegetables — carrots, turnips, radishes. Radish: from *radix*, root; for example the square root of two, an irrational number, that is, *alogos*, absurd. They masticate the absurd; they live *on* as well as *in* the irrational. The more Gogo eats the worse it gets, but Vladimir gets used to the muck as he goes along (WFG, 14a). And it is Gogo who is the one who usually says "Let's go," whereas Vladimir says they can't because they're waiting for Godot. In spite of the absurdity of their situation, Didi tends to keep up hope in the appearance of the Absolute, while Gogo is more pessimistic.

Inasmuch as they are waiting for and so dependent on Godot, they can be thought of as "tied" to him, but when Gogo asks if they are tied down to him Didi rejects the notion. "Tied to Godot! What an idea! No question of it. (*Pause*.) For the moment." Indeed, the posture already characterized as "simian" ("*They remain motionless, arms dangling, heads sunk, sagging at the knees*") can also be seen as the posture of puppets whose strings have been relaxed or cut. However Godot is thought of — as God or the Absolute or perhaps even a Kantian categorical imperative — his "meaning" is that of a principle normative for being and action. Paradoxically, the two men are not free with regard to Godot, for their future is contingent upon his "offer," yet they are free, for they are not "tied" to him. But their freedom is the freedom of puppets without a puppeteer: it is the freedom of "motionlessness."

What it means to be tied to the Absolute — or to one kind of Absolute — is now exhibited to the two men: "*Enter Pozzo and Lucky. Pozzo drives Lucky by means of a rope passed round his neck . . .*" Pozzo exercises much the same kind of power over Lucky as the interventionist God of the Occasionalists exercised over man. He manipulates Lucky's body the way he would a marionette. "Stop! (*Lucky stops.*) Forward! (*Lucky advances.*) Stop! (*Lucky stops.*) . . . Back! (*Lucky moves back.*) Turn! (*Lucky turns . . .*)" (WFG, 28). He can also order him to "Think, pig!" But he cannot tell him what to think, for in his Geulincxian mind Lucky is free to think what he wants to think, and the only way to stop him from thinking is to attack him physically and remove his hat. Lucky's "thinking" is a pseudo-theologico-scientifical inquiry into the causes of things, and of old it has been held that *Felix qui potuit rerum cognoscere causas.*

This is the dilemma. Man tied to the absolute is a puppet to a puppeteer, a slave to its master, a circus animal to its trainer, and perhaps a character to its author; yet in his dependence and suffering he has at least the slight consolation of knowing who he is and what he is to do and be, and the very fact of his suffering lends him a minimal dignity which cannot be taken away from him, as the sentimental Gogo tries to do when he starts to wipe Lucky's tears away. Man not tied to the absolute, however, is "motionless," paralyzed by the absence of any cause or value or good to which he can give himself and which will validate his existence in a world which — lacking the absolute — is a meaningless void. Man not tied to the absolute is free, as the slave is not, but what is he free for? What is he free to do? What is he free to be? Is he free only to wait for the appearance — or reappearance — of the absolute?

Didi and Gogo are not tied to Pozzo, nor are they tied to each other except by such intangible bonds as a vaguely remembered but still common history, by common needs of nourishment and rest, by common sufferings (though Didi, the intellectual, suffers from an ailment of the urinary tract, and the somatic Gogo from bad dreams). The result of their sharing the common condition of being-human is that they have developed an inconsistent but still genuine compassion for each other. Their relationship can hardly be dignified by the word "love," but it is one of occasional concern, of fellow-feeling and compassion. "Does it hurt?" is a question that Pozzo never asks Lucky, even in mock sympathy.

This does not mean that Didi and Gogo are models of Christian charity. They are both self-centered, Gogo perhaps more than Didi, and are frequently cruel to each other as well as to Pozzo and Lucky. Indeed, one of the bitterest moments in the play comes in the second act when Didi, in a burst of eloquence, replies to the fallen Pozzo's pathetic plea for help.

VLADIMIR. Let us not waste our time in idle discourse! (*Pause. Vehemently.*) Let us do something, while we have the chance! It is not every day that we are needed.

This stern resolution is immediately enervated by careful reasoning, however. "Not indeed that we personally are needed. Others would meet the case equally well. . . ." Then again a declaration of intended help; which is lost in further weighing of the pros and cons of helping; all of which is finally concluded, not by an act of aid, but by a self-righteous claim to integrity:

VLADIMIR. . . . What are we doing here, *that* is the question. And we are blessed in this, that we happen to know the answer. Yes, in this immense confusion one thing alone is clear. We are waiting for Godot to come —
ESTRAGON. Ah!
POZZO. Help!
VLADIMIR. Or for night to fall. (*Pause.*) We have kept our appointment and that's an end to that. We are not saints, but we have kept our appointment. How many people can boast as much?
ESTRAGON. Billions.

(WFG, 51–51a)

In vanity and emptiness Didi waits for someone who does not come to bring something that may not be in his power to give; while at his feet, immediately present, lies the occasion for making of his life something more than a series of exercises in passing or killing time. Blinded by the dazzling spectacle of the future possibility of leading a significant existence, deafened by the roar of distant Godot's promise, the two men can neither see nor hear that there are two other human beings in need of help.

I want to explore this situation a little further, and in doing so I shall use Martin Heidegger's language and concepts again. But at the outset I must once more insist that I am not imputing a knowledge of Heidegger to Beckett (though I would not deny it either), and am not supposing that Beckett's works are puzzles or allegories explicable only by reference to *Sein und Zeit*. I am, rather, trying to get at the "meaning" of the scene, and am using Heidegger as only one of several possible ways of doing so.

As in the case of the trilogy, the problem at issue is that of Dasein's existence. Like the Unnamable, Didi and Gogo are "guilty" of inauthentic existence, of living in the "they-self" and hence of being in a condition of "lostness." Dasein — again, Didi and Gogo, or perhaps Didi-Gogo — is lost in the "they" and in the talk of the "they" — Godot's promises, the voices of dead thoughts, and their own idle chatter and time-passing. Thus lost, Dasein "fails to hear its own self in listening to the they-self." "If Dasein is to be able to get brought back from this lostness of failing to hear itself, and if this is to be done through itself, then it must first be able to find itself — to find itself as something which has failed to hear itself, and which fails to hear in that it *listens away* to the 'they.' This listening-away must get broken off. . . ." [3]

It is the voice of conscience which is able to break off the attachment to the "they-voice"; for conscience makes its appeal to the very center of Dasein, to that Self which is, in Heidegger's terminology, "Being-in-the-world." "The call of conscience has the character of an *appeal* to Dasein by calling it to its ownmost potentiality-for-Being-its-Self; and this is done by way of *summoning* it to its ownmost Being-guilty." [4] Thus conscience calls Dasein out of its lostness in the they, calls it forth into its own possibilities.

So far, so good. But now Heidegger goes on to identify the caller and to describe the content of the call. "*In conscience Dasein calls itself.* . . . The call comes *from* me and yet *from beyond me.* . . . In its 'who,' the caller is definable in a 'worldly' way by *nothing* at all. The caller is Dasein in its uncanniness: primordial, thrown Being-in-the-world as the 'not-at-home' — the bare 'that-it-is' in the 'nothing' of the world. The caller is unfamiliar to the everyday they-self; it is something like an *alien* voice." [5] And yet it appears that the voice which is most alien to the they-self is exactly the Self which Dasein is. Hence, in conscience, Dasein calls itself.

And what is said in the discourse of conscience? "*What* does the conscience call to him to whom it appeals? Taken strictly, nothing. The call asserts nothing, gives no information about world-events, has nothing to tell. . . . 'Nothing' gets called *to* . . . this Self, but it has been *summoned* . . . to itself — that is, to its ownmost potentiality-for-Being. . . . The call dispenses with any kind of utterance. It does not put itself into words at all. . . . *Conscience discourses solely and constantly in the mode of keeping silent.*" [6]

Now not even so ingenious a playwright as Samuel Beckett has yet been able to devise a dramatic technique for representing a discourse whose content is nothing and which originates from "nothing at all." If the drama is anything, it is "worldly," public. It is, if one may put it so, the art form whose dealings are exactly with the "they-self"; and Heidegger lends himself rather more readily to discussions of the novel of the interior life than to discussions of the interrelations of persons on a stage. Consequently, if the voice of conscience is to be dramatized, it must be "externalized," and it must be given an audible if minimal content. Allow the speculation, if only momentarily and conditionally, that the Heideggerian voice of conscience is articulated by Pozzo, and that the content of the call is the one word, "Help."

(In parentheses an interesting correspondence between Beckett's play and the philosophical argument may be noted. In the second act, when all four characters are down, and Pozzo has crawled a little way away from the rest, Didi and Gogo call him by name, but since he does not respond they decide to call him by other names. It would be amusing, says Gogo, "to try him with other names, one after the other. It'd pass the time. And we'd be bound to hit on the right one sooner or later" [wfg, 53a]. He calls out "Abel! Abel!" Pozzo replies, "Help!" and Gogo exalts, "Got it in one!"

> The caller maintains itself in conspicuous indefiniteness. If the caller is asked about its name, status, origin, or repute, it not only refuses to answer, but does not even leave the slightest possibility of one's making it into something with which one can be familiar. . . . On the other hand, it by no means disguises itself in the call. That which calls the call, simply holds itself aloof from any way of becoming well-known. . . . The peculiar indefiniteness of the caller and the impossibility of making more definite what this caller is, are not just nothing. . . . They make known to us that the caller is solely absorbed in summoning us to something, that it is *heard only as such*, and furthermore that it will not let itself be coaxed.[7]

So when Gogo calls Lucky by the name of Cain, Pozzo responds to that name too with the same word, "Help." Whereupon Gogo concludes, "He's all humanity" [wfg, 54].)

I intend not to construct a brief in defense of Beckett's reliance on Heidegger, but simply to draw attention to a similarity of "shape" or "function" between Pozzo's call for help and Heidegger's "call of conscience." There are indeed important dissimilarities between the play and the argument as well as similarities. In Heidegger, the call of conscience is the call of "care" (*Sorge*); and as such it does not lead to repentance in any theological sense, nor does it necessarily lead to "ethical" behavior. Care is wholly "self-centered," inasmuch as it is concern for one's own potentiality-for-being, and it is to this that conscience calls the self. The relations among persons is not of primary interest in *Sein und Zeit*.

But in the play, Pozzo's plea for help is the call of one Dasein to another Dasein. After procrastinating for an unconscionably long time, Gogo and Didi eventually act in accordance with the content of the call.

pozzo. Help!

. . . .

vladimir. He wants us to help him to get up.
estragon. Then why don't we? What are we waiting for? (*They help Pozzo to his feet, let him go. He falls.*)
vladimir. We must hold him. (*They get him up again. Pozzo sags between them, his arms round their necks.*)

(wfg, 54–54a)

The eye looking for such a thing may see in this tableau the composition of a Pieta or a Deposition. But it takes no special insight to recognize that the relationship which the three men establish is quite a different thing from the relationship of, say, Pozzo and Lucky. The call for help has resulted in the development of a community of interdependence among men. In this moment when action has at least the shape of charity we have a "now" whose content is of the very stuff of human Being; it is at long last a "now" that is not simply another compartment of the void. But Didi and Gogo do not recognize this. They help Pozzo to his feet, and continue their conversation in an ordinary way, as if nothing had happened.

Why do the two tramps help Pozzo? They are not "tied" to him any more than they are to Godot. He certainly has done nothing to deserve their help. In his treatment of them he has been condescending, intimidating, scornful, supercilious. He does promise them a reward of two hundred francs; but by the time they help him they seem to have forgotten the promise, and make nothing of it. Is it out of obedience to religious or ethical principle? In the first Act, Vladimir berates Pozzo for treating Lucky so badly: "To treat a man . . . like that . . . I think that . . . no . . . a human being . . . no . . . it's a scandal!" (wfg, 18a). Didi seems to have some vaguely Kantian notion of man as an end in himself. When he hears Pozzo tearfully complain about Lucky's behavior, however, Didi attacks the slave with equal ferocity: "How dare you! It's abominable! Such a good master! Crucify him like that! After so many years! Really!" This is the rhetoric of a sentimental, sanctimonious humanism that responds with bathos and righteous anger to the evil nearest at hand and most emotionally publicized. There is nothing in it of conviction or real devotion to the human good. Inevitably, then, Didi responds to Pozzo's call for help with mere eloquence.

And yet, in the event he and Gogo do come to Pozzo's aid — not because Pozzo deserves it, not because they will receive a reward, and not really out of any moral conviction. Once up, Pozzo asks if the two are his friends, to which Vladimir replies that they've proved they are by helping him. Gogo agrees: "Exactly. Would we have helped him if we weren't his friends?" Didi replies, "Possibly," thereby undermining this reason too.

In other words, their helping Pozzo get up is an act as arbitrary as their getting themselves up after having themselves fallen:

> *They get up.*
> ESTRAGON. Child's play.
> VLADIMIR. Simple question of will-power.
> (wfg, 54)

There is no suggestion of moral or any other value to helping Pozzo. It is not something one needs to do for this or that compelling reason. It is something one can do, it is something to do, to pass the time, until Godot comes. The act changes nothing. The two men have no sense of having done well, of having obeyed a categorical imperative, of having played the Good Samaritan. They are not different for having done what they did. Pozzo too is the same as before. Ready to leave, he tells the men to get Lucky on his feet by pulling on the rope as hard as they like, short of strangling him; and if this doesn't move him, they should give him a taste of the boot, "in the face and the privates as far as possible."

Then what of the call of conscience summoning Dasein to its own-most potentiality-for-Being-its-Self? Do we see in Didi and Gogo that authentic existence which is initiated by Dasein's acknowledging of its guilt? By no means. They are not other than they were: "the essential doesn't change." And Didi and Gogo are *essentially* pseudo-persons, imitation human beings, mere characters in a play, who the following night, like automata, will go through the whole process over again. The issue is not whether they will change. The issue is whether the only Dasein that is real, the only Dasein that is important, will change; and that is the Dasein seated in "that bog," the auditorium.

So the real call of conscience is not Pozzo's cry for help. The real call is the soundless image of two men helping a third, the three locked in the embrace of human compassion, "his arm round their necks." The image is all but lost in the business that precedes and follows it. It is there, and then gone. But it is the moment to which the whole of the play leads, and which, in its simplicity and purity, stands in judgment on the meaningless waiting, the tyrannical abuse of one's fellow man, and the ravings of a maddened intellect which in the play pass for "entertainment." And it stands in judgment on those same actions and events in the "real" world in which the "real" Dasein dwells, and which, in that world, pass for "living." It is the counterpart, infinitely more subtle, of Hamm's screamed command to the Dasein watching him, "Get out of here and love one another!" (E, 68)

Given this moment of positive value, and one or two others, how are we to assess the play as a whole? Are the pessimism and despair of the two tramps overcome by those instances of charity and compassion that are also represented? Does not Didi's act of covering the sleeping Gogo's shoulders with his own coat somehow compensate in the total economy for Pozzo's abuse of Lucky?

I think in fact it does. The "weight" of despair is exactly counterbalanced by the "weight" of optimism; the meaningfulness of compassion equalizes the meaninglessness of isolation and ennui. Echoing the sentiment expressed by Neary in the figure of the "two buckets" (M, 58–59), Pozzo declares, "The tears of the world are a constant quantity. For each one who begins to weep somewhere else another stops. The same is true of the laugh" (WFG, 22). This is Newton brought to bear on passion. The third of his laws of motion declares that for every action there is an opposite and equal reaction. The loss and decay suffered by Pozzo and Lucky suggest a tragic view of history, but the appearance of a few leaves on the tree suggests life and rebirth and a "comic" view. Both of these views, however, are countervailed by the "cyclical" theory of history suggested by the similarity of the two acts and the round that Didi sings. The play is subtitled "Tragicomedy in 2 Acts," and comedy and tragedy, hope and despair, optimism and pessimism, are engaged in a dialectic of affirmation and negation whose issue is left in doubt. Each of the two acts ends when the opposites are balanced in an ephectic stasis: *"They do not move."*

II

◄ ► If *Waiting for Godot* is "difficult," *Endgame* (*Fin de Partie*, 1957) is no less so. In both cases, one of the important reasons for the difficulty is that the antecedents and the consequences of what is happening on stage are obscure. We do not know very much about the characters' past, and can only speculate on what their future will be. All we have is a Present. In the case of *Endgame*, that Present is more or less intelligible. There are four characters: Hamm — blind, aging, apparently paralyzed from the waist down, seated stage center in a wheelchair; Clov, his servant and adopted son, indifferently obedient to his master's orders but continually threatening to leave, afflicted (like Cooper in *Murphy*) with acathisia, a disease which prevents him from sitting; also Nagg, Hamm's father, and Nell, his mother (this is not certain), each stowed in ashbins, lids down, front left. They enter into conversation, mostly with one another; they tell jokes and stories: Nagg tells a joke more ancient than his ancient self about the tailor who compares to his own advantage the trousers he has made with the world God has made; Hamm narrates the next installment of a story he has been telling over a long period of time. Toward the end we learn that Nell has probably died — this loss offset in the universal economy, however, by the appearance off-stage, if we credit Clov, who reports the phenomenon, of a small boy.

This and much more is intelligible. It is the common lot of the aged that they die; it is in the nature of servants to be surly; it is typical of the weak, or of the once-powerful, that they tell themselves stories celebrating their imagined strength or their lost power. But the playgoer or reader wants more than this. Being curious and an inquirer into the causes of things, he wants to know how it came to pass that Hamm and his colleagues got themselves into such a fix, and wants to know as well — so given is he to prying, so aboriginal as to hold that causes have effects — wants to know whatever is to become of the remaining three? Is Nagg really dead? Is Hamm finally finished? Will the small boy join the group? Will Clov leave, and if so, where will he go?

In a more considerate age, when men and nations had histories and destinies, questions such as these did not go unanswered.

> Our last king,
> Whose image even but now appear'd to us,
> Was, as you know, by Fortinbras of Norway,
> Thereto prick'd on by a most emulate pride,
> Dar'd to the combat; in which our valiant Hamlet —
> For so this side of our known world esteem'd him —
> Did slay this Fortinbras; . . .[8]

Horatio rehearses the developments in recent military and political history not in order to brief Bernardo and Marcellus on current events, but to lay out for the audience the causal agencies which will be operative during "stage Time Present." Similarly at the end: the chaos of the final scene is imminently to be ordered, for there are causes in "stage Time Present" which will bring this about in "stage Time Future."

> I cannot live to hear the news from England
> But I do phophesy th' election lights
> On Fortinbras; he has my dying voice. . . .[9]

The particulars of implementation are irrelevant. It suffices to know that a whole sequence of energies and counterenergies has been exhausted, and that a causal and moral stasis or plateau has now been or is shortly to be achieved.

It is otherwise in *Endgame*, as it is in *Waiting for Godot*. The origin as well as the outcome of the situation on stage is but dimly perceived. Some things we know. Nell recalls an April afternoon when she and Nagg went rowing on Lake Como. The water was deep, but you could see to the bottom, "So white. So clean." She and Nagg lost their legs in a bicycle accident as they were travelling through the Ardennes on their way to Sedan. Clov had wept to have a bicycle, but Hamm refused him. There was a doctor, the source perhaps of Hamm's "pain-killers," but he is dead. So is Mother Pegg who at one time besought Hamm for oil for her lamp. He refused, though he had some; and she died, according to Clov, "of darkness." Hamm's estate has declined severely from the time when he could send out Clov, sometimes on foot, sometimes on horse, to inspect his "paupers." The world was at one time full of a great number of things — pap, sugarplums, bicycles, tides, pain-killers, coffins — but now it must be said of all these, "There are no more."

Of the future we know almost nothing. Clov has spotted a small boy, "a potential procreator," but Hamm distrusts the report. Whom are we to believe? If there is such a boy, ponders Hamm, he will either die out there or he will come "here." It is the second alternative that is perplexing. If he comes "here," will he be adopted by Clov as he himself had been adopted by Hamm? Will Clov then take Hamm's place and the dreary endgame begin anew? Is Hamm dead at the final tableau, or is he just lying doggo, like the flea in Clov's trousers? Will Clov actually make good on his promise to leave Hamm? If so, why is it that during the final moments of the play, and dressed against any weather (*"Panama hat, tweed coat, raincoat over his arm, umbrella, bag"*), he only stands by the door and watches Hamm? Is this in fact the end of the quartet, the ending end, or is this an end which contains yet another beginning? Is life finished, or only nearly finished? And what does it all mean? (Hamm: "Ah the old questions, the old answers, there's nothing like them!")

Those questions have a familiar ring. They sound like the questions posed by the alarmed baritone voice at the end of a fifteen-minute soap opera, or flashed glaringly across the screen at the end of an installment of one of the old movie serials. But if indeed we "tune in" tomorrow, or return next week to the neighborhood theater, we shall not in any way be advanced in our understanding, for we shall begin at the beginning (or at the end: "The end is in the beginning . . .") with the paradoxical opening words spoken by Clov, "Finished, it's finished, nearly finished, it must be nearly finished." What happens next in stage Time Future seems to be an unanswerable question, for the playwright has hidden these things from us. In *Endgame*, as in *Waiting for Godot*, there are fragments, obscure but visible, of Time Past. Of Time Future, there is nothing to be perceived except a void.

There are two versions of Time Past in *Endgame*. For Nell, it is something to be sighed over. "Ah yesterday." Yesterday is when one went rowing on Lake Como, and the bottom of the lake, like time itself, was white and clean. By the end of the play she is dead: so perish all sentimentalists. For Clov, yesterday is "that bloody awful day, long ago, before this bloody awful day." He continues to the end of the play, spiritually exhausted. Of Time Future also two versions: (1) there isn't any; (2) if there is, there will be sharks.

> HAMM (*with ardour*). Let's go from here, the two of us! South! You can make a raft and the currents will carry us away, far away, to other . . . mammals!
>
> .　.　.　.　.　.　.　.　.　.　.　.　.　.　.　.　.
>
> CLOV (*hastening towards door*). I'll start straight away.
> HAMM. Wait!
> (*Clov halts.*)
> Will there be sharks, do you think?
> CLOV. Sharks? I don't know. If there are there will be.
> (*He goes towards door.*)
> HAMM. Wait!
> (*Clov halts.*)
> Is it not yet time for my pain-killer?
>
> (E, 34–35)

Thus it is that the native hue of resolution is sicklied o'er with the pale cast of thought, etc. For as men were once immobilized by the threats of purgatory and Hell's fire, now they are immobilized by the mere possibility of threats — the shadow of shadows. Nor are the Platonic resonances of the situation wholly lost on the insightful blind man.

> HAMM. Did you ever think of one thing?
> CLOV. Never.
> HAMM. That here we're down in a hole.
> (*Pause.*)
> But beyond the hills? Eh? Perhaps it's still green. Eh?
> (*Pause.*)
> Flora! Pomona!
> (*Ecstatically.*)
> Ceres!　　　　　　　　　　　　　　　　(E, 39)

However, one cannot get "beyond the hills" merely by thinking about it. One must build rafts and launch them into the Heraclitean currents, sharks or no. But the dread of Time Future — that undiscover'd country from whose bourn no traveller has ever yet returned — puzzles the will and makes us rather bear those ills we have — with the help of a little pain-killer — than fly (or float) to others we know not of.

The fact that Beckett has suppressed the antecedent causes which give rise to the situation on stage, as well as the probable consequences of that situation, raises serious problems for the critic of *Endgame*. We may note two examples of another way in which the play's significance is obscured.

Early in the play there occurs the following passage:

HAMM. Why don't you kill me?
CLOV. I don't know the combination of the cupboard.
    (*Pause.*)
HAMM. Go and get two bicycle-wheels.
CLOV. There are no more bicycle-wheels.
HAMM. What have you done with your bicycle?
CLOV. I never had a bicycle.
HAMM. The thing is impossible.

(E, 8)

The first two lines remind us that a playgoer may be defined as a privileged eavesdropper. For the price of admission, he is permitted to observe and overhear some more or less interesting people doing and saying more or less important things. But he ought not to suppose that he can stretch his privilege to a guarantee that he will understand everything he overhears; for even characters on stage have something corresponding to private lives. I am not defending the validity of such questions as, How many children had Lady Macbeth? I am simply remarking the observable fact that characters on stage have a mystery about them analogous to the mystery which is a part of any man or woman in the world. I would also remark the obvious fact that the playwright can manipulate the dimensions of the mysterious attaching to a character or — as in the present case — attaching to a relationship, as this relationship has developed in time. To Hamm's question, "Why don't you kill me?" Clov replies "I don't know the combination of the cupboard." Beckett has deliberately amplified our awareness that we do not know all that there is to know about these two men. For Clov's reply makes no sense. What has the cupboard to do with killing Hamm? Is this where the instrument of murder is hidden? If so, why keep us in the dark about it?

Immediately following Clov's reply the stage directions call for a pause. Hamm's next words are, "Go and get two bicycle-wheels." It is reasonable to ask what train of thought leads Hamm from his question to his command. Here, by contrast with the example just noted, we may see order. For Hamm, death is a way out of the anguish he is enduring. But it is a way out that is locked. But if not death, then escape: he can leave. But his wheelchair has only small wheels, castors, very inefficient. As he himself notes a little later, "We'd need a proper wheel-chair. With big wheels. Bicycle wheels." If one is to escape, one must have better transportation. Hence the command to Clov to get bicycle wheels.

The other example of Beckett's deliberate suppression of intelligibility is very like the first. Hamm has dispatched Clov to open the window which looks out on the sea.

HAMM. You swear you've opened it?
CLOV. Yes.
    (*Pause.*)
HAMM. Well . . . !
    (*Pause.*)
    It must be very calm.
    (*Pause. Violently.*)
    I'm asking you is it very calm!
CLOV. Yes.
HAMM. It's because there are no more navigators.
    (*Pause.*)
    You haven't much conversation all of a sudden. Do you not feel well?
                                                                      (E, 65)

Clov's earlier answer — that he did not know the combination of the cupboard — had the air of mutual intelligibility and appeared to satisfy Hamm. But Hamm's speculation as to the reason for the calmness of the sea seems to engage no conversational gears in Clov. He seems to be stumped by his master's comment. We must suppose that Hamm knows what he means by the statement, "It's because there are no more navigators." But its meaning seems to elude Clov — he makes no reply, anyway — and it eludes the audience and reader as well.

The point I am making is this. *Endgame* is a difficult text to understand because the author appears to have suppressed evidence which it is important to have. He has obfuscated the causal relationships which support the plot, and he has tucked into the interstices of its structure data which we should very much like to have in the open. In the latter case, he has hidden particular meanings behind the intimacy which has developed between characters over the period of their association, so that the characters know what they mean, but the audience does not. Or he has made intelligibility dependent upon the correct interpretation of a character's train of thought or habits of association, neither of which is clearly discernible. It is probably to this tactic of deliberately suppressing the connections between statements, or between statement and significance, or between cause and effect, that Beckett referred when he spoke of the play as "rather difficult and elliptic." [10] He might well have said, "Rather difficult *because* elliptic."

The play is difficult, but by no means impossible, provided that we respect its elliptical quality and its multifaceted character. Richard M. Eastman has pointed out how *Endgame* operates on several "planes of reality": the characters inhabit a kind of limbo; they are pieces in a chess game; and they are actors who call attention to the fact that they are only actors. [11] Ruby Cohn notes the several correspondences between the play and the Gospel of John and Revelation. [12] Hugh Kenner says of the opening moments of the work that this is "so plainly a metaphor for waking up that we fancy the stage, with its high peepholes, to be the inside of an immense skull." [13] There are still others. Instead of referring to these several facets of the play as "planes of reality," however, I should prefer to call them dramatized metaphors for human existence. We may briefly describe five of the most important of these metaphors.

The stage set represents a portion of the board on which the last stage (endgame) of a game of chess is being played. Hamm is king, Clov a more mobile piece (knight, perhaps — he sometimes inspected Hamm's paupers [pawns] "on horse"), and Nagg and Nell two enemy pieces which have been taken and put out of the action (their faces are "very white" whereas Hamm's and Clov's are "very red"). (Parenthetically, we may note the language of other games. "Deuce": existence is like that point in tennis where advantage is to neither player and the game is at a stalemate. "Discard. . . . A few more squirms like that and I'll call": existence is like a hand of poker — you can't know if you are a winner unless you take the chance ["I'll call"] that you are a loser.) The chess metaphor concludes the play, for Hamm "remains motionless" in the brief tableau at the end: having sacrificed every piece in his own defense — pain-killer, coffins, bicycle wheels — he is now in check.

Checkmate (from Arab., shāh mātah, "the king is dead") reminds us of the second metaphor. The stage represents a throne room, Hamm a king, Clov a courtier (prince?). Kenner tentatively compares Hamm with Hamlet, Richard III ("My kingdom for a nightman"), and Richard II.[14] But Hamm is ruler over an empty and dying kingdom, his authority absolute and meaningless. He knows it, and quotes another king to show he knows it: "Our revels now are ended." The metaphor now attaches king to actor. The stage set represents a stage set, Hamm is a star actor, Clov has a supporting role. Existence — we have heard this before — is a game, like chess or tennis or poker, or like a play; and Hamm and Clov would agree with Jacques that

> All the world's a stage
> And all the men and women merely players:
> They have their exits and their entrances,
> And one man in his time plays many parts,
> His acts being seven ages. . . .[15]

The last of the seven scenes that Jacques describes is "second childishness" — when for example, one plays with toys again (Hamm: "Is my dog ready?") — and "mere oblivion,/ Sans teeth, sans eyes, sans taste, sans everything." From this, Hamm's catalog of losses varies a little: "We lose our hair, our teeth! Our bloom! Our ideals!"

Prospero's speech too is apposite to the metaphor, but the last lines seem especially applicable to the world described by *Endgame*:

> the great globe itself,
> Yes, all which it inherit, shall dissolve
> And, like this insubstantial pageant faded,
> Leave not a rack behind.[16]

It would seem reasonable that of clouds too it must be said, "There are no more."

The human being who plays Hamm plays the role of a man who believes that to exist is to play a role, or several roles — one of which is that of storyteller. Hamm tells himself — and Nagg — the story of a man who once appeared to Hamm to beg a favor. Hamm is narrator, plays the role of the beggar, plays the role of Hamm. He drops his roles and says to himself that he will soon be done with this story unless he finds other characters.

HAMM. . . . But where would I find them?
(*Pause.*)

Where would I look for them?
(*Pause. He whistles. Enter Clov.*)
Let us pray to God.

(E, 54)

The stage set now represents the narrator-writer's study, his "scriptorium." Hamm is a writer, Clov a character created by the writer (Hamm to Clov: "It was I was a father to you. . . . My house a home for you"), Nagg and Nell characters who once were alive for the writer but now are useless, manuscripts chucked into the wastebasket. Time was when the writer had only to whistle and out would pop a character ready to "play." Malone, in the trilogy, suffered the same decline of powers. "All went well at first, they all came to me, pleased that someone should want to play with them. If I said, Now I need a hunchback, immediately one came running, proud as punch of his fine hunch that was going to perform. . . . But it was not long before I found myself alone, in the dark" (TN, 245). So it is with Hamm. His "character," the man begging, is the last to be created in the imagination. He can whistle Clov out of the kitchen as he used to be able to whistle a character out of nowhere, but now "There are no more characters," or if there are, they will have to be supplied out of the grace of the Divine. Hence Hamm's behest, "Let us pray to God." Worse yet, even the one character who remains obedient to his master's every wish is now getting very tired of the "goings-on."

CLOV (*imploringly*). Let's stop playing!
HAMM. Never!

(E, 77)

The writer, we may recall, is bereft of everything but the "obligation to express." It is the act of ultimate desperation, then, when Hamm discards his gaff, for in *Endgame* as in *Malone Dies*, the gaff (equivalent to Malone's stick, later, his axe-pencil) is the author's instrument for expressing whatever he has left to express.

Already at the beginning of the work Clov-as-character displays the qualities of recalcitrance and uncooperativeness which will result in his being quite unavailable to Hamm-as-artist at the end of the work.

HAMM. All right, be off.
(*He leans back in his chair, remains motionless. Clov does not move, heaves a great groaning sigh. Hamm sits up.*)
I thought I told you to be off.

CLOV. I'm trying.
(*He goes to door, halts.*)
Ever since I was whelped.
(*Exit Clov.*)

(E, 14)

But in this multifaceted work, Character is to Author as Body is to Mind, and Clov carries out his master's orders with all the verve and dispatch we have been led to expect from bifurcated Cartesian man. And now the stage set represents, as Kenner suggests, the interior of a skull, Hamm being un-extended thinking substance, Clov the Body-Sensory apparatus which is extended and unthinking. Hamm knows of the "without" (the term used in *Murphy* to apply to extramental reality) only what Clov tells him; Clov, as Body, can initiate no action on his own but can only obey his master. Neither can exist without the other, but neither one can abide the other.

HAMM. . . . Why do you stay with me?
CLOV. Why do you keep me?
HAMM. There's no one else.
CLOV. There's nowhere else.
(*Pause.*)
HAMM. You're leaving me all the same.
CLOV. I'm trying.
HAMM. You don't love me.
CLOV. No.

(E, 6)

Despite his pretensions to casualness, Hamm is very concerned about his location in the room. His chair must be placed ever so carefully ("Put me right in the center! . . . Bang in the center!"). The maneuver is a delicate one ("I feel a little too far to the left . . . to the right . . . a little too far forward . . . too far back . . .") since Hamm must be located such that "the animal spirits in its [the brain's] anterior cavities have communication with those in the posterior, . . ." and so on. Hamm's seat is the pineal gland, the mediator in Descartes' system between mind and body; and the fact that Hamm is paralyzed from the waist down is symptomatic of advanced atrophy of the conarium. The fate suffered by Murphy is close at hand, for Hamm.

At least these five metaphors are to be discerned in the structure of *Endgame*. The stage set represents a chess board in the last moments of play, the throne room of a dying king, a stage set on which the last scene of a drama is being enacted, the study of a writer who no longer is able to create, and the interior of the skull of a man who is dying of dichotomy. Moreover, Ruby Cohn is surely correct in urging that the stage also represents a Golgotha; and we may perhaps also see in it a prison and a man condemned to die in a gas chamber or an electric chair.[17]

It takes nothing more than a recitation of these metaphorical dimensions of the play to indicate their common theme. The world is coming to an end: ". . . time is over, reckoning closed and story ended." Time is over for kings and actors and writers and all who play the game of human existence. It is the end of the Self whose body and mind we have seen continually abrading each other. It is the end of the World which lies on the other side of those hollow bricks which represent Skull. The final tableau ends in stillness and motionlessness. Nagg and Nell are locked in their ashbins, Clov has stood through the last minutes "impassive and motionless," Hamm's last act is to lower his arms to the armrests of the wheelchair, whereafter he "remains motionless." Clov's dream has come true.

> HAMM. . . . What are you doing?
> CLOV. Putting things in order.
> (*He straightens up. Fervently.*)
> I'm going to clear everything away!
> (*He starts picking up again.*)
> HAMM. Order!
> CLOV (*straightening up*). I love order. It's my dream. A world where all would be silent and still and each thing in its last place, under the last dust.
>   (E, 57)

The final tableau shows exactly this — each thing in its last place. To the long list of things of which there are no more, we add the two last: there is no more speech; there is no more motion. It is the condition of maximum entropy.

I realize, of course, that I have just used "entropy" as a synonym of "order," whereas in fact the term ought to be used of its opposite, "disorder" or "randomness." But in connection with Clov's speech it makes sense to use the term in this way, for by "order" Clov means the disposition of things in such a way that they will not interact with one another. This, roughly, is what entropy means as well, for entropy is the unavailability of energy for work. Anatol Rapoport supplies a clear example.

For instance, if we have two bodies at different temperatures, we can rig up a heat engine between them. . . . But if the bodies are left alone, say in contact with each other, eventually the hotter one will cool off and the cooler one warm up, and they will settle down to the same temperature. Then no heat engine can be rigged up between them because a heat engine must work between two temperatures. No heat has disappeared; it was only redistributed. But now no heat is available for doing work, because of this distribution. The physicist says, "The entropy of the system has increased. . . ." [18]

In a heat engine (automobile engine, steam locomotive engine) a fuel — gasoline, diesel oil, coal — is converted into heat in the form of a gas or steam which expands and drives a piston which turns a wheel. In a perfect engine, the amount of work done is equal to the amount of energy expended, in accordance with the First Law of Thermodynamics (the conservation of energy). But the Second Law of Thermodynamics qualifies this by saying that in any such system a certain amount of energy is "degraded," made unavailable for work. This energy is not lost or destroyed; it is simply shunted off, useless. The cosmological implication is obvious. The universe itself is an energy system, and in the course of time will gradually have less and less "useful energy" available to do work. Entropy — energy unavailable for work — will increase, and the universe itself will finally "run down."

Moreover, the process whereby entropy increases in any given energy system is a process that is unidirectional and irreversible. As Rudolph Clausius put it in one of the early formulations of the Second Law of Thermodynamics, "Heat cannot, of itself, pass from a colder to a hotter body." The only "direction" is from hot to cold, from energy to work. The cold body cannot pass whatever little heat it retains to the hot body. (If it could, a "perpetual motion" machine could be constructed.) Hence, time's arrow is pointed at the bullseye of cosmic stasis. History is running downhill to the point where the original impetus peters out and everything takes its last place under the last dust. The universe itself will eventually come to its rest, its own *apatheia*, its own peace.

Man too is an energy system, fueled by the food he eats, converting this to work, doomed eventually to the condition of maximum entropy called death. So is a society a heat engine, for they are "hot" who command, and they are "cold" who obey. By his orders to Clov, Hamm "drives" him as steam drives a piston. Exactly the same holds for the relationship between Pozzo and Lucky. If we generalize, we may call it the "master-slave" relationship, where master is heat or energy, slave is cold or work. In good time, and with the increase of entropy, "master" will run down: Pozzo loses all his paraphernalia; Hamm loses the little enthusiasm or drive that he has left at the opening of the play. Again, the two units in a system, hot and cold, if left "touching" one another will gradually become the same temperature, colder than the "hot" unit, warmer than the "cold" unit, for the heat of the "hot" unit will "of itself" pass over into the "cold" unit. In terms of capacity for work, however, the system will have achieved a high degree of entropy, and will be wholly dead, wholly cold.

Nagg and Nell, of course, in their ashbins. Their faces are "very white," not simply because they are pieces in a chess game, but because they at one time composed an energy system which was a going concern, but is now dead, or nearly dead, their faces white and cold as ice. (Lucky's hair is white, too.) As befits energy systems which are younger, Hamm's face and Clov's face are "very red." They are still active, each after his fashion; though it is clear that the metaphor of the chess game here takes precedence of the metaphor drawn from thermodynamics, else their faces would be described rather as a fading pink in token of the subsidence of their late strengths.

Man, society, the universe itself are all heat engines, obedient to the laws of thermodynamics. But even the life of the spirit may be comprehended in this fashion. The heat of hope may cool to tepid doubt, and doubt may become the ice of despair. Courage may decline to policy, and this to cowardice and fear. Love may become toleration, then hatred. In all other realms this decline is irreversible. Is it possible that in the realm of the spirit it is *not* irreversible? Is it possible that the source of a man's spiritual energy can be renewed? Perhaps so. It is just possible, it is barely but really conceivable, that when the heat of life in a man is dying, it may be restored to him.

HAMM. . . . Give me a rug, I'm freezing.
CLOV. There are no more rugs.
(*Pause.*)
HAMM. Kiss me.
(*Pause.*)
Will you not kiss me?
CLOV. No.
HAMM. On the forehead.
CLOV. I won't kiss you anywhere.
(*Pause.*)
HAMM (*holding out his hand*). Give me your hand at least.
(*Pause.*)
Will you not give me your hand?
CLOV. I won't touch you.   (E, 67)

Significantly, Hamm asks first for a rug, in the expectation that he will be able to insulate himself and prevent what warmth he has from escaping. Only after he learns that there are no more rugs does this thermodynamical solipsist turn to his fellow man to be "recharged," as it were, with the warmth of human compassion — and then it is an act of the utmost selfishness. Equally selfish, Clov denies Hamm even this one gesture of friendship.

So it is natural that only a few lines later Hamm should speak in direct address to the audience which is attending the death-by-freezing of this actor-king-author-energy system: "Get out of here and love one another! Lick your neighbor as yourself!" It is the proclamation of one who has learned too late that the decline of the world of men into a frozen wasteland of the spirit can be restrained only if man will reach out to touch the hand of his neighbor — if, indeed, he will permit himself the sympathy which dogs show to one another when they lick one another's wounds.

So in *All That Fall*:

> MISS FITT. Is it my arm you want then [as support in climbing stairs]? (*Pause. Impatiently.*) Is it my arm you want, Mrs. Rooney, or what is it?
> MRS. ROONEY (*exploding*). Your arm! Any arm! A helping hand! For five seconds! Christ, what a planet!
>
> . . . .
>
> MISS FITT (*resignedly*). Well, I suppose it is the Protestant thing to do.
> MRS. ROONEY. Pismires do it for one another. (*Pause.*) I have seen slugs do it.
>
> (KLT, 57)

Halfway through the play, Hamm prophesies to Clov — though coming from the mouth of the one who takes obvious delight in the story about the man who came pleading on behalf of his starving son, Hamm's prophecy is intolerably hypocritical; but even hypocrites can speak the truth: "Infinite emptiness will be all around you, all the resurrected dead of all the ages wouldn't fill it, and there you'll be like a little bit of grit in the middle of the steppe. (*Pause.*) Yes, one day you'll know what it is, you'll be like me, except that you won't have anyone with you, because you won't have had pity on anyone and because there won't be anyone left to have pity on" (E, 36). It is an accurate picture of the man who in lovelessness and pitilessness has isolated himself from those sources of spiritual heat and energy and life which are available to him in the relationship of compassion between one man and another. Martin Buber once wrote: "A newly-created concrete reality has been laid in our arms; we answer for it. A dog has looked at you, you answer for its glance, a child has clutched your hand, you answer for its touch, a host of men moves about you, you answer for their need. . . ." [19] You either answer for it, in love and pity and respect, or you end up a "little bit of grit in the middle of the steppe," remembering and forgetting and forgotten in an ashcan, dying from the unavailability of life, alone on a planet as cold and white and silent as the moon.

III

◄ ► Beckett's work is eschatological. It deals with the last things — the end of a man (*The Unnamable, Krapp's Last Tape*), a woman (*Happy Days*), a social order (the bourgeois culture represented by Pozzo), or the whole world (*Endgame*). As the novels in the trilogy move from "the last but one but one" (*Molloy*, TN, 5; cf. 29: "Yes, let me cry out, this time, then another time perhaps, then perhaps a last time") to the last but one (*Malone Dies*) to the last (*The Unnamable*), so three of the dramatic works advance to what is perhaps the ending end. *Waiting for Godot* deals with the early or middle stage of history in which time may be thought of either as cyclical or as just beginning to run out. *Happy Days* is next, for in its two acts it represents first the antepenultimate time, then the penultimate. Time is drawing to an end, its prisoners soon to be extinguished. *Endgame* is last, its one act the last act in the human comitragedy.

In his contribution to *Our Exagmination Round His Factification for Incamination of Work in Progress*, Beckett expounded with enthusiasm the cyclical theory of history developed by Giambattista Vico and from him adopted by James Joyce and used in *Work in Progress* (*Finnegans Wake*). Beckett notes the three stages through which, according to Vico, every civilization or society must pass. The first is the theocratic age, the second the heroic age, the third the human age. To each of these ages there corresponds an institution and an abstraction: the institutions are Religion, Marriage, and Burial; the abstractions Birth, Maturity, and Corruption. There is also a fourth stage in which the transition is made to the beginning of the cycle again, the abstraction here being Generation (OERH, 7–8). The extent to which Beckett has employed Viconian theory in his own work is a matter yet to be investigated, and I do not mean to go into it here, but there seems to be a possibility that this scheme helps shape the structure of the trilogy. Moran and his easy Catholicism represents the first or theocratic age; Malone through his surrogate Macmann represents the heroic age, and the institution of marriage; the Unnamable represents the human age, the institution of burial, and the abstraction corruption; Molloy's story is "the day beginning again" (TN, 8), and represents the abstraction generation.

The dramatic works perhaps follow a similar order. *Waiting for Godot,* with its biblical imagery and Gogo's comparison of himself with Christ, suggests the theocratic age and religion; Winnie and Willie in *Happy Days,* the heroic age and marriage; *Endgame,* the human age, corruption, and burial in a vault. There seems to be no counterpart in the drama to the fourth stage of Generation and rebirth.

Of course Beckett's vision of history is neither simply cyclical nor simply linear. As we have seen, *Waiting for Godot* incorporates three theories of history. But there does seem to be a tendency toward compounding a cyclical theory with the linear theory which is the corollary of the Second Law of Thermodynamics. Time moves to an end by way of a cyclical repetition of events. The progress of time is exactly analogous with the progress of the Cartesian Centaur, for though with respect to the axis of the Centaur's bicycle wheel any given point on the rim moves in a circle, yet the total effect is that of motion toward a terminus. Beckett's cycles, however, are not Vico's nor those of any other historian, for in the usual way of speaking an historical cycle covers years, decades, centuries. Beckett's cover days, hours, minutes, and seconds. His creatures are prisoners and victims upon whom the seconds and minutes and hours and days drop continuously, unhurriedly, maddeningly. "Moment upon moment," muses Hamm, "pattering down, like the millet grains of . . . (*he hesitates*) . . . that old Greek, and all life long you wait for that to mount up to a life" (E, 70). These lines, coming late in the play, repeat the theme of Clov's first speech:

> CLOV (*fixed gaze, tonelessly*). Finished, it's finished, nearly finished, it must be nearly finished.
> (*Pause.*)
> Grain upon grain, one by one, and one day, suddenly, there's a heap, a little heap, the impossible heap.
>
> (E, 1)

The little heap, in fact, is what Winnie, of *Happy Days,* finds herself buried in. The stage directions call for "*Expanse of scorched grass rising centre to low mound. Gentle slopes down to front and either side of stage. . . . Imbedded up to above her waist in exact centre of mound, WINNIE*" (HD, 7). At the beginning of the second act Winnie is imbedded up to her neck. She can no longer turn, bow, or raise her head: she can move only her eyes. The Unnamable uses the same image. He is reaching the end of his long recitation:

. . . the question may be asked, off the record, why time doesn't pass, doesn't pass from you, why it piles up all about you, instant on instant, on all sides, deeper and deeper, thicker and thicker, your time, others' time, the time of the ancient dead and the dead yet unborn, why it buries you grain by grain neither dead nor alive, with no memory of anything, no hope of anything, no knowledge of anything, no history and no prospects, buried under the seconds, saying any old thing, your mouth full of sand, oh I know it's immaterial, time is one thing, I another, but the question may be asked, why time doesn't pass, just like that, off the record, en passant, to pass the time. . . . (TN, 541–42)

Time in Beckett's universe is running short. His titles say as much: *Endgame*; *Krapp's Last Tape*; *Embers*. From Malone onward his characters are mostly senile, decrepit, dying. Their world is dying too, the light waning, the heat dissipated, the sky light black from pole to pole. Winnie and Willie, Hamm and his roommates — these are the last inhabitants of a world that is finished, nearly finished, must be nearly finished. The last days have arrived, the eschaton is upon us. So infused with this sense of the imminence of the end of things is Beckett's art that, in addition to being called eschatological, it properly deserves to be called apocalyptic.

Now the apocalyptic vision is not typically characterized by joy, moderation, or timidity. It is a vision of destruction unlimited, of death by fire, sword, famine, and pestilence. Its advent is recognized with horror and published abroad in a voice hoarse with terror. Except, of course, by Beckett's creatures. To the Unnamable, for example, the end is something to be hoped for. "Yes, the hope is there, once again, . . . of ending here, it would be wonderful. But is it to be wished? Yes, it is to be wished, to end would be wonderful" (TN, 417). Clov looks forward to the day when each last thing will be each in its last place under the last dust. Winnie, enervated, looks forward to the end with equanimity: "Ah well, not long now, Winnie, can't be long now, until the bell for sleep. (*Pause.*) Then you may close your eyes, then you *must* close your eyes — and keep them closed" (HD, 59).

But after all, what else should we expect from characters who, like Gogo, have compared themselves to Christ, in the sense that their lives are a Via Dolorosa, a passion without form or stations or meaning? If existence is utter torment, who would not look forward to its end? Beckett's *Act With-*

out Words I is a parable of man's life, and is in form simply a version of the Tantalus story.

> Desert. Dazzling light.
> The man is flung backwards on stage from right wing. He falls, gets up immediately, dusts himself, turns aside, reflects. (KLT, 125)

Whistles from wings and fly call the man's attention to various objects, notably a carafe of water. The carafe is just out of reach. A large cube descends, of a height sufficient to let the man climb up and reach the carafe. He climbs up, reaches, the carafe is whisked up just beyond his finger's grasp. A second cube, smaller than the first, is let down from above. The man places it on top of the first, climbs to the top of his little pyramid, is about to reach the carafe when it is jerked up again. "We are rather in the position of Tantalus," wrote Beckett in *Proust*, "with this difference, that we allow ourselves to be tantalised" (PTD, 13). It is not so much a matter of allowance in the later works as it is a requirement, a condemnation, a condition of existence.

In Beckett's eschatology, peace is the peace of frozen silence. It is the motionlessness of Clov's dream, Winnie buried silent under the grains of time. It is the world conjured up by Henry as he tells of the encounter between Holloway and Bolton: "Not a sound, white world, bitter cold, ghastly scene, old men, great trouble, no good. . . . Nothing, all day nothing. (*Pause.*) All day all night nothing. (*Pause.*) Not a sound" (KLT, 121). Nothing: it is the word for what is to be, for what is to be hoped is to be. And why not? There is no other way of dealing with a world which is irrational, senseless, and absurd. There is no other way of escaping the mortifying recurrence of empty hours and days and years. And though the world and time are both inhospitable to man, his condition is only exacerbated by the fact that he has nowhere to turn, no one to turn to, for help. The nature of man is such that the Ego has no identity from moment to moment: we are not merely wearier because of yesterday; we are other, different. I cannot know who I am, though I spend my life looking into myself, looking for myself. Nor can I expect assistance from another, for between him and me is fixed an untraversable gulf. Watt cannot know Knott, the Unnamable cannot find himself, to say nothing of any other. Winnie counts it a happy day when Willie vouchsafes a word or two to her. Love is a mockery, an obscene ritual which machines go through. Man in his most urgent need can cry to another, but there is no reply. Henry is telling his

story of Bolton and Holloway, the first asking the second for something —
it makes no difference what. Henry narrates:

Bolton: "Please!" (*Pause.*) "Please!" (*Pause.*) "Please, Holloway!" (*Pause.*)
Candle shaking and guttering all over the place, lower now, old arm tired, . . .
night, and the embers cold, and the glim shaking in your old fist, saying, Please!
Please! (*Pause.*) Begging. (*Pause.*) Of the poor. (*Pause.*) Ada! (*Pause.*) Father!
(*Pause.*) Christ! (KLT, 120–21)

But Bolton's world, like Watt's, is of such a nature that one cannot say
Christ, Christ, and be comforted; and the people who inhabit the world are
spiritual paupers, bankrupt in the inner man.

For in and through his art, Beckett has brought forth a world which is
cheerless, grey, and cold, evacuated of meaning, truth, joy, love. In his essay
on Joyce, Beckett compared Dante's Purgatory with the purgatory that
Joyce fashioned in *Finnegans Wake.* As he did in his comments on Proust,
Beckett speaks as much about himself as about the man whom he discusses.
In Dante's Purgatory, he writes, there is an "absolute progression and a
guaranteed consummation"; in Joyce's (and Beckett's) purgatory there is
merely "flux" and an apparent consummation. In Dante, "movement is unidirectional, and a step forward represents a net advance." In Joyce, movement is nondirectional or multidirectional, and a step forward is "by definition" a step backward. Nonetheless, Joyce's work is "purgatorial," in the
sense that it represents "the absolute absence of the Absolute" (OERH, 21–
22). The phrase could stand as the ultimate judgment upon Beckett's own
work. Nowhere do we find a Ground or Presence which either supports
man's life or stands over against it as judgment. As Nathan A. Scott has observed of the image of man which Beckett presents to us, "Man is nothing
because there is Nothing either in or beyond existence that sanctions or
gives any kind of warrant or dignity to the human enterprise." [20] In Beckett's art, Being is reduced to the least possible, history is a torture, existence
is pointless and absurd, and man is a senile robot in search of a self — his
own or another's — which he can never find and which, if he found it, he
could not know, and if he knew it, could not love.

Or have we gone too far? Have we, perhaps, misunderstood Beckett? Is
he nothing but the connoisseur of the impasse, the craftsman of the absurd,
a magician who with a wave of his wand (in his quick hands it looks like a
short pencil, sharpened at both ends . . .) and a few hundred thousand
painfully extruded words can reduce Something to Nearly Nothing, can
work the metamorphosis of Life into Rhetoric and transmogrify the bread

of high literary art into the cold stone of despair? He is all this, of course —
clown, artist, magician.

But we have also called him an Apocalyptic, a prophet of the Eschaton,
and it has always been true of the apocalyptic visionary that the city whose
destruction he foretells is the same city over which he weeps. If it is true, or
even partly true, that Beckett has been speaking out of the apocalyptic tradition, then our assessment of his significance as a modern writer must be
modified. For we should not then be able to think of him as one who is
morally disengaged from the world and simply reporting upon the death
of man, but as one who is very much a part of the world, and who is calling
upon man to acknowledge the extremity of his present situation.

Like his precursors in the tradition, Beckett incarnates his vision in parables. "The kingdom of earth is like unto two hoboes who wait to be given
something which only they themselves can supply . . ." Or "The kingdom
of man is like unto the last stages of a game of chess . . ." Or again, "The
kingdom of earth is like unto a woman buried in sand up to her diddies
. . ." The parable is one of the major tactics employed by the prophet, but
it is also a principal instrument of the poet as well, for a parable is a metaphor or simile enlarged. Whether used by poet or prophet, its function is
always the same — to reveal, to disclose, to illuminate. In the case of Beckett, what is being revealed in and through his art is simply the condition of
man. And what hinders man from apprehending his condition, according
to Beckett, is habit.

Beckett makes a great deal of habit in his essay on Proust. Habit, he says,
is "a compromise effected between the individual and his environment, or
between the individual and his own organic eccentricities, the guarantee of
a dull inviolability, the lightning-conductor of his existence. Habit is the
ballast that chains the dog to his vomit" (PTD, 18–19). The effect of habit is
to keep the world at arm's length; it is a "screen" which spares its victims
"the spectacle of reality," and its purpose and effect is to reduce phenomena
to the condition of a "comfortable and familiar concept," or to hide "the essence — the Idea —" of the phenomenon or object in the "haze of conception — preconception." Fifteen years after *Proust*, Beckett created Watt, the
creature of habit, and set him in the domain of Knott, where, in the language of the essay, an object "is perceived as particular and unique and not
merely the member of a family," where it is "independent of any general
notion and detached from the sanity of a cause, isolated and inexplicable in
the light of ignorance" (PTD, 22–23). And six years after *Watt*, in *Waiting*

for Godot, Beckett presented his audience with a Knott-world, and the effect on the audience was exactly the same as that on Watt.

It was what Beckett had no doubt intended. For since *Watt*, Beckett has been trying to find the metaphors, the parables, which will paralyze habit and expose his readers and audience to "the essence — the Idea —"; in short, to reality. His mission as prophet has been to set before those who will attend to him images of human existence which will not yield to our habitual patterns and procedures of analysis and evaluation — images which rather will shock, insult, mystify, and will work upon us in such a way that "the boredom of living is replaced by the suffering of being" (PTD, 19). Suffering, said Beckett in *Proust*, "opens a window on the real" (PTD, 28), and he expands the phrase "suffering of being" to mean "the free play of every faculty." In the light of these comments, Beckett's mission can be seen as the attempt to awaken man to the grim facts about his life. And what he said in *Proust* he only repeated to Tom Driver some twenty years later. To Driver he said, "The confusion is not my invention. . . . It is all around us and our only chance now is to let it in. The only chance of renovation is to open our eyes and see the mess." [21] Beckett is the prophet of the mess, the prophet of the absolute absence of the Absolute. If he holds out any hope at all for the human experiment, it is a hope founded on man's capacity to endure a world in which the light is dying, the temperature is dropping, meaning has long since dissipated, and existence is a painful slogging from station to station of a Via Dolorosa that has no *telos* but merely a terminus.

And perhaps there is one other ground for hope. We recall the tableau in *Godot* or Hamm's almost hysterical command, "Get out of here and love one another." If the world's temperature is to rise again and the world's light to be renewed, it is by reason of the fire of love. Of course, love in Beckett's world is impossible, for man is alienated from man. An act of charity would establish a life's significance, but meaning is by definition not an element in the constitution of the world. So it is difficult to understand Hamm's imperative. Kindness — at least, the instinct to assist — is innate in pismires and slugs, if we are to believe Mrs. Rooney; but as a virtue or even capacity, it seems to have died out in the human species, along with most of the rest of man's resources. This fantastic race of the deprived — a-theist, a-gnostic, hopeless, and dis-integrated — manages to endure, manages somehow to retain the obligation to endure. It is almost unbelievable — it is indeed irrational and absurd — to believe that there could be in such a world the possibility of more than mere continuance. Beckett's principal witness to the condition of man and his ability to survive even in this most unpromising and empty time seems to be contained in the last proud, feeble, desperate words of the Unnamable: ". . . where I am, I don't know, I'll never know, in the silence you don't know, you must go on, I can't go on, I'll go on."

But is man's life no more than this, a passion without form or stations, a purgatory without consummation but only termination, a solitary and agonizing striving for the peace of nonbeing? Is there nothing more to human existence than simply this "going on"? If there is more, if there is meaning or kindness or even love, it is not to be had by an exertion of will, for man's will is exhausted, his self an infinite regression into itself. In the situation of ultimate privation, alienation, and despair, man's posture must be that of Bolton, his word Bolton's word: please. Please! It is absurd, of course, but may we not see in this word, this prayer, man's plea to the Absolute — or if not that, then to simple human decency and compassion — not, for God's sake, to be absolutely absent?

> veronica mundi
> veronica munda
> give us a wipe for the love of Jesus
> ("Enueg II")

VI REDUCTION, REFLECTION, NEGATION: SOME VERSIONS OF CONSCIOUSNESS

Noli foras ire, in te redi, in interiore homine habitat veritas.

Augustine

The phenomenological reduction thus tends to split the ego. The transcendental spectator places himself above himself, watches himself, and sees himself also as the previously world-immersed ego. In other words, he discovers that he, as a human being, exists within himself as a *cogitatum*.

Husserl

Consciousness is a reflection (*reflet*), but *qua* reflection it is exactly the one reflecting (*réfléchissant*), and if we attempt to grasp it as reflecting, it vanishes and we fall back on the reflection. . . . But reflection is *one being* . . .; it is a *being which has to be its own nothingness*. . . . The one who is reflecting on me is not some sort of non-temporal regard but myself.

Sartre

In Stoicism, self-consciousness is the bare and simple freedom of itself. In Scepticism, it realizes itself, negates the other side of determinate existence [*bestimmten Daseins*], but, in so doing, really doubles itself, and is itself now a duality. In this way the duplication, which previously was divided between two individuals, the lord and the bondsman, is concentrated into one. Thus we have here that dualizing of self-consciousness within itself, which lies essentially in the notion of mind; but the unity of the two elements is not yet present. Hence the *Unhappy Consciousness* [*das unglückliche Bewusstsein*], . . . which is the consciousness of self as a divided nature, a doubled and merely contradictory being.

Hegel

Consciousness is a disease.

Dostoevsky [1]

I

◀ ▶ In his Introduction to *Adventures of Ideas*, Alfred North Whitehead writes: "In considering the history of ideas, . . . we must remember that there are grades in the generality of ideas. Thus a general idea occurs in history in special forms determined by peculiar circumstances of race and of stage of civilization. The higher generalities rarely receive any accurate

verbal expression. They are hinted at through their special forms appropriate to the age in question." [2] One of the "general ideas" that has intermittently engaged the attention of serious thinkers for the last century and a
half has been the idea of consciousness. One of the important shifts in the
history of Western thought came about when, instead of talking about
"mind" and "thinking substance," or about "pure reason" and "judgment,"
Hegel began talking about "consciousness" and "self-consciousness." Ironically enough, two of the men who understood Hegel best, Karl Marx and
Soren Kierkegaard, took his concepts and methods and used them against
Hegel, the one in the interests of the material well-being of the proletariat,
the other in the interests of the spiritual well-being of the individual. After
the middle of the nineteenth century, however, the idea of consciousness
was not of primary interest to philosophers until — again ironically —
Freud's concept of the "sub-conscious" called attention once again to the
fact of consciousness. As a theme for philosophical speculation, the idea had
of course occupied Fichte and Henri Bergson and William James and
Franz Brentano, among others. But it was not until Edmund Husserl published his *Ideen* in 1913 that it again received what Whitehead refers to as
"accurate verbal expression." As of now, the idea of consciousness, investigated by means of phenomenology, is one of the principal topics of intellectual concern, and two of the giants of our time, Martin Heidegger (Husserl's student) and Jean-Paul Sartre, are intimately connected with the phenomenological movement.

In the same period of time, consciousness was being tentatively explored
through one of the "special forms" appropriate to the age — the form of the
novel. One thinks of the Dostoevsky of *Notes from Underground*, of Virginia Woolf, Proust, Joyce, the Faulkner of *The Sound and the Fury*, and
most recently of the French "New Novel" — of Alain Robbe-Grillet, Nath-
alie Sarraute, Michel Butor. One thinks as well of Samuel Beckett.

It will be our business in this chapter to consider three versions of consciousness — those of Husserl, Sartre, and Hegel — and to relate these to
themes and methods used by Beckett. I undertake this examination in the
conviction that an understanding of philosophical treatments of the concept of consciousness will enhance our understanding of Beckett's artistic
achievement. I recognize that this conviction is not shared by all students
of literature, for here and there the idea is still alive that poets are strictly
non-thinkers. This may be true of some poets (though I cannot think of
any offhand), but it is patently not true of Beckett. He has thought, and

thought hard, about the problems of his art and the problems of his time: and consciousness is a problem common to both art and existence.

From time to time in this chapter Beckett's work will seem to disappear from view. I can only say that I have tried to remember that, for the literary critic, the purpose of climbing the Pisgah of philosophy is to get a better look at the Gilead of art. To put it more abstractly, the art of interpretation is a constant moving between the general and the special, the universal and the particular. Speaking again of "the principle that dominates the history of ideas," Whitehead says: "There will be a general idea in the background flittingly, waveringly, realized by the few in its full generality — or perhaps never expressed in any adequate universal form with persuasive force. . . . But this general idea, whether expressed or implicitly just below the surface of consciousness, embodies itself in special expression after special expression." [3] Consciousness is such a general idea, and Beckett's art is one of its "special expressions." This means that it is not necessary to impute to Beckett a close acquaintance with any of the philosophical systems to be dealt with here. It is sufficient for our purposes that the general idea is in the background. Our task now is to bring it to the foreground. We begin with the founder of phenomenology.

II

◀ ▶ In 1938 Beckett published *Murphy*, and in that same year Edmund Husserl died. This historical coincidence is about the only concrete connection that can be made between the Irish writer and the German philosopher, for though Beckett has alluded to or cited by name Heraclitus, Democritus, Augustine, Bruno, Descartes, Geulincx, Berkeley, Leibnitz, Spinoza, Vico, and Schopenhauer, among others, he has never mentioned Husserl. Yet between Beckett and Husserl there are similarities of concern and even of method or procedure that are of more than passing interest. Certainly, it would be out of place here to try to present a detailed analysis of Husserl's thought, especially since he altered and refined his ideas and terms throughout his working life. But we can try to get at those ideas which seem relevant for our study of Beckett's art; and we shall use one of his concepts — that of the transcendental Ego — to make the transition from Husserlian phenomenology to Sartrean existentialism.

Like Descartes, whose thought his own resembles in many respects, Husserl set for himself the task of establishing philosophy as a rigorous and self-grounded "science." Again like Descartes, he sought to do this by clearing philosophy of the accumulated rubble of doctrines, traditions, prejudices, formulas, and anything else that would prevent the serious thinker from encountering reality. If he had a slogan, it was "Zu dem Sache selbst!" "To the things themselves!" In order to get back to "the things themselves," one must start from the beginning. In an early essay, *"Philosophie als strenge Wissenschaft"* (published in 1911), Husserl writes, "Philosophy . . . is essentially a science of true beginnings, or origins. . . . The science concerned with what is radical must from every point of view be radical itself in its procedure. Above all it must not rest until it has attained its own absolutely clear beginnings." [4] Getting back to the beginnings is not an easy task, however, for it requires the philosopher to "set aside all previous habits of thought, see through and break down the mental barriers which these habits have set along the horizons of our thinking, and in full intellectual freedom proceed to lay hold on those genuine philosophical problems still awaiting completely fresh formulation." [5] Two of the habits which Husserl might have had in mind when he wrote this are the Kantian and the Positivistic. To the extent that the Kantians of his time were content to explore only the logically necessary conditions of experience they failed to deal with the world, which is presumably what one has experiences *of*. To the extent that the positivists (especially psychological positivists) attempted to define reality in objective and naturalistic terms, they failed to deal with the human being through whom the world comes into being and for whom it has meaning. Husserl's philosophical endeavors can be interpreted as the effort to ground philosophy in a union of subjectivity and objectivity — that is, in the knowing, experiencing Self or Ego. As he wrote in the first of the *Cartesian Meditations*, "The Objective world, the world that exists for me, that always has and always will exist for me, the only world that ever can exist for me — this world, with all its Objects . . . derives its whole sense and its existential status, which it has for me, from me myself, *from me as the transcendental Ego*." [6]

In the most general sense, then, my business as a phenomenological philosopher is to return to the Beginnings of thought in the effort to see the world as it appears or gives itself to me. This is hard to do, however, because in the course of my life I have learned facts about the world and have constructed systems for its interpretation. In my sophistication I "see through" the world to its physical or chemical or economic or religious basis and structure. I am also immersed in values and commitments, and these too obscure my vision and prevent me from seeing the world as it simply appears or presents itself. When I look out upon the world I look at it from the "natural standpoint." I see real things — trees, furniture, people; I see also a world of values and goods, of beauty and ugliness. Things are *vorhanden*, at hand to be used, and I use them. This is the spatio-temporal fact-world (*räumlich-zeitliche Wirklichkeit*).[7]

But now, in order to look at the world anew I re-enact the Cartesian *cogito*, not indeed to establish a realm of mind which is epistemologically immaculate and free of doubt, but in order to establish a standpoint radically different from the Natural Standpoint. The Natural Thesis concerning the world — that it is there, and there in the fullness of its being — is not negated in the manner of the sceptics; it is simply put out of action. I "disconnect it" (*schalte sie aus*), "bracket it" (*klammere sie ein*). I disengage the thesis of the natural standpoint, and I put in brackets whatever it includes concerning the nature of Being. What remains as the "phenomenological residuum" when I have performed the reduction is a new region of Being, the realm of "pure experiences" (*Erlebnisse*), or "pure consciousness." This is the realm of Being which I as a practitioner of phenomenology am to study and describe. My task is to "see" what appears in consciousness, and describe it simply as it appears or gives itself. I am not to try to account for what appears, in the sense of saying whether "that which appears in consciousness" has an "Objective" counterpart in the Objective or Natural World, for I have already "bracketed" this question. I am rather simply to describe what gives itself simply as it gives itself. Succinctly put, my task is that of becoming conscious of consciousness.

Husserl thought of himself as the first to inquire rigorously and systematically into the field of consciousness, but he recognized that Augustine, Descartes, Hume, Kant, Brentano, and others had been there before him. Maurice Merleau-Ponty, one of the second-generation phenomenologists, says that as a style of thinking it was practiced before Husserl by Hegel and Kierkegaard, by Marx, Nietzsche, and Freud.[8] The literary critic and historian would certainly see it employed by Dostoevsky in, for example, *Notes from Underground* or *The Possessed*, as well as by Proust and Joyce. Indeed, when a New Critic disengages a poem, play, or novel from its historical and biographical "causes" and tries simply to describe the work as it gives itself in his consciousness, he is practicing the phenomenological method. Writers and critics are not engaged in the Husserlian task of establishing philosophy as an apodictic and rigorous science of course, but if Merleau-Ponty is right when he says that "True philosophy consists in relearning to look at the world," [9] then writers and critics contribute to the larger philosophical enterprise. Herbert Spiegelberg has characterized phenomenology as "a philosophy which has learned to wonder again and to respect wonders for what they are in themselves." [10] He was alluding to Husserl's description of the "pure ego and pure consciousness" as "the wonder of wonders," but as Merleau-Ponty would insist, the philosopher does not have a monopoly out on that human commodity. Merleau-Ponty writes: "If phenomenology was a movement before becoming a doctrine or a philosophical system, this was attributable neither to accident, nor to fraudulent intent. It is as painstaking as the works of Balzac, Proust, Valéry, or Cézanne — by reason of the same kind of attentiveness and wonder, the same demand for awareness, the same will to seize the meaning of the world or of history as that meaning comes into being." [11]

And to Merleau-Ponty's list of artists must we not add Joseph Conrad? He said: "The artist appeals to that part of our being which is not dependent on wisdom; to that in us which is a gift and not an acquisition — and, therefore, more permanently enduring. He speaks to our capacity for delight and wonder, to the sense of mystery surrounding our lives; to our sense of pity, and beauty, and pain." [12] And in speaking of the "creative task," Conrad, too, justified the artist's mission by an appeal to "awareness," though he used slightly different language. "The sincere endeavour to accomplish that creative task, to go as far on that road as his strength will carry him, to go undeterred by faltering, weariness or reproach, is the only valid justification for the worker in prose. . . . My task which I am trying to achieve is, by the power of the written word to make you hear, to make you feel — it is, before all, to make you *see*. That — and no more, and it is everything." [13]

But then, when you think about it, of which of the great writers, of the serious "workers in prose" (and in poetry for that matter: Conrad draws a tight net) would it be false to say, "He sought to increase our awareness; he sought to show us the world more clearly"? Is it not the case that in describing the purpose and method of systematic phenomenology Husserl and Merleau-Ponty have in some sense described the purpose and method of art? What is it that we do, when the lights go down and the curtains begin to separate, if we do not perform the "phenomenological reduction," if we do not "bracket" the Natural Standpoint and its Natural Thesis? Is not the act of picking up a novel, opening it, and reading the words which appear on the page at the same time the act of disengaging ourselves from the practical world? Edward Bullough has described the frame of mind which art seems to require and generate for its apprehension as "psychical distance." "Distance" is that quality of our relation to a work of art which permits us to look upon it "objectively" or "impersonally." It has both a negative and a positive function: "It has a *negative,* inhibitory aspect — the cutting-out of the practical sides of things and of our practical attitude to them — and a *positive* side — the elaboration of the experience on the new basis created by the inhibitory action of Distance." [14] It is the "inhibitory aspect" which seems familiar after having attended to the workings of the phenomenological reduction. Distance, says Bullough, is obtained "by separating the object and its appeal from one's own self, by putting it out of gear with practical needs and ends." [15] "Putting it out of gear": it is an apt description of the epoché, the phenomenological reduction.

We must not try to stretch a similarity into an identity, however. Phenomenology in its strictest or Husserlian sense is not art and not art criticism but a disciplined inquiry into the field of consciousness as the ground of all knowledge whatsoever. There is a sense in which the dimming of the lights in a theater corresponds to the action of the epoché, as the frame around a painting or the pedestal on which a statue stands "brackets" the circumambient world of our practical concerns and asks us to look "here" where the painting or the statue is. But in these cases we do not so much refrain from judgment of the natural world as we shift the focus of our intention or awareness. We concern ourselves with (we "intend" or "posit") not the everyday world of our lives but this special world which actors and stage props, for example, are bringing into being "there on stage." Certainly these several kinds of pseudo-bracketing do not have the purpose of fixing my intellectual "gaze" on the field of my consciousness, but serve rather to direct and focus my attention on a particular portion of the "natural" world. In short, I cannot get to the realm of the transcendental Ego by way of the usual methods of aesthetic contemplation.

But who would argue that Samuel Beckett employs the usual forms of art or requires of his readers the usual forms of attention and contemplation? When he said to Tom Driver, "One can only speak of what is in front of him," he was speaking in the phenomenological idiom.[16]

Here is a passage from Husserl in which, with a determined naiveté, he describes the world as it is seen "from the natural standpoint."

I am aware of a world, spread out in space endlessly, and in time becoming and become, without end. I am aware of it, that means, first of all, I discover it immediately, intuitively, I experience it. Through sight, touch, hearing, etc., in the different ways of sensory perception, corporeal things somehow spatially distributed are *for me simply there*, in verbal or figurative sense "present," whether or not I pay them special attention by busying myself with them, considering, thinking, feeling, willing. Animal beings also, perhaps men, are immediately there for me; I look up, I see them, I hear them coming towards me. . . . They too are present as realities in my field of intuition, even when I pay them no attention.[17]

And here is a passage from *The Unnamable*:

Where now? Who now? When now? Unquestioning. I, say I . . . I shall have company. In the beginning. A few puppets. . . . And things, what is the correct attitude to adopt towards things? . . . Malone is there. . . . He passes before me at doubtless regular intervals. . . . He passes close by me, a few feet away, slowly, always in the same direction. I am almost sure it is he. The brimless hat seems to me conclusive. . . . Oh, look, there is the first thing, Malone's hat. I see no other clothes. . . . Dim intermittent lights suggest a kind of distance. (TN, 401, 402, 403, 404)

This is the Unnamable occupying the standpoint (should we risk "*der Sitzpunkt*"?) of the Natural Thesis. "What am I to do," he asks, "What shall I do, what should I do, in my situation, how proceed? By aporia pure and simple? Or by affirmations and negations invalidated as uttered, or sooner or later? Generally speaking. . . . Can one be ephectic otherwise than unawares? I don't know" (TN, 401, 402). Whether by "aporia pure and simple" or by the dialectic of affirmation and negation, the Unnamable's procedure will ultimately produce the same effect — that of bracketing his *Umwelt*. For here, in the third part of the trilogy, Beckett does indeed attempt to enter the field of the transcendental Ego and explore it as no one else in the history of letters has done before him. The trilogy as a whole is his analysis of what he called in the essay on Proust "the only world that has reality and significance, the world of our own latent consciousness." As such, the three novels represent the end of the new road which he took in preference to the old "dreary road" of expressionism.

It took Beckett a long time to discover this road, however, and finding his way into the world of consciousness was not an easy task. Recall the opening lines of *Murphy*:

The sun shone, having no alternative, on the nothing new. Murphy sat out of it, as though he were free, in a mew in West Brompton. Here for what might have been six months he had eaten, drunk, slept, and put his clothes on and off, in a medium-sized cage of north-western aspect commanding an unbroken view of medium-sized cages of south-eastern aspect. (M, 1)

Here is a world chock-full of things: of mews and clothes and aspects and directions and months and cages; we will later discover "animal beings also, even men," as Husserl (a hint almost of surprise in his voice) so quaintly puts it. It is indeed more than just a world — it is an entire universe, with sun and all. Not that Murphy takes the least interest in it. He has long since rejected this big world for the little one of his mind. Nor does Murphy doubt this world, after the Cartesian or Husserlian fashion. Plainly and simply, he does not like it, for in the big world he is not free; whereas in the third zone of his mind he is so free that free is not the word for it: "he was but a mote in the dark of absolute freedom."

The philosophical assumptions which underlie this novel do not admit Beckett into the realm of subjectivity, however, for these assumptions define man as a mind in a body rather than as a kind of subjective unity of experience or consciousness. In spite of Descartes' definition of mind as unextended thinking substance, mind is treated in both the philosophical tradition and in the novel as a "place." Murphy is built in a way that lets him retreat into his mental "place," and he can even lose himself there in the absolute freedom of non-consciousness. Using Berkeley's terms, Beckett can describe Murphy's trance as "the absence of *percipi*," even though Beckett probably knew quite well that the Bishop insisted on the indivisible unity of *percipi* and *percipere*. Because Murphy's mind is interpreted as a place, it can be thought of as "containing" certain things — ideas, no doubt, as well as the three "zones." When we examine these zones, however, we find nothing corresponding to the streaming or flowing of conscious experience that Husserl discovered when he performed the phenomenological reduction. We find instead in the first zone a puppet theater, with Murphy as the puppeteer; in the second zone an intellectual pastry shop; and in the third a near vacuum of absolute freedom with a Murphy-mote floating free in it. What we do not find, either in the zones or in the trance, is the consciousness which, for purely practical purposes, we call by the name of Murphy.

Nor do we find a phenomenological concept of the ego in *Watt*. Beckett's second novel, like his first, is founded on a dualism, but where this dualism in *Murphy* is ontological and divides being into mind and body, in *Watt* it is epistemological and separates things known from the knowing subject. One's notion of the way things are obviously is going to have an important influence on one's notion of how one knows what is, or how one knows the way things are; and one's notion of the way one knows and the limits (if any) to that knowledge will help shape one's notion of what is; and Watt's way of walking is a clear reminder that man is a ghost in a machine. Still, Watt's great grief is the result of his inability to know, not his inability to be. Among the things he tries to know or understand or make sense of are the famous pot, Erskine's picture, the incident of the Galls, the way in which Mr. Knott's garbage is disposed of, and finally, Mr. Knott himself. Of the many things, persons, and events available for his scrutiny, the one thing Watt does not try to understand is himself. He is firmly rooted in what Husserl called the Natural Standpoint, and Watt's investigations are always directed *out* upon things and events in the world, and never *in* upon his own experience or consciousness of those phenomena.

The purpose of the phenomenological reduction ("reduction" meaning not "diminution" but "leading back" — namely, back to the Beginning), as we have seen, is to bracket or disengage the Thesis of the Natural Standpoint so as to bring into view the event as it gives itself in experience or consciousness. In effect, what Husserl is trying to do by means of the epoché is to get at the experience of experience or the consciousness of consciousness. This is no easy task, obviously, because one is asked to investigate neither the thing known (which is simple enough for the empirical or positive sciences working from the Natural Standpoint), nor the structure of knowledge (which is the task of logic), but some nebulous, intermediate province or region. Even supposing that one could become conscious of his own consciousness, what could he say to someone else about what he had "seen" there? How would he get it down on paper? These objections were brought against Husserl, and in *Ideas* he quotes a paragraph written by one of his critics. We might suppose that the hero of Beckett's second novel abstained from examining himself for the very reasons which the critic sets out. Husserl quotes his philosophical antagonist as follows: "It is scarcely possible even to form opinions concerning the way in which one comes to a knowledge of immediate experience. For it is neither knowledge nor the object of knowledge, but something different. One cannot see how a record concerning the experience of experience, even if it has been taken, could be put on paper." [18] The name of this critic, who is so sceptical of the purpose and method of Husserl's phenomenology, is (would it were not so!) H. J. Watt.

It is a difficult question that H. J. asks. How can you put on paper the record of an experience of an experience? Husserl himself, in fact, rarely tried to make such a record, and devoted himself mainly to the propaedeutics of phenomenology. Still, we can get an idea of what would be required in order to get the experience of an experience down on paper from the following excerpt from the first of the *Cartesian Meditations*. Husserl writes:

> This universal depriving of acceptance, this "inhibiting" or "putting out of play" of all positions taken toward the already-given Objective world . . . therefore does not leave us confronting nothing. On the contrary we gain possession of something by it; and what we (or, to speak more precisely, *what I, the one who is meditating*) [italics added] acquire by it is my pure living, with all the pure subjective processes making this up, and everything meant in them, *purely as* [Husserl's italics] meant in them. . . . The epoché can also be said to be the radical and universal method by which I apprehend myself purely: as Ego, and with my own pure conscious life.[19]

The clue is in the shift from the first person plural to the first person singular, from the general We to the specific I. In the case of Samuel Beckett, this means a shift from the third person to the first, from "Watt snited" to "I am in my mother's room." *Watt* of course is narrated in the first person, as we learn after getting well into the text, by Sam; but Sam is so diffident and unobtrusive that he might just as well not be there. The first-person mode of narration does not make a serious difference in the novel, and it could just as well have been written entirely from the third-person perspective. But after *Watt* there is no more third-person narrative.[20]

More than a simple change in narrative technique is required if Beckett is to enter into the realm of transcendental subjectivity, however. What is required is nothing less than a total redefinition of the self and its cognitive structure. What Beckett must do is replace the Cartesian concept of mind as place with the Bergsonian or Husserlian concept of mind as the continuously living process of consciousness. Bergson's testimony on this score has already been heard: "At the very instant that my consciousness is extinguished, another consciousness lights up — or rather, it was already alight: it had arisen the instant before, in order to witness the extinction of the first; for the first could disappear only for another and in the presence of another. . . . So, do what I will, I am always perceiving something, either from without or from within." [21]

William James, one of Bergson's admirers, argues for the same notion of consciousness as continuous, and supplies the figure which is finally to stick: "Consciousness, then, does not appear to itself chopped up in bits. Such words as 'chain' or 'train' do not describe it fitly as it presents itself in the first instance. It is nothing jointed; it flows. A 'river' or a 'stream' are the metaphors by which it is most naturally described. *In talking of it hereafter, let us call it the stream of thought, of consciousness, or of subjective life.*" [22] If consciousness is nothing jointed, if it has no lacunae, no interstices, then it is "there," and always there at every moment. Whenever I look for it I find it; I cannot lose my consciousness and I cannot escape from it. As James puts it, under the subheading "The Fundamental Fact": "The first and foremost concrete fact which every one will affirm to belong to his inner experience is the fact that *consciousness of some sort goes on.* 'States of mind' succeed each other in him.* If we could say in English 'it thinks,' as we say 'it rains' or 'it blows,' we should be stating the fact most simply and with the minimum of assumption. As we cannot, we must simply say that *thought goes on.*" [23]

This, then, is the lesson Beckett had to learn if he was ever to be able to deal with the world that is real and significant, the world of consciousness. He learned it, of course, and after *Murphy* we do not see again an Ego like Murphy's that is capable of denying itself or losing itself in the gaps within consciousness. For James is right: thought goes on. It goes on, as the Unnamable realizes, and on and on and on and . . .

Still supposing that the phenomenological reduction, or something very like it, does in fact operate in Beckett's work and particularly in the trilogy, it is evident that it does not and cannot operate in the same way as a literary device and as a philosophical method. In Husserl the reduction operates totally and immediately. As soon as I bracket the Objective world I am in the presence of the subjective field of intentional consciousness. In Beckett's case the reduction operates slowly and progressively. Each of the characters must work through the Objective world of bodies and beds and sticks and pots in order to get at his own consciousness, and in the last analysis it is only the Unnamable who actually makes a clean break with the Objective world. Allowing for this difference, we can, I think, continue to speak guardedly about the reduction in Beckett's three major novels.

It is in the trilogy that the Husserlian reduction properly begins. Each of the four parts of the work (counting *Molloy* as two, Molloy's story and Moran's) is narrated in the first person: "I am in my mother's room." "I am calm." "I shall soon be quite dead at last in spite of all." "I, say I." By using this device the narrator is spared the embarrassment of having to deliver to his readers (or auditors) the kind of world they are used to (including human beings replete with "the comic relief of features," as Beckett called the human physiognomy in *Proust*) but which neither Beckett nor his creatures can take seriously any longer. What Beckett presents in *Molloy* is a character remembering; what the character remembers is as it were his business, not Beckett's. Whatever world does appear in *Molloy* appears at second hand, and is a vague, ambiguous place. We are sure of nothing about it, not even of names (Mrs. Lousse or Loy? Was Molloy's old lover called Ruth or Edith?). The events which occur, the things described, are important only as occasions for eliciting Molloy's reminiscences. What is under scrutiny here is not the world but Molloy remembering.

The second half of *Molloy* is Moran's story, and this too is a first-person narrative, although Moran's remembrance of the past is ampler and more detailed. There are "animal beings" — a grey hen, a swarm of bees, for example — and even men — Moran, his son, Verger Joly, Father Ambrose, to name just these four. There are places with names (Hole, Bally) and things (keys, umbrella, bicycles) almost too numerous to mention. When you get right down to it, Moran's world is a dense place indeed — until the last four sentences of the book. There he denies the truth of the first two sentences of his story, and in so doing as much as confesses that his account is neither autobiography nor history but fiction, a tissue of lies. The artist has failed again. And yet, something remains. Consider Moran under the species Author. His retraction simply calls attention to the fact that he has been practicing his craft, the craft of writing fiction. Now consider him under the species Character. Moran is the product of yet another writer, the Author of *Molloy*, but he is a Character who is an Author. The story which he as Author tells is a fiction, a lie, and though it purports to talk about the world it does not, for, being a fiction, it cannot. But the mistake which we as readers make is that we take up with reference to his story what Husserl might call the Natural Standpoint. That is, we take his story as true. In his last four sentences Moran invites us to take up the Phenomenological Standpoint. He asks us, that is, to "bracket" the "facts" which he has related — the facts about his family, his home, his search for Molloy. He requires us to bring all of this under the phenomenological epoché and reserve our judgment about it all so that we may consider his story *as story*.

Recall Beckett's aversion, expressed in his dialogue with Georges Duthuit, to all forms of art grounded in expressionism and which therefore never stir from the field of the possible; and his commitment to an art which is the expression (even Beckett has to use words) that "there is nothing to express, nothing with which to express, nothing from which to express, no power to express, no desire to express." Two things are established, he goes on to say, the "aliment" and its manner of dispatch. "All that should concern us is the acute and increasing anxiety of the relation itself." Moran's denial of the truth of his story brackets the whole "Objective" world of his adventures — his son, his housekeeper, Gaber, his keys and hen, everything — and insists that we view his recital neither as history nor as autobiography but as art, the art of fiction, the art of telling what is not so. As such, it is disengaged from the principles of expressionism, for it is not Moran's "interpretation" of a segment of his life, it is not "expressive" of his version of reality. It is simply a story floating free in an aesthetic field which is not connected with any other psychological, ethical, historical, scientific, or religious field. It goes nowhere, it means nothing. At the most it is what Moran (whoever he is) does in order to "kill time." All we can see in it is the acute anxiety of the relation between the artist (Moran) and the materials of his story, his "aliment."

And yet this is not all Moran's story is. For on philosophical grounds supplied by Bergson, James, and Husserl, it is necessary to say that the story is in some sense tied to or even expressive of that consciousness of which it is the product — call that consciousness what you will, Moran's, the Author's, even Beckett's consciousness. If it is nothing else, it is the kind of story that kind of person would tell. It is even more than that. It is the kind of story an Author would tell if he lacked any Characters to tell a story about, and had therefore to tell a story about himself as Author searching for a Character.

In the second volume of the trilogy, *Malone Dies*, these intricacies do not appear to survive, and we have, very simply, the death of the Author. Again, because of the first-person point of view, what of the world exists does so by virtue of the consciousness of Malone. It is not much: a room, a bed, a cupboard, a long stick, a dish, a chamber pot, a window with a glimpse of roofs, sky, and street. Compared with the traversable world enjoyed (it is the wrong word) by Molloy and Moran, it is very little. The epoché is bringing more and more of the Objective world into its grip.

Malone is the Author reduced to the least possible. He is at his last gasp, at the end of both literary career and life. We are reminded of Hamm — that is, of Hamm as Author; and the two have much in common. Each is semi-imprisoned, mostly inert, in a condition of advanced paralysis. Each has a servant who attends to the basic needs; each tells himself stories. Importantly, each one is coming to the end of his career because he has no more stories to tell, and he has no stories because he has no characters to tell about. Malone speaks of his writing as a game, as play.

People and things ask nothing better than to play, certain animals too. All went well at first, they all came to me, pleased that someone should want to play with them. . . . But it was not long before I found myself alone, in the dark. That is why I gave up trying to play and took to myself for ever shapelessness and speechlessness. (TN, 245)

Similarly Hamm, at the end of the story he tells Nagg, is at a loss for *dramatis personae*.

> HAMM: . . . I'll soon have finished with this story.
> (*Pause.*)
> Unless I bring in other characters.
> (*Pause.*)
> But where would I find them?
> (*Pause.*)
> Where would I look for them?
> (*Pause. He whistles. Enter Clov.*)
> Let us pray to God.
>
> (E, 54)

Malone, as we have seen, is the Author responsible for the fictitious characters we have met with in Beckett's writing thus far. "Live," he says, "and cause to live"; as he had caused Murphy and the butler and Molloy and Watt and the rest to live—and to die. "I watched them come and go, then I killed them [as he killed Murphy by setting him on fire], or took their place [as he does by becoming a Character to himself as Author], or fled [as he does when he replaces Sapo, the hero of his story, with Macmann]." After each failure, "I began again, to try and live, cause to live, be another, in myself, in another" (TN, 265–66). The last three phrases are difficult. Malone apparently means that the only way he could cause another to live, a Moran, say, or a Molloy, is for himself to become another—*the* Other, the Character—while still remaining in himself as Author, though as Character he is also "in another." If this is a correct reading, then Malone is taking responsibility only for the first-person narratives—that is, only for the two parts of *Molloy*. However, he also claims to have killed the butler in *Murphy*. Perhaps this is why he immediately comments on the passage, "How false all this is. No time now to explain." Malone seems to be saying that his career as an author has had something to do with his life as a person; that he can be an author only if he writes about himself; that his being as a person is his being as an author, but his being as an author is dependent upon himself being the character about whom he writes. Hence we draw the conclusion that his being as a person is merely fictitious, for it is the being of a character. The intricacies have been resuscitated.

And when we come to *The Unnamable*, they are compounded. But lest we lose our way entirely in these various mergings and separations, let us make a brief summary of identities.

Molloy is a character looking for an author; finding none, he himself turns author and writes his own story.

Moran is an author who is sent in search of a character; finding none, he himself turns character and writes about himself.

Malone is an author who, when he tried to cause others (characters) to live, could do so only by writing about himself.

The Unnamable is the ultimate author and the ultimate character. It is for him as Author that Molloy sought, for him as Character that Moran sought, in whose stead Malone wrote and about whom he wrote — or tried to write — as well.

We have already noted that in *The Unnamable* the Husserlian epoché achieves its intended universality. Beginning with a very limited world, the novel steadily reduces it all, brings it all into question and doubt, until toward the end there is nothing but the pure flow of consciousness. Now let us attend to another passage from Husserl in order to see what develops from this.

The purpose of the phenomenological reduction, Husserl says, is to open up or disclose the realm of Transcendental Subjectivity or consciousness. When the Objective world is brought under the epoché, when we reserve our judgment about its existence, there is still left the "phenomenological residuum," that is, consciousness. This consciousness is of course the consciousness of him, the Ego, who is performing the phenomenological reduction. At the end of the reduction, then, there is left only the Ego and the consciousness which is the Ego's but to which the Ego may direct its attention and concern. Husserl writes of this stage in the reduction:

If the Ego, as naturally immersed in the world, experiencingly and otherwise, is called *"interested"* in the world, then the phenomenologically altered — and, as so altered, continually maintained — attitude consists in a *splitting of the*

Ego: in that the phenomenological Ego establishes himself as *"disinterested on-looker,"* above the naively interested Ego. That this takes place is then itself accessible by means of a new reflection, which, as transcendental, likewise demands the very same attitude of looking on *"disinterestedly"* — the Ego's sole remaining interest being to see and to describe adequately what he sees, purely as seen, as what is seen and seen in such and such a manner.[24]

Since Consciousness is "one's own" or Ego's consciousness, and yet the contents of consciousness can be perceived and described, it becomes necessary to posit a "something" which perceives and describes. But this perceiving and describing is also "mine" or "Ego's," as it is "my" or "Ego's" consciousness. Hence, it is necessary to say that the Ego is "split off" from itself and can examine itself, can examine its own consciousness. Thus far Husserl.

But the logic of his argument does not let us stop here. Grant the monadic Ego; grant the self-reflective ability of the Ego, whereby the Ego may examine its own consciousness. Now why not grant a second "splitting off," so that the process of consciousness which is the act of the Ego examining its own self becomes itself an object to a yet higher Ego? We then would have:

Consciousness being examined by Ego; which is itself a
Consciousness' being examined by Ego'; which is itself a
Consciousness'' being examined by Ego''; which is itself a
Consciousness''' being examined by Ego'''; which is . . .

There is an infinite regression of Egos examining consciousnesses. Moreover, the shape of this process is the shape of the process whereby one pursues the aboriginal surd, *the* Alogos, the square root of 2; the process, as Hugh Kenner[25] points out, looks like this:

$$1 + \cfrac{1}{2 + \cfrac{1}{2 + \cfrac{1}{2 + \cfrac{1}{2 + \dots}}}}$$

And this in turn looks like the relation of Author and Character we have been watching develop through the trilogy. For in this work

a Character is the creation of an Author; but the Author is himself
a Character who is the creation of an Author; who is himself
a Character who is the creation of an Author; who is himself
a Character who is the creation of an Author . . .

III

◄ ► I am not asserting in this argument that in order to understand Beckett one must understand Husserl's phenomenology. I am saying that this philosopher and this writer are concerned with the same realm of human experience — the realm of consciousness; and the way Beckett gets to that realm bears a remarkable similarity to the way in which Husserl gets there. Anyone acquainted with Husserl's thought will, indeed, recognize what an extraordinary liberty I have taken with it in order to suggest what may be judged a dubious relation. For nowhere does Husserl suggest that the phenomenological reduction entails an infinite regression of Ego reflecting upon Ego reflecting upon Ego . . . Rather, he insists upon the identity of the Ego through time and the several stages of the reduction. My purpose in adverting to Husserl is twofold: to suggest a certain similarity of purpose and method between Husserl and Beckett; and to prepare the way for the transition from phenomenology to existential ontology. The first of these now having been fulfilled as well as may be, let us turn to the second.

In both *Ideas* and the later *Cartesian Meditations*, Husserl holds that the Ego is immune to the phenomenological reduction. In the former, he himself asks whether the Ego is brought through the reduction to transcendental nothingness, and then replies: "After carrying this reduction through, we shall never stumble across the pure Ego as an experience [*Erlebnis*] among others within the flux of manifold experiences which survives as transcendental residuum. . . . The Ego appears to be permanently, even necessarily, there. . . . The pure Ego appears to be *necessary* in principle, and as that which remains absolutely self-identical in all real and possible changes of experience, it can *in no sense* be reckoned *as a real part or phase* of the experiences themselves." [26] In the fourth of the five Meditations, Husserl regards the Ego as the "substrate of habitualities." "The ego grasps himself not only as a flowing life but also as *I*, who live this and that subjective process, who live through this and that cogito, *as the same I*." [27] With every act emanating from the Ego and having a new sense, he acquires a new abiding property; so if I decide something, I am abidingly the Ego who has so decided. Accordingly, the Ego constitutes himself as identical substrate of Ego-properties, and also constitutes himself as a fixed and abiding personal Ego. [28]

Now it is just this immunity of the Ego from the phenomenological reduction, and the Ego's consequent permanence and self-identity, that Jean-Paul Sartre attacks in his *La Transcendance de l'ego: Esquisse d'une des-*

cription phénoménologique (1937). The unity of consciousness, Sartre argues, is not the result of a transcendent subject or Ego, but the unity of a transcendent object. "The unity of a thousand active consciousnesses by which I have added, do add, and shall add two and two to make four, is the transcendent object 'two and two make four.'" [29] Sartre retains the fundamental principle that consciousness is always intentional—that is, consciousness is always *consciousness of* something. But he concludes from this that there is no room in consciousness for an Ego, for the Ego is simply another of the things consciousness is *consciousness of*. Thus the Ego is expelled into the world, to take its place with all the other objects of consciousness. For Sartre it is improper to say "I am conscious of this or that," for this suggests that a substantive Ego is qualified in a certain way, namely, by being conscious; and the implication is that I might be otherwise than conscious. Nor is it correct to say that "I have consciousness," for again this suggests that consciousness is a thing which "I" can possess and hold on to. Even such locutions as "I am conscious of" or "I am consciousness of," though sometimes grammatically necessary or useful, are misleading, for they suggest that the Ego is the subject of consciousness, when in fact the Ego is its object. Reversing the common view of things, Sartre holds that in order of time consciousnesses are first; these constitute states; and through the latter the Ego is constituted. [30]

When Sartre expelled the Ego from consciousness, he "purified" it of the last element of opacity. In consciousness all is now "clear and lucid." Consciousness is only itself, and as such, it does not "contain" anything. If I say that I am conscious of this typewriter, I do not mean either that the typewriter is "in" my consciousness, or that there is some mysterious, ghostly inhabitant of my mind that perceives the typewriter. "All that there is of *intention* in my actual consciousness is directed toward the outside." [31] That is to say, there is nothing *in* consciousness.

But we must take the expression very seriously. If there is nothing *in* consciousness, then everything is *in* the world. Everything that *is* is in the world. That which *is* is Being, and it is everything that is. But if Being is everything, then consciousness must be precisely Nothing. How consciousness can be Nothing and what this means for living in the world is what Sartre undertakes to explain in *Being and Nothingness*.

Early in that text, Sartre makes a neo-Cartesian distinction between being and consciousness, and since the distinction is the basis of everything that follows, we must try to grasp it well as we can. Being is everything that is

— this typewriter, these books, my body, my Ego, other persons, the whole world. Over against this stands consciousness as that which is aware of beings and of being. The primordial act of consciousness is negation as interrogation and opposition. Consciousness can extricate itself from being and can ask questions of it; and it can do so because it is aware that it is not identical with being. I am not this typewriter. I am not even my own ego, nor am I identical with my body, for both Ego and body are beings of which consciousness is or may be conscious.

The crucial distinction, then, is between consciousness and that of which consciousness is conscious. The complications — grammatical, intellectual, and existential — arise from the fact that one of the beings of which consciousness may be conscious is itself. Clearly, consciousness *is*, and therefore must in some sense be a being. But it is a being whose business in the whole economy of being is to be opposed to being. But since being is everything, nothing can be opposed to it, or that which is opposed to it is nothing. The being of consciousness must therefore be a paradoxical being, for it must both be and not be, must be both being and nothingness.

Our task is now to explicate the paradoxical being which self-consciousness is. Let us move step by step, rehearsing and complicating as we go along. (Follow me carefully, God send I don't make a balls of it.)

Consciousness is nothing. Being is, and is all that is. Consciousness is not being and is not in being, but stands outside being and interrogates and "nihilates" being. Since everything that is is being, and since consciousness is not being, consciousness is nothing.

Consciousness is intentionality. Consciousness cannot exist other than as consciousness *of* something. It intends or posits, for example, this typewriter, this poem, this feeling. The totality of consciousness is employed in an intentional act.

Consciousness is reflexivity. One of the things consciousness may be conscious *of* is itself, and in this case it is spoken of as reflexive — that is, it reflects upon itself. Consciousness is both positional and non-positional: it is consciousness *of* and conscious that it is consciousness *of*. Consciousness does not exist except as both positional and non-positional, or as pre-reflective and reflective.

Consciousness is freedom. In virtue of its ability to oppose being, consciousness can stand out of the causal nexus which otherwise is the law of being. The only limitation to the freedom of consciousness is that it is not free not to be free. Consciousness *has to be free*, not in the sense that it is obedient to some law higher than itself, but in the sense that it cannot exist other than as free.

Consciousness is not in-itself (en-soi) but for-itself (pour-soi). Being is it-self, or in-itself, or is what it is. This typewriter is, and is only what it is. As in-itself, it does not aim to be anything other than itself, so it is not intentional. Therefore it cannot oppose or nihilate itself or call itself into question; for not being intentional it cannot be reflexive. Since it is not reflex-ivity, it is only what it is, and as such it cannot escape itself, so it is not free.

Consciousness, however, is for-itself, in that it is separated from itself by virtue of its reflexivity. As intention, consciousness is always consciousness *of*. At the same time, it is never just that. For in order to be truly conscious, it must in some sense be conscious that it is conscious. Consider the act of belief, for example. I believe this or that. In the act of belief, is consciousness anything other or more than belief? It must be, for if someone were to ask me to do so I could give an account of my belief: "I believe this or that." Similarly in the case of counting or being sad, or any other activity of con-sciousness: consciousness is always aware of itself. "What are you doing?" "I am counting; I am sad." "I am trying to be sincere." "I am not telling the truth. . . ." Consciousness is always and at the same time consciousness *of* and consciousness of being consciousness *of*.

Are we not initiating anew the infinite regression? Consciousness is consciousness of consciousness of . . . No, says Sartre, for the type of ex-istence of consciousness is to be consciousness of itself. It is both "positional" and "non-positional." "Every positional consciousness of an object is at the same time a non-positional consciousness of itself." [32] Or again, "Every con-scious existence exists as consciousness of existing. . . . At one stroke it de-termines itself as consciousness of perception and as perception." [33] Sartre distinguishes this second order of consciousness by writing "conscience (de)." Consciousness (of) is not a new or different consciousness, how-ever; consciousness cannot exist except as both consciousness *of* (some ob-ject) and consciousness (of) consciousness *of* (some object).

When consciousness posits some transcendent object in the world, it is accompanied by the pre-reflective cogito, but when it posits itself it becomes the reflective cogito. When consciousness reflects upon itself, it structures itself as reflecting and reflected. The reflecting consciousness is positional with regard to the reflected, but is always accompanied by a non-positional consciousness (of), for if it were not, it would not be conscious that it is conscious of consciousness (as reflected). But the reflecting consciousness cannot be conscious of itself *as reflecting*. In reflection, the consciousness which reflects is not the consciousness reflected on. Hence, the consciousness which says "I think" is precisely not the consciousness which thinks.[34]

This reflexive structure of consciousness is what constitutes the "self," for the term indicates a duality-within-unity. The self is nothing other than itself, but is itself as the reflecting-reflected dyad. The self is not in-itself, in the sense that being is in-itself, for if it were it would not be capable of reflecting upon itself. It must rather be "present to itself," as the reflected is present to the reflecting. And yet the very fact that it is present to itself indicates that within the self there is a gap, an impalpable fissure; and this fissure is Nothingness. "Nothingness lies coiled in the heart of being — like a worm."[35]

The for-itself is the instrument by which nothingness is "made to be." It is the foundation of nothingness, and as such it is the continual nihilation of being in-itself. In self-consciousness, however, the for-itself apprehends itself as not being its own foundation. As for-itself it is continually fleeing from the self which it no longer is to the self which it is not yet. In anguish it understands itself as freedom, and recognizes both that the things which it has been in the past do not accumulate to determine what it is or shall be, and that the future does not present itself as anything but an infinity of possibilities any one of which the for-itself may freely grasp as its own.

In the region of self-consciousness the for-itself is the nihilation of the in-itself: it is perpetually determining itself not to be the in-itself, for the in-itself is precisely what the for-itself is not. This implies that the for-itself is lacking something. The fact that it understands itself as "lack" indicates that the for-itself has an intuition of what it is that is lacking. What is lacking to the for-itself is nothing other than its self — or itself as in-itself. "Human reality is its own surpassing toward what it lacks; it surpasses itself toward the particular being which it would be if it were what it is."[36] It seeks an absolute coincidence with itself, because only so can it be its own foundation. The formulation of the goal toward which the for-itself is continually surpassing itself is: the For-Itself-In-Itself.[37]

Similarly in the region of temporality: As nothingness separates the reflecting from the reflected, the self from itself, so nothing separates the Past from the Future. The name of this nothing is Present, and Presence is what the for-itself is in temporality. The past is the in-itself which the for-itself as Presence is not; the future is the possibility of the for-itself surpassing itself toward that which it is not yet. "The Future is the ideal point where the sudden infinite compression of facticity (Past), of the For-itself (Present), and of its possible (a particular Future) will at last cause the *Self* to arise as the existence in-itself of the For-itself." [38]

Let the instance of suffering provide both an illustration of the goal of being for-itself-in-itself and the transition to what is, after all, our major concern.

Fate has dealt me a grievous blow. I am sad, I suffer. I weep, I gnash my teeth, tear my raiment. I am in transports of grief and rage and misery. So much do I suffer that suffering is what I am, I am become suffering. But not quite, for the structure of consciousness requires that while I suffer, I must be conscious that I suffer. Consciousness *of* is always accompanied by consciousness (of). Between me and my suffering there is a distance, and I am aware that I suffer. Indeed, being free, suffering is what I choose now to be, and I cannot be suffering unless I create and sustain myself as suffering. My calamity being so stupendous and astonishing, I do so choose, and I desire that my being be the being of suffering itself. I choose to dissolve my being in the being of suffering, to be one with it as the stone is one with itself, as the in-itself is one with itself. At the same time, I desire that it be I that is one with suffering, else it would not be I that suffers; for if it is not I that suffers, there would be only Suffering. So the I which is For-Itself desires to be the Suffering which is In-Itself: I seek to be For-Itself-In-Itself. Only so shall I achieve the foundation of my being.

My desire is vain, the project impossible. As intention I cannot be other than consciousness *of*; as reflexivity I cannot be other than consciousness (of) consciousness; as freedom I cannot be other than free; as self I cannot be other than presence-to-self; as Presence I cannot be other than nihilation of what I was and flight to what I am not yet. What I am as consciousness both creates my desire to be other than I am and prevents me from achieving that goal. The human reality is what it is not, and is not what it is.

So I cannot *be* suffering; I can only play at it, thereby bringing suffering into being and keeping it there. I weep and cry out and wring my hands, and in so doing I create weeping-itself and crying-itself and wringing-itself. Could I *be* suffering, I should not have to play at it; I should not have to weep and cry and wring. Could I be suffering, I should be For-Itself-In-Itself.

If then I cry out, it is because I cannot be silent and still be suffering. But my ideal is to be silent — the silence of him who is Suffering-itself. "Each groan, each facial expression of the man who suffers aims at sculpturing a statue-in-itself of suffering. But this statue will never exist save through others and for others. My suffering suffers from being what it is not and from not being what it is. . . . It is loquacious because it is not adequate, but its ideal is silence, — the silence of the statue, of the beaten man who lowers his head and veils his face without speaking." [39] Hamm appears to achieve the ideal of silence. The last lines of *Endgame* are his: "Since that's the way we're playing it . . . (*he unfolds handkerchief*) let's play it that way. . . . and speak no more about it . . . (*he finishes unfolding*) . . . speak no more . . . Old stancher! (*Pause.*) You . . . remain. (*Pause. He covers his face. . . .*)" But even the act of veiling the face, of speaking no more, is just that — an act, a playing at suffering — whose purpose is to keep my suffering alive by exhibiting it to others, including myself as reflecting on myself as suffering. Suffering does not come into being by itself. It is made to be or brought into being by my decision to suffer or to be suffering, and it is maintained in its being by my continued willing to be suffering. It is I who am the foundation of my suffering, but as its foundation I am still not suffering-itself. Between the I as the ground of my suffering (or of any other mode of being) and suffering-itself there is always the Distance — the same Distance as that between the I that is reflected upon and the I that reflects.

The reflexive structure of consciousness as laid out by Sartre is, I believe, the philosophical "model" or "type" of the interpretation of the self to which Beckett comes in the later works, and especially in the third volume of the trilogy. It is congruent with the other metaphors of the self we have already examined. The mathematical metaphor is that of the process of finding the square root of 2; the autobiographical metaphor is that of the character who is an author, who in turn is a character to another author, etc.; the "phenomenological" metaphor is that of a consciousness which is examined by a conscious Ego, which in turn is a consciousness examined by a conscious Ego, etc. In Sartre's case, the reflecting ego reflects upon the reflected ego. Put thus, it looks like the beginning of another infinite regression: the reflected ego is examined by a reflecting ego, which becomes in turn a reflected ego to the next reflecting ego, *ad infinitum*. The ego reflected upon would then stand to the reflecting ego as character to author, and after *The Unnamable* there would need to be another novel which stands to it as *The Unnamable* stands to *Malone Dies*. But this is not the way I read the trilogy, and it certainly is not Sartre's idea of the structure of consciousness. As we have seen, Sartre explicitly rejects the notion that the consciousness of consciousness is morphologically identical with the knowledge of knowledge or Spinoza's *idea ideae ideae* . . .[40] It is of course true that if I define consciousness as knowing, then I must also say that self-consciousness is knowing that I know; and then I must go on to say that if I know that I know, I also know that I know that I know, etc. But the Sartrean consciousness is not capable of such an infinite extension. The reason is that the consciousness which reflects is the same consciousness which is reflected upon. The two are not identical, since identity would prohibit a reflection at all; but they are not different either. Sartre writes, "The reflected-on is an *appearance* for the reflective without thereby ceasing to be witness (of) itself, and the reflective is *witness* of the reflected-on without thereby ceasing to be an appearance to itself." [41] Both the reflective (or witness) and the reflected (or appearance) are affected by the reflection, for each strives to be autonomous and establish itself as for-itself-in-itself. But the reflective can have its being only in and through the appearance, so it is not and cannot be the ground of itself; and the reflected can have its being only in and through the witness, so it cannot be the ground of itself. It is the state of the reflected-on that is especially interesting. Sartre writes: "The reflected-on is profoundly altered by reflection (reflexion) in this sense that it is self-consciousness as the consciousness reflected-on *of* this or that transcendent phenomenon. The reflected-on knows itself observed. It may best be compared — to use a concrete example — to a man who is writing, bent over a table, and who while writing knows that he is observed by somebody who stands behind him." [42] There cannot be a second observer standing behind the first observer, however, and another behind him, etc. For the structure of consciousness as the reflective–reflected-on dyad admits only two terms, not three or an infinite number.

Reflection is the for-itself conscious *of* itself. But just as the for-itself attempts to found its own being by becoming the for-itself-in-itself, and finds that it is always separated by a nothingness from itself, so the reflective tries to found itself in reflection, but finds that it is also separated from the reflected-on by a nothingness.

Reflection (reflexion) remains for the for-itself a permanent possibility, an attempt to recover being. By reflection the for-itself, which has lost itself outside itself, attempts to put itself inside its own being. Reflection is a second effort by the for-itself to found itself; that is, *to be for itself what it is*. Indeed if the quasi-dyad the reflection-reflecting were gathered up into a totality for a witness which would be itself, it would be in its own eyes what it is. The goal in short is to overtake that being which flees itself while being what it is in the mode of not-being and which flows on while being its own flow, which escapes between its own fingers.[43]

Sartre speaks of the reflected-on as a writer who knows he is being observed, but from our point of view the reflected-on is precisely the Character, whereas the reflective is the Author. To be an Author is to bring into being a Character, and if or when the Author is not bringing a Character into being he is not himself being an Author. His being an Author is then dependent on the act: "bringing a Character into being." Hence his being is dependent upon the being of the Character, just as the being of the reflective is dependent upon the being of the reflected-on, and the for-itself is dependent upon the in-itself. In the "autobiographical" trilogy, the Author is the Character, as the reflective is also the reflected-on, but the Author is never identical with the Character, as the reflective is never identical with the reflected-on or the for-itself with the in-itself. The first term in each pair is separated from the second by the nothingness which, simply by being what it is (by being Author, etc.), it interpolates between itself and the second term. To be for-itself is precisely not to be in-itself; to be reflective is precisely not to be the reflected-on; to be author is precisely not to be character. And this is true even though the goal in each case is, as Sartre says, "to overtake that being which flees itself while being what it is in the mode of not-being." "Live and cause to live," says Malone. "After the fiasco, the solace, the repose, I began again, to try and live, cause to live, be another, in myself, in another" (TN, 266). The Unnamable realizes that in order to stop speaking he must speak of himself. But he can no more speak *of himself* than the reflective can reflect upon itself and not upon the reflected-on. It is as if a man were to ride in a railway train, his back to the engine, his sight limited to the semicircular field in front of him. He is always ahead of what he is looking at, and he can see only where he has been. He cannot say where he is "now," only where he was "then." This is the way the narrator of Beckett's story "The Expelled" (1946) rides in his cab: with his back to the horse (STN, 17). And I amuse myself by supposing that this story is Beckett's version of the eviction of the Ego from consciousness, as Jean-Paul Sartre described that eviction nine years earlier in *The Transcendence of the Ego*.

IV

◀ ▶ Philosophical systems which take their departure from the Known are analogous to narrative fiction written from the omniscient point of view, whereas systems which begin with the Knower are like novels written in the first person. The former are congruent with a version of the world which lays stress upon the many particular things that exist, what the causes and interrelations of these are, and how they do or do not cohere together to compose a certain kind of unity. In the latter case, when thought or art begins with the Knower, the richness and variety of the world are typically subordinated to the complexities of subjectivity, and the question of the coherence of the many to form a one is replaced by the question of the congruence of perceptions and ideas to what is. In particular, intellectual systems which begin with the problem of knowledge and fiction which adopts a first-person narrative encounter similar difficulties in moving from the knower to the known and from "I" to "He." A novel which makes this shift stands in danger of being faulted for inconsistency, and its author may be accused of having failed to develop a strategy for handling the problems which his scheme would inevitably develop. When a philosopher tries to move from a discussion of the nature of knowledge to the nature that is known, he sometimes encounters great difficulties, and needs to call upon some mediating principle or mechanism (as did Descartes) or upon some larger concept which can contain and integrate the perceiver and the perceived (as did Malebranche and Berkeley in their notions of the relation of ideas to God's vision or mind). The writer who stays within the limits of his original viewpoint is usually commended for his technical ability; but the philosopher who from his situation in subjectivity cannot or will not move, or who does not appear to his critics to move, may be condemned as a sceptic, an idealist, or even a solipsist, and may have to suffer the ignominy of having commonsensical men punt stones at his fragile house by way of refutation.

Philosophical subjectivism has usually been encouraged by the conviction that the World Out There cannot be known, or is not worth knowing, or is less important to know than the inner world of ideas and feelings. In its concern with the structure and operations of the Self, subjectivism tries to turn away from the world and other people, but in the course of time there are fewer and fewer places for an Augustine or a Descartes, an Arsenius or a Climacus to flee to; there are more and more people, and by the nineteenth century thinking is done in populous cities where the Other is a fact that cannot be done away with. It is indeed with Hegel's *Phänomenologie des Geistes* (first edition 1807) that the Other becomes a principal philosophical theme. It is also indicative of Hegel's genius that he gives that theme its characteristically modern tone, and at the same time reveals aspects of the Self which had gone unnoticed or unemphasized in earlier thought. It is to the *Phenomenology* that we turn now, to consider briefly Hegel's concept of the Other and some of his terminology, and to get a feel for his dialectical method.

Whether we talk of man or the self or God or Reason or the Absolute, we must talk in terms of a process of becoming. Reason is purposive activity; and although the human embryo is in-itself (*an sich*) it is not for-itself (*für sich*), for man is for-itself only as the educated reason has made itself that which it is in-itself.[44] As the power of becoming, the for-itself is negativity, for it is continually negating what it is as in-itself, but at the same time it preserves what it negates and takes it up into itself in its process of becoming.

It is not enough for the self to be conscious, however. It must be conscious *of itself*, for only so will it attain to a scientific knowledge of itself and of the Spirit. In order to know itself, it must become an object to itself, but it can do so only by encountering another self-consciousness. "Self-consciousness exists in itself and for itself, in that, and by the fact that it exists for another self-consciousness; that is to say, it *is* only by being acknowledged or 'recognized.' "[45] Hegel is working here without the help of Sartre's "nonpositional consciousness (of)," so he must hold that the self can understand itself as such only by recognizing it in the Other. In doing so, however, the Self loses itself in the Other, for it discovers itself only as Other. So in order to recover itself, the self must sublate [*aufheben*] its being-Other in order to return to its being-for-itself [*Fürsichsein*]. Consciousness cannot view the Other simply as a thing, for in so doing it would miss precisely what it is aiming at — the recognition of itself as being-for-itself. It must recognize the Other as another being-for-itself. At the same time, self-consciousness is being-for-itself in that it excludes every Other from itself; so that the Other is marked with the character of the Negative. Thus, in the view of the One, the Other is the negative, though at the same time in the view of the Other (who is also self-consciousness or for-itself) the One is negative. In the encounter of the One and the Other, then, each attempts to sublate his opponent, and simple recognition develops into a life and death struggle for existence as for-itself. Either the One or the Other will prove the stronger, and he will emerge as independent for-itself, whereas the weaker will become the dependent for-another. The former is the Master, the latter the Slave.[46]

When Karl Marx came upon this passage, he interpreted it as a description of the class conflict, the Master being the bourgeoisie, the Slave the proletariat. Inevitably, contemporary critics who know Marx but do not know Hegel read *Waiting for Godot* as a parable of the struggle between the exploiters and the exploited. Although the play will sustain this interpretation, it is hardly exhausted by it.

Sartre is more faithful to Hegel's intent, and in *Being and Nothingness* he asserts that the original meaning of being-for-others is conflict, and treats the conflict in several ways, one of them in terms of sadism and masochism, another in terms of the Look. When I am looked at by the Other, I am to him an object, mere in-itself. As such I have lost the freedom which as for-itself I primordially am. The Other is, then, a threat to my freedom, and I can recover myself as for-itself only by negating the other in himself as for-itself. As freedom and nihilation, consciousness must negate what is not itself in order to be itself.

Transposing freely, we might say that just as consciousness cannot be consciousness absolutely but must always be consciousness *of*, so mastery cannot be itself absolutely but must be mastery *of*. This sets master and slave in a dialectical and paradoxical relationship, for the master cannot be what he is unless there is a slave for him to be master *of*. Hence, his mastery is dependent upon slavery, and that means that it is no mastery at all. Conversely, the slave cannot be what he is unless there is a master for him to be the slave *of*. Hence the slave must create his master and sustain him in his mastery, and this of course means that the slave is master of the master, and this is no slavery at all.

This paradoxical structure is evident in the relationships of Pozzo and Lucky, and Hamm and Clov. The Pozzo who drives Lucky before him with a whip, who treats him as a beast of burden — a slave — is the same who declares that Lucky is killing him. Although Clov can no longer live with Hamm he cannot leave him either, for apart from him he cannot be what he is — a slave — and with him he cannot be what he is — a free consciousness. Hamm can be what he is — Master — so long as Clov stays, but his mastery is dependent on Clov's being a slave, so he is not really Master either.

In Hegel's terms, the Master has got himself into the situation of having destroyed in the Slave the very thing he sought to find there — that for-itself which will exhibit to him what he is. He has indeed become an independent self-consciousness, but at the cost of destroying the independence of the Slave. He does not see in the Slave what he himself is, so he does not have the truth of his existence. The Slave, for his part, sees an independent self-consciousness in the Master but does not and cannot see it in himself, since the Master has destroyed it in him. Hegel's universe is as restless as an almost perfectly adjusted balance (or as a well with two buckets), however, and the enslavement of the Slave is the beginning of his liberation. For in the encounter, the Slave has been nihilated by the independent self-consciousness which the Master is, and this experience of nihilation is the fear of "death, the sovereign master." But consciousness is nothing other than absolute negativity, so in being nihilated by the Master the Slave achieves self-consciousness. Moreover, the Slave must serve and labor; but this now proves to be the means for transcending slavery. For the structures which the Slave creates by his labor are both autonomous [*selbständige*] and the product of consciousness which the slave recognizes as his own. So in his work the Slave acquires what he had been denied by the Master — independent self-conscious existence. We should note a qualification, however. If fear does not find its expression in work, it will remain inward and mute, and if work is not the expression of absolute fear, the slave will not discover that he has a "mind of his own" [*eigenen Sinn*] but will simply become stubborn [*Eigensinn*].

The effect of the encounter of two independent self-consciousnesses is their polarization into Master and Slave, each of which is isolated from the other. The Master can therefore neither continue in the development which as for-itself he should do, nor can he rest in his condition as in-itself which in the encounter he achieved. The Slave sees in the products of his labor the objectification of his consciousness, but does not perceive (as Slave — before the beginning of his transformation) that it is his own consciousness that is responsible for the object he has made. Both Master and Slave are then fixed at a moment of development in which neither is complete. In a difficult transitional passage, Hegel apparently argues that the Slave retires into himself as thinking being, for it is here that he can be the autonomous self-consciousness which he cannot be in the perspective of the Master. "In thinking I am free, because I am not in an other, but remain simply and solely in touch with myself; and the object which for me is my essential reality, is in undivided unity my self-existence [*Fürmichsein*]." [47] This freedom of self-consciousness Hegel calls Stoicism. Hegel doesn't say so, but he probably has had in mind throughout the discussion of the Master and Slave two of the most famous stoics, the Emperor Marcus Aurelius and the slave Epictetus.

Stoicism is not really freedom, however, but merely the notion of freedom, for in retiring into the mind Stoicism disengages itself from life. It is free, but only in the sense that it is free to "maintain that stolid lifeless unconcern which persistently withdraws from the movement of existence, from effective activity as well as from passive endurance, into the simple essentiality of thought." [48] A passage from Epictetus may illustrate the attitude being criticized: "Exercise yourself then in what lies in your power. Each man's master is the man who has authority over what he wishes or does not wish, to secure the one or to take away the other. Let him then who wishes to be free not wish for anything or avoid anything that depends on others; or else he is bound to be a slave." [49] Stoicism as thinking consciousness is, then, only abstract freedom and only an incomplete negation of otherness, for it has not given itself to the total negation of existence.

The style of thought that continues the movement begun by Stoicism is Scepticism. If Stoicism is the concept of independent self-consciousness, Scepticism is its realization: "In Scepticism, the entire unessentiality and unsubstantiality of this 'other' becomes a reality for consciousness. Thought becomes thinking which wholly annihilates the being of the world with its manifold determinateness, and the negativity of free self-consciousness becomes aware of attaining, in these manifold forms which life assumes, real negativity." [50] As radical negativity, sceptical self-consciousness achieves the freedom which Stoicism merely strived for. By the negation of the "manifold determinateness" of the world, Scepticism establishes itself as totally free.

But this freedom is purchased at the cost of permanence and identity. Thought itself has nothing "fixed" to which it can attach itself, and it spins in disorder through its own categories and the structures of the world. Ultimately it must negate even itself, and then it must acknowledge itself as a fortuitous, individual consciousness which "is empirical, which is directed upon what admittedly has no reality for it, which obeys what, in its regard, has no essential being, which realizes and does what it knows to have no truth." [51] It is its own contradiction. In its sceptical form, consciousness is "thoroughgoing dialectical restlessness, [a] mêlée of presentations derived from sense and thought, whose differences collapse into oneness, and whose identity is similarly again resolved and dissolved. . . . This consciousness

. . . instead of being a self-same consciousness, is here neither more nor less than an absolutely fortuitous embroglio, the giddy whirl of a perpetually self-creating disorder." [52]

In Scepticism, consciousness attains to actual freedom, but it is the freedom of pure negation: "If sameness is shown to it, it points out unlikeness, non-identity; and when the latter, which it has expressly mentioned the moment before, is held up to it, it passes on to indicate sameness and identity. Its talk, in fact, is like a squabble among self-willed children, one of whom says A when the other says B, and again B, when the other says A, and who, through being in contradiction with themselves, procure the joy of remaining in contradiction with one another."

Thus the two children in *Godot*:

VLADIMIR. When you seek you hear.
ESTRAGON. You do.
VLADIMIR. That prevents you from finding.
ESTRAGON. It does.
VLADIMIR. That prevents you from thinking.
ESTRAGON. You think all the same.
VLADIMIR. No, no, impossible.
ESTRAGON. That's the idea, let's contradict each other.

(WFG, 41)

And just as, in the play, Didi and Gogo are in some sense the antitheses of one another and hold themselves apart, so too, in the sceptical consciousness the two moments of individuality and universality, difference and identity, are held apart; and this form of consciousness is split within itself.

But at the third and still higher stage of self-consciousness, Scepticism comes to the realization that the split is precisely within itself, and that it is, for all its infinite variety and indeterminateness, still one self-consciousness. At this stage, consciousness realizes that it is freedom and nothing else, and so is self-identical with itself and determinate; but its freedom is negativity and the destruction of everything that is, including itself in its own determinateness. It is both free and determinate, independent and dependent, *für sich* and *an sich*, negation and affirmation, itself and not itself. It is a union within one consciousness of the two forms of consciousness which were earlier described under the heading of Master and Slave. This consciousness, which is a unity of contradiction, Hegel calls *"das unglückliche Bewusstsein,"* the consciousness which is unhappy, unfortunate — even "unlucky." [53]

It may be that Beckett took Lucky's name from Hegel, just as (and with a higher degree of probability) he may have taken Pozzo's name from Sartre.[54] Certainly, in Lucky's long effort at thinking we see the sceptical consciousness at work, affirming only to deny, predicating only to negate, hypothesizing only to destroy the hypothesis by qualification. In Lucky's speech, thought drifts free from any stable or fixed concepts, rushes on to no goal, and carries with it no principle of proof or completion by means of which it can determine when it can or should stop — except the principle of physical exhaustion. Moreover, there would be a nice irony in calling him "Lucky," for it suggests that he has not yet arrived at that stage of self-consciousness where the antithetical moments are recognized to be moments of *one* consciousness, and has not, therefore, arrived at the condition of *"das unglückliche Bewusstsein."* That condition is reserved for the narrators of the later fiction, and in its purest, most agonizing form, for the Unnamable.

v

◄ ► In Hegel's scheme, the "Unhappy Consciousness" is the synthesis, in one sense, of the two antithetical moments of the sceptical consciousness, and in another of Stoicism and Scepticism as the preliminary and opposed structures of self-consciousness. But of course the dialectic does not stop with the Unhappy Consciousness. Split as it is, this third stage is still aware of itself as a single consciousness, and so will seek to be reconciled with itself. "Its true return into itself, or reconciliation with itself, will, however, display the notion of mind endowed with a life and existence of its own, because it implicitly involves the fact that, while being an undivided consciousness, it is a double-consciousness. It is itself the gazing of one self-consciousness into another, and itself is both, and the unity of both is also its own essence; but objectively and consciously it is not yet this essence itself — is not yet the unity of both." [55] "Aber es für sich ist sich noch nicht dieses Wesen selbst, noch nicht die Einheit beider." It is precisely here, in just two words, that the difference between Hegel and Sartre, indeed their irreconcilable opposition, comes clearly into view. For Hegel, the unity of the doubled consciousness, the reconciliation of the *für sich* and the *an sich* is *"noch nicht"*: yet, in the stately, irresistible procession of Reason through history it will surely come. For Sartre, however, the coincidence of the *pour-*

soi and the *en-soi*, the grounding of the nihilating freedom of consciousness in being, is an event which is a logical, phenomenological, and eschatological impossibility: its advent is not *"noch nicht"* but *"jamais."*

For Hegel in a preliminary and temporary way, and for Sartre in a continuing and permanent way, the Other is a threat to the being of the self-consciousness which the I is. For Hegel, the conflict of the Master and the Slave is a struggle to the death, but a struggle which will issue in a still higher and more refined self-consciousness; for Sartre, the meaning of being-for-others is conflict, and the freedom which the Other as *pour-soi* is presents a limit to the freedom which I am. What Hegel described as the dynamics of the Master and the Slave, Sartre, drawing on more recent terminology, can describe as sadism and masochism. And in one of his most celebrated lines, Sartre defined hell as "other people," or simply as "the others." [56]

This attitude toward the Other, however, is characteristic of all those thinkers, of whatever age, whose style of thought invites the adjective "existential." It is there in the fear and contempt of Kierkegaard for the universal, of Nietzsche for the herd, of Dostoevsky's Underground Man for the Crystal Palace and the rule of reason, of Heidegger for *"das Man."* Wherever freedom, subjectivity, uniqueness, individuality are lauded as the highest good for man, there the Other, as limitation or objectivity or law or the common good or simply as another human being, is viewed with suspicion, contempt, and fear. The world being what it is, however, there is no escape from "Him" or "Them," so every "existentialist" is at least potentially a shivering mass of paranoia.

The dreadful discovery made by Hegel, however, is that the Other is not located only "out there" in the world, but is also "in here," as an integral and essential element of the self. The "Unhappy Consciousness" is exactly the doubling of itself into itself and the Other, and the Other is the principle of contradiction and negation interior to the self. The struggle between the Master and the Slave is the struggle within consciousness of the active and the passive, of overcoming and undergoing, of motion and rest, life and thought, for-itself and in-itself, the one and the many, determinacy and indeterminacy. If consciousness attempts to rest in any of these paired terms as the One, it is confronted with and negated by its opposite and Other. And wherever the reality of the self is understood in this dialectical fashion, as in Hegel, Kierkegaard, Sartre, and in Beckett, there the self must be viewed not only as potentially paranoid but as essentially schizophrenic.

That psychosis or an advanced state of neurosis is the condition of Beckett's major characters is a suggestion that hardly needs elaborate documentation. As one moves from *Murphy* through *Watt* and the short pieces *La Fin*, *L'Expulsé*, *Le Calmant*, and the *Textes pour Rien*, to the trilogy, the plays, and *How It Is*, one recognizes that the ergophobia, introversion, megalomania, and paranoia which seemed so uniquely to be Murphy's are indeed endemic to the whole of the Beckett country. The "mercantile Gehenna" means to Murphy what the language of the "they" means to the Unnamable, and the "they" who beat Gogo are comparable to the unidentified and unidentifiable "person" who extorts the fragments of speech from the narrator of *How It Is*. The situation is hardly surprising, though; for whether one emphasizes the Cartesian or the "existentialist" aspect of the various characters, the fact remains that the "I" is the sole support of the Being of both the world and the self; and the realization of the fact carries with it both a megalomaniac pride in providing the cause and support of Being, and a paranoid terror of those who would threaten this absolute ground.

We do not need detailed clinical and theoretical analysis by medical authority, either. Almost any description will serve. This happens to be Jung:

> The picture of personality dissociation in schizophrenia is quite a different matter [from that in hysteria]. The split-off figures assume banal, grotesque, or highly exaggerated names and characters and are often objectionable in many ways. They do not, moreover, co-operate with the patient's consciousness. They are not tactful and they have no respect for sentimental values. On the contrary, they break in and make a disturbance at any time, they torture the ego in a hundred ways; all and sundry are objectionable and shocking either in their noisy and impertinent behavior or in their grotesque cruelty and obscenity. There is an apparent chaos of inconsistent visions, voices, and characters of an overwhelmingly strange and incomprehensible nature. If there is a drama at all, it is certainly far beyond the patient's understanding. In most cases it transcends even the physician's mind.[57]

If in place of "patient's understanding" we read "the Unnamable's understanding," and in place of "transcends even the physician's mind" we read "transcends even the critic's mind," we shall not be far from the truth.

No critic wants to believe that the drama of Beckett's art transcends his mind, however, and he may be tempted by Jung's mention of "an apparent chaos of inconsistent visions, voices, and characters" to identify the narrators of the later fiction as a series of avatars the original of which is to be found in Mr. Endon's unobtrusive and melodious inner voice (M, 186). Is it not this voice, amplified to a level of audibility, diminished as to sense, enlarged and complicated as to its emotional range—is it not this voice which, having gone out of Mr. Endon and seeking rest but finding none, wanders through the dry places indifferently identified as a person or as a novel—through *Molloy*, say, or Malone? Is not this voice the continuo which supports and unifies the single, massive polyphonic score we call "the later fiction," all of which was composed [*sic*] in French? Unheard by Murphy or by us but heard by Mr. Endon, this voice is later heard by us who listen to what it narrates but is unheard by him in whom and for whom it is narrated, for he is far, sunk deep in the mud of his psychosis.

I think we must take seriously the notion that the narrative voice is indeed the audible remainder of a dissociated psyche. But if we take it so seriously as to exclude every other consideration, our analysis of the fiction will no longer be literary criticism but psychoanalysis. The assumption to which the critic must cling, even at the risk of having it all transcend his mind, is that what we are dealing with here is, in spite of everything, still art; and Beckett's art will no more reduce to the lore of psychoanalysis than it will to the propositions of philosophy. Moreover, if Hegel is right, psychopathology merely recapitulates ontology, and our ontological analysis of self-consciousness has already revealed that both schizophrenia and paranoia are latent in the very structure and dynamics of the "I." Let us suppose, then, that the pathological or clinical element is really there in Beckett's work, but it is there as one of the possibilities which reside in the very make-up of consciousness as doubled or reflective and as the sole ground of the being of itself and the world.

In addition to psychological hazards there are also philosophical hazards which threaten the one who seeks the Beginning in his own interiority. The reason for starting there is as old as the realization that a straight stick half immersed in water appears bent. Sensory perception is unreliable, and what it tells me of the world must be doubted. When Descartes purged the room of his mind of everything that sense and education had furnished it with, he discovered that he could eliminate everything except the room itself. The very act of doubting verifies the being of an agent of doubt. This was good enough for Descartes, and took him as far as he needed or wanted to go. In more recent times, however, the search for certitude has been replaced by the search for the self, and the agent of doubt which was for Descartes an end became for Hegel and Husserl and Sartre a new Beginning. Again, doubt in the hands of Descartes was a controllable instrument or method; for the later dialecticians it is itself a topic or problem. For the act of doubting is the act of negation, and as such it is treated at the ontological level as the principle of non-being or nothingness. The primordial and ownmost act of the self is the act of nihilation: "That is not I." All that remains to the being of the "I" in the extreme case of Sartre is its being as non-being or as nihilation. The doubt which for Descartes was an epistemological instrument has become the very being of the "I." Scepticism is no longer a preliminary and finite stage in the pursuit of apodictic truth but is the condition of man — for Hegel the antepenultimate condition, to be superseded by the Unhappy Consciousness and then by the resolution of its antitheses; for Sartre the final condition, hopeless and absurd.[58]

In addition to being threatened by Scepticism, the one who looks for the Beginning in himself is threatened by Solipsism. Husserl was perfectly aware of this:

Without doubt the sense of the transcendental reduction implies that, at the beginning, this science can posit nothing but the ego and what is included in the ego himself. . . . Without doubt [it must at first parenthesize the distinction (evinced within the ego) between "me myself" with my life, my appearances, my acquired certainties of being, my abiding interests, etc., and others with their lives, their appearances, etc.; and thus, in a certain sense,] it begins accordingly as a pure egology and as a science that apparently condemns us to a solipsism, albeit a transcendental solipsism. As yet it is quite impossible to foresee how, for me in the attitude of reduction, other egos — not as mere worldly phenomena but as other transcendental egos — can become positable as existing and thus become equally legitimate themes of a phenomenological egology.[59]

Husserl believed, however, that the solipsism which the transcendental reduction seemed to entail was only a preliminary stage, and would be followed by a "phenomenology of transcendental intersubjectivity." Sartre on the other hand, never one to compromise, rejects this idea of the possibility of a phenomenology of transcendental intersubjectivity as flatly as he rejects Hegel's idea of the reconcilability of the bifurcated Unhappy Consciousness. For Sartre, the "me" is simply the noematic correlate of a reflective intention — that is, the "me" is that of which consciousness is or may be conscious. My "me" is available to my intuition, and so is the Other's "me," although in both cases inadequately and incompletely; but that is as far as I can go. For the Other's consciousness — that is, very inexactly, his "I" — is *radically* impenetrable," not only to intuition but to thought, for

I cannot conceive his consciousness without making an object of it. That is to say, Paul cannot conceive Peter's consciousness without making it into a being or a thing; and this is precisely what it is not, for as consciousness it is not being but nothingness. Hence Paul cannot *know* Peter — at least not Peter's consciousness — for Peter is "impenetrable." [60] The "being" of consciousness denies man access to his fellow man. That fact is what drove Watt mad.

Schizophrenic and paranoid, sceptical and solipsistic — these are the terms that define the unhappy consciousness, the modern consciousness, the Beckettian consciousness. They apply, moreover, not simply to the extreme case, to the psychopath and the philosophical eccentric, but to anyone who has the courage to look at what is in front of him and listen to the voices within and all about him. Schizophrenia is the destiny of reflecting, as paranoia is the destiny of living, scepticism of thinking, and solipsism of speaking. The Absolute Identity — "I am that I am" — which has grounded the speculative tradition from Parmenides and the Elohist of Exodus 3:14 through the German idealists and Coleridge to the present time, an Identity which is still threefold in omnipotence, omniscience, and omnipresence, is negated by Sartre; and this negation becomes the formula for the absurdity of existence, for the human reality is what it is not, and is not what it is.

Thrown into existence, the self is powerless to become what it thinks it wants to become and ought to become. Its being gets frittered away in idle talk, reminiscence, story telling. The Other stands over against it, objectifies it, and denies it its freedom. Knowing nothing for sure, it listens in to what the Others say in the hopes of finding the truth about itself, but what They say is said in Their words and does not apply. When it listens to itself, it hears only the stories of what it was and how it failed in its self-appointed task of being itself. Never having been itself, it has no experience of what it would be like to be itself, and knows not what it is called upon to do and be. When, finally, in its powerlessness and ignorance it turns for help and solace to some other, it discovers a thing, a machine, with which intercourse — either sexual or verbal — is governed by the laws of physics or the patterns of stimulus-response.

table of basic stimuli one sing nails in armpit two speak blade in arse three stop thump on skull four louder pestle on kidney
five softer index in anus six bravo clap athwart arse seven lousy same as three eight encore same as one or two as may be (HII, 69)

Identity, power, wisdom, and love are eliminated as real possibilities by the fact that to be is to be conscious. Consciousness alienates me from myself, sets me at the mercy of the Other, negates every statement of my being, and isolates me from every other consciousness.

That is how it is.

VII

DIALECTIC AND THE ABSOLUTE ABSENCE

When facts disagree, but the contradictory statements have exactly the same weight, ignorance of the truth is the necessary consequence. But even this statement has its corresponding antithesis, so that after destroying others it turns round and destroys itself, like a purge which drives the substance out and then in its turn is itself eliminated and destroyed.

Diogenes Laertius

Nature presents to me nothing which is not a matter of doubt and concern. If I saw nothing there which revealed a Divinity, I would come to a negative conclusion; if I saw everywhere the signs of a Creator, I would remain peacefully in faith. But, seeing too much to deny and too little to be sure, I am in a state to be pitied. . . . In my present state, ignorant of what I am or of what I ought to do, I know neither my condition nor my duty.

Pascal

That the subjective existing thinker is as positive as he is negative, can also be expressed by saying that he is as sensitive to the comic as to the pathetic. As men ordinarily live, the comic and the pathetic are divided, so that one person has the one and another person has the other . . . But for anyone who exists in a double reflection, the proportions are equal: as much of the pathetic, so much also of the comic. The equality in the relationship provides a mutual security, each guaranteeing the soundness of the other. The pathos which is not secured by the presence of the comic is illusion; the comic spirit that is not made secure by the presence of pathos is immature.

Kierkegaard

Ein Gott vermags. Wie aber, sag mir, soll
ein Mann ihm folgen durch die schmale Leier?
Sein Sinn is Zwiespalt. . . .
. . . .
Gesang ist Dasein. Für den Gott ein Leichtes.
Wann aber *sind* wir? . . .

Rilke [1]

I

◄ ► In his essay on Joyce, Beckett contrasted Joyce with Dante with respect to the presence and absence of "the Absolute." In Dante, Hell is an Absolute, for it is "the static lifelessness of unrelieved viciousness"; Heaven is an Absolute for it is the "static lifelessness of unrelieved immaculation." Even Dante's Purgatory is an Absolute, for it is conical and implies a culmination: movement is "unidirectional, and a step forward represents a net advance" toward the culmination. Joyce's work (*Finnegans Wake*) contains no Absolute, however. It represents neither Heaven nor Hell but Purgatory, and even this Purgatory is spherical, not conical, so movement is merely "flux — progression or retrogression," and there is only an apparent consummation. Virtue and Vice, which for Dante are Absolutes, are for Joyce simply a series of stimulants. Nonetheless, Joyce's work is purgatorial, for "the vicious circle of humanity is being achieved," and this achievement is the result of the "recurrent predomination of one of two broad qualities" — Virtue and Vice or any other pair of "large contrary human factors" (OERH, 21–22).

In this early essay (he was twenty-three when it was published), Beckett touches on two motifs which become central in his own later work. I have mentioned (Ch. V) the theme of the absolute absence of the Absolute. The dialectical relation between any pair of "large contrary human factors" has been implicit in all the discussion of his work. Both themes need now to be dealt with at greater length.

In traditional Western thought, "the Absolute" is one of the ways of speaking of God. As Absolute, God is not contingent upon or conditioned by anything other than himself. His being is the being of aseity. We have already had occasion to quote Aristotle on this score: "And thought thinks on itself because it shares the nature of the object of thought; . . . And life also belongs to God; for the actuality of thought is life, and God is that actuality; and God's self-dependent actuality is life most good and eternal. We say therefore that God is a living being, eternal, most good, so that life and duration continuous and eternal belong to God; for this *is* God." [2]

In Aristotle and classical Greek thought, God in his self-dependent actuality transcends the world. The Judaeo-Christian tradition adds two dimensions to God which bring him into relation to the world. God created the world and man, and he loves what he created. The creation is contingent upon the being of God, but as created it is good, and as good it is lovable by God. Thus the world is "theomorphous"; and as man was created in the image of God, he too is deiform. God, world, and man, therefore, are all mutually congruent with one another. The importance of the geocentric cosmology is that the center of the cosmos is man's home, the earth. And when Dante beheld the beatific vision, the Absolute Itself seemed to him "pinta de la nostra effige," "limned with our image." [3]

In Aristotle, God is Thought thinking upon Itself. In the Judaeo-Christian tradition God is Love. "We love him," writes John (I John 4:19), "because he first loved us." These two traditions are brilliantly fused by Spinoza in a passage we have already noticed. "The intellectual love of the mind towards God is that very love of God whereby God loves himself, not in so far as he is infinite, but in so far as he can be explained through the essence of the human mind regarded under the form of eternity; in other words, the intellectual love of the mind towards God is part of the infinite love wherewith God loves himself." [4] Understood either as Mind or as Love, the divine life is a going out and a returning into itself. Its "shape" is a circle: *Deus est sphaera cujus centrum ubique.* In its multeity and activity the Godhead is still one and in repose in itself. Going out from itself, it is still complete in itself. In later terminology, it is For-Itself-In-Itself.

In the sixteenth and seventeenth centuries, the new cosmology reduced God to the status of the First Efficient Cause. At creation he wound up the cosmic Machine and set it in motion, and it has run smoothly ever since, without his further interference. In the new cosmology, God is unnecessary as a continuing Presence in the universe. "I cannot forgive Descartes," wrote Pascal. "In all his philosophy he would have been quite willing to dispense with God. But he had to make Him give a fillip to set the world in motion; beyond this, he has no further need of God." [5] This means that the world itself is an Absolute, however, for its being is in no serious sense dependent on any being other than its own. But the being of the world is still of two kinds, extended, unthinking substance (body), and unextended, thinking substance (mind). We have not one but two Absolutes, coordinated by the pineal gland, the pre-established harmony, or — in some unenlightened quarters — by the intervention of God. But the way is now prepared for two of the dominant intellectual forces in modern thought: scientism, with its emphasis on the Absolute World, and Romanticism, with its emphasis on the Absolute Ego. As late as Kant these two Absolutes are still in gear with one another, for the categories of reason mesh with the events taking place in the phenomenal world.

Hegel's analysis of the Absolute Ego or Self, however, reveals that the Self is not in fact an Absolute. The structure and dynamics of its life threaten to tear it apart, and set it in conflict with the Other. In opposition to Parmenides, and in agreement (at least in principle) with Democritus, Hegel declares:

The Eleatics are celebrated as daring thinkers. But this nominal admiration is often accompanied by the remark that they went too far, when they made Being alone true, and denied the truth of every other object of consciousness. We must go further than mere Being, it is true: and yet it is absurd to speak of the other contents of our consciousness as somewhat as it were outside and beside Being, or to say that there are other things, as well as Being. The true state of the case is rather as follows. Being, as Being, is nothing fixed or ultimate: it yields to dialectic and sinks into its opposite, which, also taken immediately, is Nothing.[6]

The being of the self, like Being as a whole, "yields to dialectic and sinks into its opposite," into Nothing. The life of the self is a life of restlessness, contradiction, opposition. It can say of itself, "I am becoming," but it can never say, as Descartes said, "I am." In Descartes the self is in fact an Absolute, for even if God is a deceiver, "He can never cause me to be nothing while I think that I am."[7] And though for Descartes the fact that I doubt implies that I am imperfect and lack something, and this in turn implies the being of the Perfect who lacks nothing, the fact of the lack does not suggest (as it does for Hegel and Sartre) that I contain within myself my own Nothing.

The point is this: the fact of the absolute absence of the Absolute necessarily entails the method of thought called "dialectic." Thought must begin where it finds itself — in the hurly-burly of being and nonbeing, self and not-self. Thought cannot begin with absolutely clear and simple ideas and proceed up the ladder of inference to general truths, for there are no such ideas. The most fundamental idea of all, the "I am," if investigated adequately, reveals that it is negated by the fact of the lack, and the lack says "I am not."

Dialectic is the only mode of thought which can deal adequately with the life of the self, for that life is itself dialectical in nature. It is dialectical in the dynamics of its own interiority and in its "public" life with the other. Thus, Hegel recognizes that "Being" and "Nothing" are empty abstractions: the truth or actuality of these abstractions is "Becoming." Since Becoming is merely the synthesis of Being and Nothing, however, it too must finally vanish, only to reappear as Dasein (Being there). Dasein is, as we have seen, both *für sich* and *an sich* in mutual opposition. Taken by and considered in itself (in a public way), however, Dasein is *Ansichsein*, Being-in-itself; but when considered (in a public way) in connection with the (public) other, where that Otherness is Negation, Dasein is *Sein-für-An-deres* or Being-for-another.[8] Being-for-another can never "rest" in itself, however, anymore than the *für sich* can rest in itself; for Being-for-another is always subject to negation by its (public) Other, and this Other is its limit. This means that Being-for-another is continually changing, continually subject to the dialectic of negation and affirmation, for it is challenged by the Other to become For-that-Other. But since that Other itself is in continuous flux, it becomes another Other, and challenges the Being-for-another to become for *that* Other, and so on *ad infinitum*. This is what Hegel calls the wrong or bad (*schlechte*) or negative infinity, for it is merely the negation of a finite — i.e., the finite For-an-Other.[9] The right or good or real infinity consists in the One "being at home with itself in its other, or, if enunciated as a process, in coming to itself in its other."[10] This mode of being is called *Fürsichsein*, Being-for-itself.[11]

Sartre's thought is also dialectical, as it must be, given the absence of the Absolute. The category of "Becoming" is not important for Sartre, for the *pour-soi* and the *en-soi* are, as Sartre recognizes, quasi-absolutes, each of which sustains the other. As Nothingness the for-itself must continually be negating the in-itself which is its own Other.

The For-itself . . . is nothing but the pure nihilation of the In-itself; it is like a hole of being at the heart of Being. . . . The for-itself has no reality save that of being the nihilation of being. . . . Thus the for-itself is an absolute *Unselb-ständig*, what we have called a non-substantial absolute. Its reality is purely *interrogative*. If it can posit questions this is because it is itself always *in question*; its being is never *given* but *interrogated* since it is always separated from itself by the nothingness of otherness.[12]

This shows, however, that what Sartre calls the *pour-soi* is not at all what Hegel meant by Being-for-itself but rather what he meant by Being-for-Another; and the result is that the structure of consciousness is for Sartre similar to what Hegel called "negative infinity." Sartre has allowed the elements of Dasein to fall asunder; but as Hegel warned: "If we let somewhat [the *pour-soi*] and another [the *en-soi*], [which are] the elements of determinate Being [Dasein], fall asunder, the result is that some becomes other, and this other is itself a somewhat, which then as such changes likewise, and so on *ad infinitum*."[13] In Sartre's case, the *pour-soi* constitutes itself as Other, then negates this its own Other in surpassing itself toward what it is not yet. The surpassing is a finite temporal process limited by death; for the *pour-soi* in unremitting restlessness negates itself, then negates the negation, *ad mortem*, but not *ad infinitum*. The ideal is of course to achieve the Absolute, the in-itself-for-itself: "The fundamental value which presides over this project is exactly the in-itself-for-itself; that is, the ideal of a consciousness which would be the foundation of its own being-in-itself by the pure consciousness which it would have of itself. It is this ideal which can be called God. Thus the best way to conceive of the fundamental project of human reality is to say that man is the being whose project is to be God." [14]

Soren Kierkegaard is also a dialectical thinker. Here is a part of the celebrated opening of *The Sickness unto Death*: "Man is spirit. But what is spirit? Spirit is the self. But what is the self? The self is a relation which relates itself to its own self. . . . Man is a synthesis of the infinite and the finite, of the temporal and the eternal, of freedom and necessity, in short it is a synthesis. . . . So regarded, man is not yet a self." [15] Or again, from the *Concluding Unscientific Postscript*: "The negativity that pervades existence, or rather, the negativity of the existing subject, which should be essentially reflected in his thinking in an adequate form, has its ground in the subject's synthesis: that he is an existing infinite spirit. The infinite and eternal is the only certainty, but as being in the subject it is in existence; and the first expression for this, is its elusiveness, and this tremendous contradiction, that the eternal becomes, that it comes into being." [16]

Hegel, Sartre, and Kierkegaard are all dialectical thinkers, but they differ greatly in their interpretations of the dialectic and its moments. For Hegel the self is composed of the *für sich* and the *an sich*; and the history of the world is the history of the Spirit moving to an ever more complete and adequate knowledge of itself. "This last embodiment of spirit — spirit which at once gives its complete and true content the form of self, and thereby realizes its notion — this is *Absolute Knowledge*. It is spirit knowing itself in the shape of spirit, it is knowledge which comprehends through notions [*begreifende Wissen*]. Truth is here not merely *in itself* absolutely identical with certainty; it has also the shape, the character of certainty of self; or in its existence — i.e., for spirit knowing it — it is in the *form* of knowledge of itself." [17] Thus, for Hegel, the contradictions and oppositions which in the Unhappy Consciousness alienate the self from itself are in the course of history to be overcome, and the self will at long last find its place.

The nature, moments, and process of this [absolute] knowledge have then shown themselves to be such that this knowledge is pure self-existence [*Fürsichsein*] of self-consciousness.

It is ego [*Ich*], which is *this* ego and no other, and at the same time, immediately is mediated, or sublated [*aufgehobenes*], universal ego. It has a content, which it distinguishes from itself; for it is pure negativity, or self-diremption [*sich Entzweien*]; it is consciousness. . . . Ego is in it, *qua* distinguished, reflected into itself; only then is the content comprehended . . . when ego in its otherness [*Andersein*] is still at home with itself [*bei sich selbst ist*].[18]

For Sartre, however, the structure of the human consciousness is such that the *pour-soi* can never achieve its self-groundedness in its *en-soi*. It seeks to become the Absolute, God in his aseity, but the project is vain.

Each human reality is at the same time a direct project to metamorphose its own For-itself into an In-itself-For-itself and a project of the appropriation of the world as a totality of being-in-itself, in the form of a fundamental quality. Every human reality is a passion in that it projects losing itself so as to found being and by the same stroke to constitute the In-itself which escapes contingency by being its own foundation, the *Ens causa sui*, which religions call God. Thus the passion of man is the reverse of that of Christ, for man loses himself as man in order that God may be born. But the idea of God is contradictory and we lose ourselves in vain. Man is a useless passion.[19]

Kierkegaard also thinks of the self as dialectic of opposites, of positive and negative; but for him the positive is the finite and the negative is the eternal or the infinite. His "formula" for the self which has been cured of the "sickness unto death" (namely despair) is: "by relating itself to its own self and by willing to be itself the self is grounded transparently in the Power which posited it." [20] That "Power" is of course God, or the Infinite. Therefore Kierkegaard attacks Hegel — or the version of Hegel taught by Danish ecclesiastics and professors — on the ground that Hegel allows the positive to prevail, thereby shutting the door on the Infinite and Eternal. Kierkegaard wants to keep that door open, for he makes the cornerstone of his thought the concept Sartre has rejected — the concept of Becoming. He repudiates the "objective" and "abstract" mode of Hegelian thought, and insists on subjectivity and concreteness. "That the knowing spirit is an existing individual spirit, and that every human being is such an entity existing for himself, is a truth I cannot too often repeat." [21] Abstract answers are wholly irrelevant to the concretely existing individual, and objective reflection is appropriate only to objects, not to living subjects. "For an objective reflection the truth becomes an object, something objective, and thought must be pointed away from the subject. For a subjective reflection the truth becomes a matter of appropriation, of inwardness, of subjectivity, and thought must probe more and more deeply into the subject and his subjectivity." [22] Becoming, concreteness, subjectivity, passion — this is where thought must begin, and it is to this that thought must lead; for thought is incomplete until it becomes real, comes alive in the thinker's existence: "For the development of the subject consists precisely in his active interpenetration of himself by reflection concerning his own existence, so that he really thinks what he thinks through making a reality of it." [23] Paraphrasing another of Hegel's students, one might say that, whereas it is philosophy's task to understand the individual, it is Kierkegaard's task to change him. But how does one go about communicating the truth if the truth is precisely subjectivity and inwardness? How does one speak to another so that the other appropriates what is said and makes a reality of it by being and living it? The answer is, by indirect communication in the form of a possibility. "Existential reality is incommunicable, and the subjective thinker finds his reality in his own ethical existence. When reality is apprehended by an outsider it can be understood only as possibility. Everyone who makes a communication, in so far as he becomes conscious of this fact, will therefore be careful to give his existential communication the form of a possibility, precisely in order that it may have a relationship to existence. A communication in the form of a possibility compels the recipient to face the problem of existing in it, so far as this is possible between man and man." [24]

How then does it stand with human being? Is the authentic existence possible? Is there hope that the bifurcated and self-contradictory Self can ever come to rest in itself and achieve that peace for which it so passionately longs?

Hegel's reply is, Yes; eventually and inevitably the Spirit will come to itself in Absolute Knowledge, which is stillness in motion, being in becoming, peace in action; and man will have become like unto God.

Sartre's reply is, No, never; for what Being has put asunder no man can join. Man desires to become God, but the idea of God is self-contradictory, and man is a useless passion.

Kierkegaard's reply is, Yes, if the Self, which is a synthesis of the finite and the infinite, gives itself in faith to the process of becoming which leads to its being grounded in the infinite and eternal.

II

◄ ► And what of Samuel Beckett? Is not all this talk of *Fürsichsein* and *Ansichsein*, of *pour-soi* and *en-soi*, of finite and infinite — is it not all far above his head? He has said, "When Heidegger and Sartre speak of a contrast between being and existence, they may be right, I don't know, but their language is too philosophical for me. I am not a philosopher." [25] When we read his fiction or see his plays, we get no disquisitions on being and nothingness, no commentary on the moments of the dialectic. We get words, rather, and usually simple words at that: "rags of life in the light I hear and don't deny don't believe don't say any more who is speaking that's not said any more it must have ceased to be of interest but words like now before Pim no no that's not said only mine my words mine alone one or two soundless brief movements all the lower no sound when I can that's the difference great confusion" (HII, 21). Sometimes we get a few actions, usually as simple as the words—falling down, getting up, or not getting up and crawling, or not crawling but lying in a ditch or bed, telling stories, waiting. These words and actions, so simple as to be nearly atomic in their irreducibility to yet simpler elements, would not seem to demand or even allow the rather elaborate philosophical commentary that has been supplied in the preceding pages. Yet it has always been the great Simples—love, hate, matter, mind, truth, goodness, beauty, freedom, justice, being—which have occasioned protracted debate, and elaborate and sometimes gaudy terminology. It is a good deal easier for me to be than it is for me to say what it means to be. The philosopher who would talk about what it means to be a human being, and the critic who would talk about the meaning of a work of art, are both compelled to devise a language suitable to the task. For being does not express itself in language (*pace* Heidegger), and the words which a poem or novel or play *is* are not the words the critic needs to say what the work is and means. The words of the trilogy or *Endgame* are there to be heard (for reading is hearing at one remove), and as I listen I hear Malone or Hamm, not the *Fürsichsein* or the *pour-soi*. And yet when I think about Malone or Hamm, when I try to interpret who they are and what they mean, I must finally give them a "price" or "value" which is roughly the same as the "price" of Hegel's *für sich* or Heidegger's Dasein or of Sartre's *pour-soi* or of Kierkegaard's "actually existing individual." In the philosophical commentary I have bought and sold in drachmas, marks, francs, and kroner because I am convinced that these are convertible into the currency of Beckett's economy.

But besides saying that he is not a philosopher, he has said something else: "I take no sides. I am interested in the shape of ideas. There is a wonderful sentence in Augustine: 'Do not despair; one of the thieves was saved.

Do not presume; one of the thieves was damned.' That sentence has a wonderful shape. It is the shape that matters." [26]

By now it should be perfectly clear that the shape of Beckett's art is the shape of dialectic. He is in the tradition of Democritus the Abderite, the laughing philosopher, for whom the Nothing was just as real as the Something; of the Zetetics and Ephectics, who sought but could not find; of the Desert Fathers who lived the absurdity of being both flesh and spirit; of the Augustine of the *Confessions*, returning into himself to find himself, confessing what he knew and what he did not know of himself; of the Pascal caught between Nothing and the Infinite; of the Hegel who analyzed the "Unhappy Consciousness"; of Heidegger's Dasein, thrown into existence, lost in *das Man*, but called by conscience to the authentic existence; of the uncompromising Sartre, who maintains his integrity by being two in one; of Kierkegaard, who seeks by main force to counter despair with faith, for whom the negative is the way to the infinite.

So in the *Concluding Unscientific Postscript*, I read this:

> But the genuine subjective existing thinker is always as negative as he is positive, and *vice versa*. He continues to be such as long as he exists, not once for all in a chimerical mediation. His mode of communication is made to conform, lest through being too extraordinarily communicative he should succeed in transforming a learner's existence into something different from what a human existence in general has any right to be. He is conscious of the negativity of the infinite in existence, and he constantly keeps the wound of the negative open, which in the bodily realm is sometimes the condition for a cure. The others let the wound heal over and become positive; that is to say, they are deceived.[27]

And in the thirteenth of the *Texts for Nothing* I read this:

> Is it possible, is that the possible thing at last, the extinction of this black nothing and its impossible shades, the end of the farce of making and the silencing of silence, it wonders, that voice which is silence or it's me there's no telling it's all the same dream, the same silence, it and me, it and him, . . . but whose, whose dream, whose silence, old questions, last questions, ours who are dream and silence, but it's ended, we're ended who never were, soon there will be nothing where there was never anything, last images. And whose the shame, at every mute micromillisyllable, and unslakable infinity of remorse delving ever deeper in its bite, at having to hear, having to say, fainter than the faintest murmur, so many lies, so many times the same lie lyingly denied, whose the screaming silence of no's knife in yes's wound, it wonders. (STN, 139)

There is no need to make much of the similarity of the two images, as extraordinary and even bizarre as they may be. For the "subjective existing thinker" whose method is dialectical, the idea of the Positive as a human body and the Negative as a wound suggests itself with a certain degree of inevitability.

But Beckett knows who he is. He is not a philosopher; he is an artist, a poet. Kierkegaard the philosopher can say that the subjective existing thinker is as negative as he is positive, but Beckett must exhibit this fact. From the ninth of the *Texts for Nothing*:

What am I doing now, I'm trying to see where I am, so as to be able to go elsewhere, should occasion arise, or else simply to say, You have merely to wait till they come and fetch you, that's my impression at times. Then it goes and I see it's not that, but something else, difficult to grasp, and which I don't grasp, or which I do grasp, it depends, and it comes to the same, for it's not that either, but something else, some other thing, or the first back again, or still the same, always the same thing proposing itself to my perplexity, then disappearing, then proposing itself again, to my perplexity still unsated, or momentarily dead, of starvation. (stn, 120–21)

Or from the eleventh:

No, something better must be found, a better reason, for this to stop, another word, a better idea, to put in the negative, a new no, to cancel all the others, all the old noes that buried me down here, deep in this place which is not one, which is merely a moment for the time being eternal, which is called here, and in this being which is called me and is not one, and in this impossible voice, all the old noes dangling in the dark and swaying like a ladder of smoke, yes, a new no, that none says twice, whose drop will fall and let me down, shadow and babble, to an absence less vain than inexistence. (stn, 130–31)

Each of his major works is, like Kierkegaard's "subjective existing thinker," a synthesis of the positive and the negative, the comic and the "pathetic," the yes and the no. Thus, in *Waiting for Godot*, the theory of history as absolute decline, represented by the disintegration of Pozzo and Lucky, is counterbalanced by the appearance of the leaves on the tree (a symbol of rebirth and growth) and by the boy's promise that Godot will come "tomorrow." The decline of Pozzo and Lucky suggests that history is closed, whereas the other images suggest that it is open. Each of these two theories is a thesis to which the other is the antithesis; but both are *aufgehoben* by the cyclical form of the drama, which suggests a cyclical view of history. Optimism and pessimism, hope and despair, comedy and tragedy are counterbalanced by one another: none of them is allowed to become an Absolute.

Similarly in the moral or interpersonal realm: none of the characters is absolutely virtuous or absolutely vicious. Lucky maintains a pathetic dignity, but he returns Gogo's favor of wiping away his tears by kicking Gogo "violently" in the shins. Didi and Gogo are alternately kind and cruel to each other. In the first act Pozzo "drives" Lucky by means of the rope, but in the second act the blind Pozzo is led by the dumb Lucky. Pozzo is of course a Master, but he is subject to the irony of the dialectic which obtains between Master and Slave: his Mastery is dependent on there being a Slave for him to be master of, and he can neither sit down (in the first Act) nor stand up (in the second) without the assistance of the slave-types Didi and Gogo.

The pair Didi-Gogo stands in opposition to the pair Pozzo-Lucky. Even though Didi is brighter and more forceful than Gogo, he does not use his advantage to exploit or enslave his companion. Their relation is much more that of mutual concern and compassion, though from time to time Gogo must defend his autonomy and independence:

> ESTRAGON. All the dead voices.
> VLADIMIR. They make a noise like wings.
> ESTRAGON. Like leaves.
> VLADIMIR. Like sand.
> ESTRAGON. Like leaves.
>
> (WFG, 40a)

Even when they become angry with each other they do so as equals, and by and large their relationship is an Affirmation which stands in opposition to the Negation which is the relationship of Pozzo and Lucky. Similarly in the case of *Endgame*: the love which relates Nagg and Nell is a positive factor which is negated by the fact that it is sentimental and senile; but even so qualified it is the antithesis of the Master-Slave relation which obtains between Hamm and Clov.

In the plays, then, virtue and vice, hope and despair, being and nonbeing, and for that matter any other pair of "large contrary human factors," are paired off against each other and balance each other out. In Beckett's world as in Newton's, for every action there is an equal and opposite reaction. Eventually the paired factors weigh equally in the scales, balance is struck, and the dialectical motion of action and reaction comes to an end: "*Krapp motionless staring before him*" (KLT, 28); Winnie and Willie look at each other, then "*Long pause. Curtain*" (HD, 64); Hamm covers his face with his handkerchief, lowers his arms to the armrests, "*remains motionless. . . .*

Curtain" (E, 84). In these works, nonbeing is not denied. It becomes, rather, one of the polar elements in a dialectic of being and nonbeing whose issue is left in doubt. Thus is achieved one of the forms which is capable of accommodating the "mess."

The exigencies of the medium being what they are, the drama almost requires the moments of the dialectic to be embodied in different characters (though in *Krapp's Last Tape* Beckett gets over even this by contrasting Krapp-now with Krapp-then by means of a tape recorder). The achieved stasis can then be represented physically and even spatially. In the monological fiction, however, this is impossible, and the dialectic takes on the form and life of either the asymptotic curve or the classically Hegelian movement of Thesis-Antithesis-Synthesis. Which of the two images more adequately represents the dialectic depends on the terms that are explicated. Thus, Vivian Mercier is certainly correct in describing the trilogy in terms of the asymptote, for as the length of the novel approaches infinity, its content (or perhaps "meaning") approaches zero.[28] This image is homomorphic with the pursuit of the square root of 2, of the numerical equivalent of pi, or of any other irrational number, and with Zeno's paradox called "Achilles and the Tortoise." This last holds that Achilles can never overtake the tortoise because by the time he reaches the point from which the tortoise began, the tortoise will have moved on to another point; and by the time he gets to that point, the tortoise will have moved still farther; and so on. Thus, Achilles can gain on the tortoise, as the curve gains on the base line, but in both cases coincidence is impossible.[29]

The image of the asymptotic curve emphasizes the transcendence of the twin goals of the monological fiction — the peace and silence which come when, in the rhetorical mode, the Speaker has spoken adequately of the being which he is, or, in the existential mode, the reflecting or for-itself becomes one with the reflected or in-itself. These are goals which are unattainable in this world, as the image itself indicates; and the image therefore also emphasizes the irrationality or absurdity of the Speaker's condition. The image does not seem to be truly dialectical, however, unless we realize that the being of the Speaker is his speaking, and his speaking is governed by the strategy enunciated by the Unnamable: "First dirty, then make clean" (TN, 413). First litter the page (and the reader's consciousness) with things (Malone's hat), facts ("I know my eyes are open, because of the tears that pour from them unceasingly"), persons (Mahood, Worm), stories, and all the rest that "literature" is made of; then eliminate them all,

one by one, until the whole is purged of everything but the essential moments of the dialectic itself — Affirmation and Negation: "I can't go on,
I'll go on."

The other major dialectical pattern in the trilogy is the Hegelian pattern
of Thesis-Antithesis-Synthesis. Whereas the asymptote implies a linear and
infinite progression toward an unattainable goal, and emphasizes the relation of form and content, speech and subject matter, the second pattern implies not only the same progression, but can also imply a satisfactory conclusion (on analogy with the completion of the dialectic in the moment of
Hegel's Absolute Knowledge) and a cyclical movement of the dialectic —
for the last Synthesis can be identical with the first Thesis. Moreover, this
second pattern emphasizes the four units of the trilogy (counting *Molloy*
as two units) as well as the characters in the units and in general the
Author-Character relation.

By this I mean that, though the trilogy can be read as a succession of
Characters and Authors, or as the history of a phenomenological Ego being
split off from itself, or as a Sartrean reflection in which the reflective is reflecting upon the reflected, it can also be read as the moments in the dialectic of a single "transcendental" self. Thus, Molloy is the thesis which is negated by its antithesis Moran, which in turn issues in the higher synthesis
of Malone. For in Malone the thesis, which is Molloy-as-Character, and its
antithesis, which is Moran-as-Author, are unified in Malone, who is himself both moments of the dialectic in one, for he is Character to his own
"Authorial" being, and Author to his own "Characterial" being. Finally,
Malone himself is negated by the Unnamable, who comprehends in himself
all the preceding moments of the dialectic.

That is to say, Molloy is the Slave (Character) who is negated by Moran
as Master (Author; *Molloy* is merely *un Roman*). They are synthesized in
Malone (Author-as-Character and Character-as-Author), who in the story
of Sapo expresses the Stoical notion of freedom and in the story of Macmann expresses the Sceptical actuality of that freedom — a freedom which
ends disastrously as "an absolutely fortuitous embroglio, the giddy whirl
of a perpetually self-creating disorder." [30] This is just how *Malone Dies*
ends:

> absurd lights, the stars, the beacons, the buoys, the lights of earth and in the
> hills the faint fires of the blazing gorse. . . .
> Lemuel is in charge, he raises his hatchet on which the blood will never dry,

but not to hit anyone, he will not hit anyone, he will not hit anyone anymore, he
will not touch anyone anymore, either with it or with it or with it or with or

. . . .

any more   (TN, 397–98)

Finally, in the Unnamable, all the preceding theses and antitheses are unified in the single but doubled self-consciousness of the Unhappy Consciousness.

But Hegel did not intend the *Phenomenology* to be the description of
some numinous, nonreal "Spirit." He intended it as an accurate account of
the development of freedom and self-consciousness through its several concrete stages in the history of Western man.

If we take that same perspective on the trilogy, behold! What vistas of
interpretation are opened to us! For Molloy is now revealed not only as a
fictional character and as standing in dialectical opposition to Moran in the
primordial state of self-consciousness, but as the Spirit in its manifestation
as the Greek world, seeking its telluric Mother, plunged in myths of dying
and rising, educated by the Homeric epics, detained in its quest of the Absolute by the "miserable molys" of sensuality, in murderous conflict with itself (or with the antithesis of itself, which is still its own self, Athens against
Sparta), collapsing finally in the ditch of its own historical self-consciousness: "It was in this ditch that I became aware of what had happened to me.
I suppose it was the fall into the ditch that opened my eyes" (TN, 120).[31]

Succeeding Molloy in time, yet searching for him in order to deliver and
preserve him — here comes Moran, Roman spirit incarnate. He is Roman
in his Mediterranean Catholicism, Roman in his obedience to his unseen
Emperor-Pope Youdi, Roman in his bureaucratic attention to detailed plan-
ning, in his respect for moderation, discipline, procedure, order. Not really
knowing what he seeks, he fails to recognize it when he discovers it, and
in the event destroys it. More and more he resembles Molloy, for one culture, in the final stage of decline and disintegration, looks pretty much like
all other cultures in that stage.

In Hegel's history, the Roman world is succeeded by the German, but in
Beckett's it is succeeded by the French. Malone is the incarnation of the
Cartesian Spirit, whether that Spirit takes up its abode in Descartes himself
or in his immediate followers or in Kant or Coleridge or Husserl. It can
also be called the Spirit of Rationalism or Subjective Idealism or Romanticism, for it begins with the "I" and generates a world out of the operations

of the Ego. So Malone, the author, externalizes himself in the Stoical Sapo and the Sceptical Macmann; and when Malone dies, the world of Macmann dies too. Malone has two "spasms," premonitions of his demise. Historically speaking, these may be the two world wars, the second of which started on the Iberian Peninsula, as Malone seems to remind us (TN, 338).

Finally, the oppositions which in the first part of the trilogy were externally embodied in Molloy and Moran, and which, in the second, were represented by Malone and his characters, are now in the third completely internalized. The Unnamable begins by talking about himself, as if he were Molloy or Moran. He soon finds that this is impossible, so he adopts Malone's technique: he tells stories about himself-named-Mahood and then about himself-named-Worm. But this indirect way of getting at himself also fails, and he settles for talking in the only way he can, in the only voice he has. This is the Unhappy Consciousness in its modern — perhaps Sartrean — form. . . .

The notion that the trilogy represents the progress of the Hegelian World Spirit through history pushes "interpretation" to its limits and beyond; and I mention it simply because it is the logically necessary conclusion to one of the lines of argument I have been pursuing. It depends for its validity more on the argument than on a careful examination of the text of the trilogy, however, and will probably prove to be another instance of the extremes to which Beckett's critics are driven by his multi-faceted art. I shall let it stand, however, if only as an example of what happens to criticism once it has fashioned a *Scala Paradisi* out of this or that piece of esoteric knowledge.

Let us then descend from the troposphere of critical speculation to the more aspirable regions of common sense and empirical evidence, to reiterate the less daring but more practical and demonstrable thesis that the shape of Beckett's mature art is the shape given it by the dialectic of action and reaction, yes and no, affirmation and qualification, and even being and non-being. There is no single pattern, of course, since the achieved form of any particular work depends on the elements which are brought into opposition. Similarly, Hegel, Sartre, and Kierkegaard, all of them dialectical thinkers, still reach different conclusions, since they elect different terms to bring into play, define identical or similar terms in different ways, and set different values on the same or similar entities. So the "shape" of *Waiting for Godot* is not identical with the "shape" of *Endgame* or of one of the fictional pieces. But the method is the same in each case. "Method" is not perhaps the right word. Neither is a word like "principle," for this suggests a commitment to some philosophical system. What is common among all the major works could rather be called a "rule of practice" which Beckett kept before him as he worked. That rule may be expressed thus: "Let every ingredient of a work cancel every other."

III

◄ ► In Dante the cosmos is the creation of God, and since man was made in God's image the cosmos is congruent with the abilities and responsibilities of man. The cosmos was created in accordance with Divine Reason, and is therefore intelligible to human reason. It was created and continues to be moved by Divine Love, so it is hospitable to human love (appropriately directed, of course, and in proper proportion). It is governed by Divine Justice, and man in his freedom may choose whether to obey or disobey the moral law; but he will be held accountable for his choice, and will be either punished or rewarded.

In our excursion into the history of thought we have seen these same terms — Reason, Love, Justice, Freedom — as well as others, treated in various ways. Since Descartes, however, they have tended to be organized under two rubrics, the Self and the World. As the theological basis of these terms has become eroded, each of them has tended to become itself an Absolute, and later becomes fragmented and relativized. From Descartes to Husserl the Self or Ego is thought of as an Absolute, for it is the basis of certitude, the unit of being, the ground of experience, the matrix of knowledge. The world or reality is that of which I can have clear and distinct ideas, or what I perceive, or have experience of, or what I feel, or what I will. Like an inverted triangle, all of Being rests on the point which is I. The I is capable of bearing the weight, moreover, for it is stable, perduring, and one with itself. So construed, the I is the ground of being and the beginning of thought. For both Hegel and Kierkegaard, however, the absolute I is the End: for Hegel, the End of the self-actualization of the Spirit, for Kierkegaard the End of the becoming of the concretely existing individual.

We have seen, however, the fate of the Absolute Ego. Hegel split it apart, expecting, of course, that it would be reunited. Kierkegaard countered its positivity with an equal amount of negativity, hoping thereby to drive the "I" into its unity with infinity. William James looked into the Ego and saw there not the solid rock of a substantial "I" but a fluid stream of consciousness. When Bergson looked he saw a succession of states of consciousness, like a series of candles, each dying out but lighting up the next. When Sartre looked, he saw Nothing.

From the very beginning the Absolute Ego has been absent from Beckett's work. Descartes, whose Cogito is the model of such an Ego, is represented in *Whoroscope* as a frightened, superstitious old man at the mercy of his enemies. The ego named Murphy is irremediably ambivalent, and the one named Neary is a Proustian succession of desires. Watt is helpless before the evanescent Knott, and each of the major figures in the trilogy is cancelled by and preserved in his successor. The personages in the dramas are dependent on one another, or are totally different from what they once were; and the voice of *How It Is* has no existence apart from its words and the Other whom it interrogates and by whom it is interrogated. Even in the "Three Dialogues," the phrase "warren of modes and attitudes," applied to the artist, suggests the plurality of selves in the Self; and "the ultimate penury" consists not in being "short" of the world and of self but of being quite without them (Dialogue III). The nearest thing to an Absolute Ego we come across in all of Beckett is the narrator of *More Pricks Than Kicks* and *Murphy*: but he is a mistake attributable to Beckett's not having thought the problem through, and neither he nor his likes appears again. There is instead only the relative, contingent, qualified Ego which is either split and in contradiction with itself (as seen mainly in the fiction), or dependent on another and not what it was (as seen mainly in the drama).

The second absent Absolute is the World — not as it is, of course, but as God made it or should have made it, and as Leibniz thought He did make it. One of the chief characteristics of such a World is justice. As it is written in Psalm 145, "The Lord preserveth all them that love him; but all the wicked will he destroy." In his providential governance of the world, God punishes the wicked and rewards the just: this is the view of the world maintained by traditional absolutist piety. It is not maintained by Beckett. Another passage from the same Psalm gave him the title of one of his radio plays. The verse reads, "The Lord upholdeth all that fall, and raiseth up all those that be bowed down." This is the text of the sermon to be preached to Mr. and Mrs. Rooney, and when she informs him of it they join together "in wild laughter" (KLT, 88). Mr. Rooney's train has been delayed because a child was killed on the way. In my reading of *All That Fall*, the child either fell from the train when Mr. Rooney tried to take its ball away, or

Mr. Rooney simply pushed it under the wheels. Mr. Rooney will not be punished for his deed any more than Watt was punished for his disobedience. In Beckett's world as in Joyce's, there is "neither prize nor penalty." As absolutes, justice and the moral order, Virtue and Vice, are absolutely absent.

A second characteristic of the absolute or ideal world is its intelligibility. An intelligible world is one whose parts are held together by some principle discernible by human reason. Time is the ground of this principle, as it is the ground of the moral order; for viewed under the aspect of Providence, time is the guarantor of justice, but when viewed under the aspect of the created order, it is the basis of causality. Taking any event E, we may find its causes in time past in D, and its effects in time future in F. Molloy knows this, for he tells us that at a certain time he set off in the direction of the sun, yet not that but toward "the least gloomy quarter of the heavens which a vast cloud was shrouding from the zenith to the skylines. It was from this cloud the above [mentioned] rain was falling. See how things hang together" (TN, 80). But it is one thing to reason from rain as effect to cloud as cause, and another to understand the world. When Watt tried it, he was disappointed.

The third characteristic of the absolute World is that it is charitable, by which I mean both that it is kind, and that it is capable of nurturing and supporting love. The very idea is enough to make one laugh, or cry.

Very well then, the Absolutes of justice, intelligibility, and charity are absent from the world. If they are not here and now, however, might they not be there and then? If so, there is yet hope, and existence can be meaningful as a striving after and an overcoming and a going on. This was enough for the magnanimous Zarathustra, but is it enough for the pusillanimous Gogo? He and Didi await Godot with the same sense of urgency that Watt sought Knott, for both these mysterious figures represent an absolute Ground capable of supporting the fractured and exhausted existence of the human Being. So important is this Other to Watt and the two tramps that without him nothing in the world is valuable or meaningful. Without him, thinking leads merely to madness, living to the grave. In him and for him they live and move and have whatever little Being they have, for he is the Absolute Essence of the contingent Ego's existence, the Ground and Authentication of its decisionful life, the purpose and very Basis of its thought. In communion with Mr. Knott is to be found that peace which is not of this relative world, for he is harbor and haven. In the concreteness of Mr. Godot's offer Didi and Gogo will have that Absolute lacking which they find it impossible to act. But just as the world and self are Absolutes which, as Beckett pointed out in the Dialogues, are absent or unavailable to the artist, so this Other is simply not there to help Didi and Gogo decide what to do with their lives; and though he is there as Watt's temple and teacher, he is not available as an object of thought. What Watt had finally to realize is that the world is not intelligible or just or charitable. What Didi and Gogo should have realized, but did not, is that, given the absolute absence of the Absolute, man is radically free.

And it is not just the *pour-soi* in general that is condemned to freedom from the Absolute but the artist and writer as such. There is no Absolute Ego, for in reality the Ego must be thought of as an indefinite succession of Egos (Bergson), or as self-contradictory (Hegel), or as a process of becoming (Kierkegaard), or as Nothingness (Sartre). The traditional kind of character who is essentially one with himself and endures basically unchanged through time is therefore a useless anachronism. Moreover, the absence of an Absolute Ego also undermines an expressionistic theory of art, as we have seen, for the artist's self is not identical with itself through as little time as it takes to write a sentence or complete a brush stroke. So which of the selves is the artist expressing in his work?

As the absence of the Absolute Ego disables expressionism, the absence of an Absolute World disables the mimetic theory of art. Recall that one of the characteristics of the Absolute World is its intelligibility and this, in turn, is a function of its causal structure, for we say that we understand a certain sequence of events only if we see how event E arises out of event D, and issues in event F. The playwright or novelist living and working under an absolutist dispensation (not political of course but intellectual) will think it necessary to supply all the relevant factors or conditions which are causally efficacious, though he may suppress some of these until the end, thereby creating suspense and enabling a happy resolution of the forces involved. By beginning at a certain point in time and by ending at another, he may isolate a temporal unit which is for all practical purposes causally self-contained and therefore self-explanatory. Such a unit is, as Aristotle said, a "whole," and as a causally self-contained whole it is an absolute, for its causal sequence is not contingent upon anything extrinsic to it. The categories of time and causality in the modality of art are then imitations of those categories in the modalities of nature or history, and the very possibility of a work of art being a whole is contingent upon an absolutist ontology which sees nature or history as a series of events which are integrated more or less closely by causality. But if the world is as essentially unintelligible as Murphy and Watt found it to be, if there is no "system of synchronisation," as Beckett put it in his essay on Proust, and if there is no absolute beginning or absolute ending, then the work of art must dispense with those devices. So if one must begin at the ending, as *Endgame* does, then that is well; and if one must end at the beginning, as the trilogy seems to do, then that is well too. And if the reason why the sea is calm is that there are no more navigators, and if that is not a "good reason" or cause for the sea being calm, then that is well too, for the intelligibility of the world is not guaranteed.

An art that imitates a formless and unintelligible world will then itself be formless and unintelligible—hence the quest for the art form that is capable of accommodating the formless. The only form that can do so is one in which the form itself is at issue. The being of the form must be negated by the nothing of the formless. Therefore the only conceivable franchise for the whole artistic venture is the one granted by dialectic, for with its help the artist does not need and cannot even use the Absolutes which govern conventional art. By seizing precisely on the principle of the Nothing which, in the "Three Dialogues," threatened to bring art to a halt, and by using it to ground his own later efforts, Beckett found a form that could accommodate the formless. Nathan Scott is right when he says that in Beckett's world "there is Nothing either in or beyond existence that sanctions or gives any kind of warrant or dignity to the human enterprise." [32] Moreover, there is Nothing that sanctions the artistic enterprise. Therefore the artist —and man—must begin where he is, as he is, in the nothingness of his freedom, and *cause to be* whatever there is to be in the way of art and the human being. There is no doubt that whatever is thereby caused to be will be negated by the Nothing which it is not. Before he sets out on his venture, man as artist and man as man knows that he is doomed to fail. But even this is not an absolute failure, for there is still left that little something which he was and which he made, and that is something, as Watt might say, is it not?

Or is it not? By means of the dialectic, Beckett achieves in his art what he observed to be true in Joyce's art and in his own confused world—the absolute absence of any Absolute at all. Nothing is left standing which could be thought to be independent, autonomous, or immune to negation. Author cancels character, circle cancels line, ending cancels beginning, question cancels answer, no cancels yes, tragedy cancels comedy, pessimism cancels optimism, pain cancels courage, suffering cancels wit, isolation cancels love, fatigue cancels action, despair cancels hope, the dark cancels the light.

Because the dialectic undercuts every conceivable Ground and commitment, Beckett's art is sprung free from the imperatives of realism or expressionism or any other theory which bases art on an Absolute other than itself. Indeed, the doctrine of the absolute absence of the Absolute operates in Beckett's work analogously with the way the phenomenological reduction operates in Husserl's. As Husserl "bracketed" the world and the natural standpoint, Beckett "brackets" the World and its Absolutes. By means of the eidetic reduction, Husserl established the autonomy of consciousness; by means of what we may call the "aesthetic reduction," Beckett establishes the autonomy of art. Liberated from theories of the relation of an extrinsic and absolute reality to itself, art no longer must conform to a supposed "essential nature" but is radically free to define itself in the very process of being itself. Absolutes which obtained in the Dantean cosmos — The Beginning and The Ending, the irreversibility of time, causality, purpose, justice, wholeness — no longer govern the work of art. Thus, as Husserl sought by means of the phenomenological reduction to gain access to pure consciousness, Beckett seeks by way of the aesthetic reduction to gain access to the realm of pure art. Already in the dialogues with Duthuit he proffered a notion as to what such art might be when he identified its parts as "the aliment" and "its manner of dispatch."

Beckett being a writer and not a painter or composer, "aliment" must mean language, words. Words, however, have a habit of meaning or saying something, and it is here that the dialectic as the "manner of dispatch" enters in. For it is the function of the dialectic to prevent the words from "meaning" an absolute self or from representing or imitating an absolute world. In the extreme case the dialectic prevents the words from "meaning" anything at all. As the Narrator of "The Calmative" says, "All I say cancels out, I'll have said nothing" (STN, 28).

"Meaning" is the final idol which the poet and the critic in their human weakness are tempted to fall down and worship. It is the last literary absolute, the one the worker in words finds it most difficult to dispense with. Yet from this extreme point of view, meaning too must be eliminated. So to ask what any of Beckett's works is "about" is to miss the point entirely, for the question supposes that there is something "out there" to which the work is subordinate or to which it refers or which it intends or "means."

But Beckett has bracketed the "out there," and has used words in such a way as to eliminate whatever meaning they may have. *Waiting for Godot* is not a play about the human condition: it is a "play," a composition in words, and tomorrow it will be played again, and then again, as long as there are players to play and audiences to attend their playing. The trilogy is not "about" a succession of authors and characters or reflective egos or anything else. It is a sequence of words which cancel out the pseudo-persons and pseudo-histories which they seem to report, and which even cancel out the statements they seem to make when, in fatigue and disgust, they have ceased trying to represent persons and things. The whole body of Beckett's work is, then, very like the various incidents in *Godot* which simply "pass the time." It is what a writer does in the middle of the twentieth century, in the time of the absence of absolutes, when he feels the obligation to write but finds that there is nothing to write, nothing with which to write, nothing from which to write, no power to write, no desire to write. The sum of even an infinite number of nothings is still Nothing, however, and that is what his art comes to.

Hence, it is the ultimate literary spoof, a practical joke played by this clowning man of letters on his readers and critics. All the learned commentaries, including this one, are seen to stand on Nothing, and with that realization are evaporated into the primal chaos out of which Beckett's own work emerges and into which it finally sinks. It is an art which, like Hegel's Unhappy Consciousness, contradicts itself and finally negates itself: and not only itself but all other art which purports to offer us Reality. In effect, art has nothing to do with reality. The art of literature is nothing more than an amusement, a playing with words and language. Telling stories is one way, and not perhaps the least amusing, to pass the time until one has no more time to pass. So is reading. So is writing commentaries on the stories that are told.

The point of view being expressed here could be called aesthetic scepticism, and though it is an extreme point of view it is one of the viable interpretations of Beckett's art. Its emphasis on the nihilating power of the dialectic leads logically to the conclusion that it all comes to nothing, or amounts to nothing more than a grand hoax. Yet such an interpretation is also very abstract and precious. It is the result of setting the critical dialectic into operation and letting it run untended, and once that process gets going it is difficult to stop. It grinds out negations and oppositions which are provocative and sometimes brilliantly witty paradoxes, but it too easily becomes fascinated with its own reflexive ingenuity, and in its narcissism loses sight of the human reality it was originally meant to disclose — as Sartre so tiresomely demonstrates in *Being and Nothingness.*

The sceptical interpretation of Beckett's art as a self-contained aesthetic exercise can be maintained, however, because it is simply there as one of the facets of his work, but it cannot be maintained as the final word on the matter. To do so would be to truncate the dialectic and elevate art to the status of an Absolute; and there is no reason to suppose that art should escape the destiny of all the other gods. And for all its dialectical brilliance, its logical elegance, its symmetrical proportions, and its painful self-consciousness, Beckett's art is profoundly and essentially human. In the very process of achieving aesthetic aseity it keeps before us the question, What does it mean to be a human being? It is ruthless in its insistence on the human facts of loneliness, emptiness, corruption, and death. His art thrusts me into the mud of existence, and against my scrubbed and tender ear it sets a foul mouth which whispers, screams, sighs, and babbles the stories of its life, and I listen to the words the voice says, and as I listen the words enter into my head, his speech fills my consciousness, his words become my words, I am no longer the hearer only but the teller, I am the one who whispers, screams, sighs, and babbles, his stories are my stories, his life my life, I am no longer I, I am he, and he is I, I no longer in here and he out there but he in here and I out there, and he and I here too and he and I there too, two persons in one word.

Existential reality is incommunicable, said Kierkegaard, so if the "subjective thinker" wants to say something to someone else about such a reality he must do so in the form of a possibility. "A communication in the form of a possibility compels the recipient to face the problem of existing in it, so far as this is possible between man and man." [33] Beckett's art is just such a compulsion, so far as this is possible for art. It requires me to face the problem of living in a world devoid of gods and devoid of the certitude and intelligibility and meaning and solace which those gods once bestowed on man and his world. It demands that I suspend for a time my habitual ways of living and thinking, for habit, as Didi observes, is a great deadener. It demands that I see with his eyes and hear with his ears. He said to Tom Driver, "The confusion is not my invention. . . . It is all around us and our only chance now is to let it in. The only chance of renovation is to open our eyes and see the mess." [34]

It does not seem to be much of a chance. In his world, as in our own, the odds seem to be on the side of the darkness which cancels the light, the loneliness which cancels love, the despair which cancels hope, the suffering which cancels joy. In his world, as in our own, all the old absolutes are absent, saving one, the absolute Master, Death.

But the dark does not quite extinguish the light, despair does not totally eliminate hope, for if they did there would be no mess. He said, "If life and death did not both present themselves to us, there would be no inscrutability. If there were only darkness, all would be clear. It is because there is not only darkness but also light that our situation becomes inexplicable." [35] In his dark world we can still see a faint glow, a distant point of light, an ember of love, a dim hope. But whether it is the last coal or the first, a receding or proceeding, a waning or a waxing, we cannot tell, because they all look alike, in the beginning, in the ending. "Where we have both dark and light," he said, "we have also the inexplicable. The keyword in my plays is 'perhaps.'"

One's sense of balance, then, is everything, and Beckett's is incredibly fine. Master dialectician and ontological funambulist, he knows just how far he can lean toward the dark of Nothing before he must right himself toward the light of Something. He knows to a hair's breadth when he is a little too far to the left, to the right, too far forward, too far back. He concludes each of his works only when he has achieved the still point, exact equilibrium: *"They do not move."*

It is the only place the dialectic can come to a rest, yet it leaves us uneasy. We want him to commit himself. Is it Yes or No? YES OR NO?

We seem to hear Beckett's voice, someone's voice speaking through Beckett, and what it says is, "Perhaps."

NOTES AND BIBLIOGRAPHY

NOTES

Preface

1. Georg Wilhelm Friedrich Hegel, *Phänomenologie des Geistes*, ed. Hermann Glockner ("Jubiläumsausgabe," 3rd ed.; Stuttgart: Fr. Frommanns Verlag, 1951), p. 541. The translation is by J. B. Baillie, *The Phenomenology of Mind* (rev. 2nd ed.; London: George Allen and Unwin, 1966), p. 716.

2. Hugh Kenner, *Samuel Beckett: A Critical Study* (New York: Grove Press, 1961); Ruby Cohn, *Samuel Beckett: The Comic Gamut* (New Brunswick, N.J.: Rutgers University Press, 1962); John Fletcher, *The Novels of Samuel Beckett* (New York: Barnes and Noble, 1964); and *Samuel Beckett's Art* (New York: Barnes and Noble, 1967); Raymond Federman, *Journey to Chaos: Samuel Beckett's Early Fiction* (Berkeley and Los Angeles: University of California Press, 1965); Josephine Jacobsen and William R. Mueller, *The Testament of Samuel Beckett* (New York: Hill and Wang, 1964).

3. Lawrence E. Harvey, *Samuel Beckett: Poet and Critic* (Princeton, N.J.: Princeton University Press, 1970); Edith Kern, *Existential Thought and Fictional Technique: Kierkegaard, Sartre, Beckett* (New Haven, Conn.: Yale University Press, 1970).

I. Problem, Theme and Style: The Beginnings

1. The first quotation from Augustine ("Our hearts are restless until they find their rest in thee") is from the *Confessions*, I, 1. The quotation from Pascal is from the *Pensées*, VII, 434, 437; the English text is from *Pascal's Pensées*, trans. W. F. Trotter, with an introduction by T. S. Eliot (New York: E. P. Dutton, 1958), pp. 121, 123. The quotation from Diogenes Laertius is from *Lives of Eminent Philosophers*, IX, 109; trans. R. D. Hicks (2 vols.; New York: William Heinemann [Loeb Classical Library], 1925), II, 519. The quotation from St. John Climacus is from *The Ladder of Divine Ascent*, trans. Lazarus Moore, with an introduction by M. Heppel (New York: Harper & Brothers, n.d.), Step 29, §14, p. 261. The second quotation from Augustine ("We ascend the stairway in the heart . . . and are raised up on high to the peace of Jerusalem") is from the *Confessions*, XIII, 9. The quotation from Arthur Schopenhauer is from the *Essays from the Parerga and Paralipomena*, trans. T. Bailey Saunders (London: George Allen and Unwin, 1951), *The Art of Literature*, "On Genius," p. 95.

2. The "Three Dialogues" originally appeared in *Transition*, V (1949), 97–103. The text is more accessible in Calder's edition, where it is published together with Beckett's essay *Proust* (London: John Calder, 1965). In Calder's edition the quotation is found on p. 103. See front matter for a list of abbreviations of Beckett's works used in this text.

3. Tom F. Driver, "Beckett by the Madeleine," *Columbia University Forum*, IV (Summer 1961), 22–23. Driver explains that he reconstructed Beckett's remarks from notes he made immediately following the conversation.

4. Driver, p. 23.

5. Kathleen Freeman, *Ancilla to the Pre-Socratic Philosophers: A Complete Translation of the Fragments in Diels, "Fragmente der Vorsokratiker"* (Cambridge, Mass.: Harvard University Press, 1957), sec. 28, "Parmenides of Elea," frag. 2, p. 42.

6. *Ibid.*, frag. 3.

7. *Ibid.*, frag. 3, n.

8. *Ibid.*, frag. 6, p. 43.

9. Freeman, Sec. 68, "Democritus of Abdêra," frag. 156, p. 106.

10. *Ibid.*, frag. 117, p. 104.

11. Climacus, Step 1, §4, p. 50; §8, p. 51; §10, p. 52.

12. *Ibid.*, Step 30, §36, p. 265.

13. I have used the translation appearing in *Basic Writings of Saint Augustine*, ed. Whitney J. Oates (2 vols.; New York: Random House, 1948), II, 168. Beckett knew the derivation of Descartes' argument, as he indicates in line 73 of *Whoroscope*.

14. "Rule V." I have used the translation appearing in *The Philosophical Works of Descartes*, trans. Elizabeth S. Haldane and G. R. T. Ross (2 vols.; n.p. [New York]: Dover Publications, 1955), I, 14.

15. Jacqueline Hoefer, *"Watt," Perspective*, XI (Autumn 1959), 180–81; Fletcher, *The Novels of Samuel Beckett*, pp. 86–87.

16. Georges Poulet, *The Metamorphoses of the Circle*, trans. Carley Dawson and Elliott Coleman in collaboration with the Author (Baltimore: Johns Hopkins Press, 1966), p. xi.

17. Martin Heidegger, *Being and Time*, trans. John Macquarrie and Edward Robinson (London: scm Press, 1962), p. 19.

18. One of the howlers in this study may well be the omission of Fritz Mauthner (1849–1923), Austrian poet, critic, and philosopher. Richard Ellmann reports (*James Joyce* [New York: Oxford University Press, 1959], pp. 661–62) that Beckett would read to Joyce passages from Mauthner's *Beiträge zu Einer Kritik der Sprache*. Edith Kern (*Existential Thought*, p. 238) quotes a passage from the *Beiträge* which connects with both Wittgenstein and Beckett: "Whoever wishes to climb the ladder of language critique — which now is the most urgent preoccupation of man — must with each step destroy the language that is behind, before, and within him. He must break every rung of the ladder as he steps upon it. Whoever follows must build his own rung only to break it in his turn."

Mauthner's position is that of a nominalism so radical that it denies the ability of language to represent not only universals but individuals. Anticipating the Wittgenstein of the *Philosophical Investigations*, he declares that language is merely a convention, a "Spielregel," which men have agreed to adopt and according to which they play their language games (*Beiträge*, 2nd ed. [3 vols.; Stuttgart and Berlin: J. G. Cotta, 1906], I, 25ff.).

Man longs for knowledge, but he has only the words of his speech to use, and these are inadequate. There can be little or no communication between man and man, for words are the names of memories, and no two men have the same memories (this is a theme Beckett pursued in *Proust*). Moreover, words are little suited to knowledge, since each word is surrounded by the undertones of its own history. Finally, words are inadequate for piercing the essence of reality, since they are merely the indicators of our memories and the things we use to express our thoughts, and these being merely contingent can no more get at true reality than a spider that has put its nest in a corner of a palace can get at the total reality of the palace (*ibid.*, III, 650). Mauthner's nominalism leads finally to both scepticism and a mystical, godless religion (*ibid.*, III, 627ff.).

19. Descartes, *Discourse on the Method*, Pt. V; Haldane and Ross, I, 116.

20. *Ibid.*

21. Fletcher, *Samuel Beckett's Art*, pp. 24–40.

22. "Samuel Beckett's Poems," in *Beckett at 60: A Festschrift* (London: Calder and Boyars, 1967), p. 55.

23. Lawrence Harvey explains: "An extensive but run-down estate that speaks of former glory, Turvey boasts several noble gateways, one of them flanked with columns surmounted by stone swans. On a nearby wall the family coat of arms repeats the motif and displays the brave motto 'Moriendo Cano,' which neatly sums up the poet's view of the relationship between life and art" (*Samuel Beckett: Poet and Critic*, p. 140).

24. Fletcher, *Samuel Beckett's Art*, p. 24. The passage is from Rimbaud's "Barbare," in *Les Illuminations*.

25. Israel Shenker, "Moody Man of Letters," New York *Times*, May 6, 1956, sec. 2, p. 3; quoted by Bell Gale Chevigny in her "Introduction" to *Twentieth Century Interpretations of Endgame*, ed. Bell Gale Chevigny (Englewood Cliffs, N.J.: Prentice-Hall, 1969), p. 9.

II. The Spectator and the Machine: *Murphy*

1. The quotation from Schopenhauer is from the *Essays from the Parerga*, "On the Sufferings of the World," *Studies in Pessimism*, pp. 7, 8. The quotation from Henri Bergson is from *Creative Evolution*, trans. Arthur Mitchell (New York: Modern Library, 1944), pp. 303, 304. The quotation from Proust ("It is not because other persons are dead that our affection for them is diminished; it is because we ourselves die") is from *A la recherche du temps perdu* (3 vols.; Paris: Bibliothèque de la Pléiade, 1954), III, 595. The quotation from Geulincx ("I am therefore merely the spectator of this machine") is from the *Ethica*, I, Cap. II, sec. ii, §2; as printed in *Arnoldi Geulincx Antverpiensis Opera Philosophica*, ed. J. P. N. Land (3 vols.; The Hague: Martinus Nijhoff, 1891–93), III: *Ethica* (1893), 33. This edition is now being reissued in a reduced facsimile format by Friedrich Frommann Verlag (Günther Holzboog). "Nudus" means "merely," but I suspect that the word accounts for Murphy's rocking chair costume.

2. Gottfried Wilhelm Leibniz, *The Monadology*, §§7, 56. I am using the English text in *Leibniz: Discourse on Metaphysics, Correspondence with Arnauld, and Monadology*, trans. George R. Montgomery (LaSalle, Ill.: Open Court, 1902 [reprinted 1962]).

3. *The Monadology*, §§7, 11, 51.

4. The tripartite structure of Murphy's mind may owe something to Schopenhauer, however. The philosopher describes three extreme forms of human life: the first is the will and strong passions; second is pure knowing, "The comprehension of the Ideas, conditioned by the freeing of knowledge from the service of will"; and finally "the greatest lethargy of the will, and also of the knowledge attaching to it, empty longing, life-benumbing languor." *The World as Will and Idea*, Bk. IV, §58. The text is that appearing in *The Philosophy of Schopenhauer*, ed., introduction by Irwin Edman (New York: Modern Library, 1928), p. 264.

5. Descartes, *The Passions of the Soul*, Pt. First, Art. XXXI; Haldane and Ross, I, 345.

6. Descartes, *Discourse on the Method*, Pt. IV; Haldane and Ross, I, 101.

7. We might remark that Geulincx anticipated Leibniz' theory of the two clocks. In this theory, the soul and the body run on separate but exactly synchronized time-systems, such that when the clock of volition strikes, the clock of the body also strikes, and body does what soul requires. Cf. Leibniz, "Second Explanation of the New System," in *Gottfried Wilhelm Leibniz: Philosophical Papers and Letters*, trans. and ed., with an introduction by Leroy E. Loemker (2 vols.; Chicago: University of Chicago Press, 1956), II, 750–52. Geulincx uses the figure in a note to the *Ethica*, I, Cap. II, sec. ii, §2, n. 19 (Land, III, 212): "Sicut duobus horologiis rite inter se et ad solis diurnum cursum quadratis, altero quidem sonante, et horas nobis loquente, alterum itidem sonat, et totidem nobis indicat horas; idque absque ulla causalitate quia alterum hoc in altero causat, sed propter meram dependentiam, qua utrumque ab eadem arte et simili industria constitutum est." In a letter to Arnauld, April 30, 1687, Leibniz uses the figure of two choirs to explain his idea of the pre-established harmony (*Leibniz*, trans. Montgomery, p. 188). In Beckett's *Watt* this image is embodied in the singing of the threne and the chorus of the frogs.

8. The quotation is from the penultimate paragraph of the third chapter (entitled "The Century of Genius") of *Science and the Modern World* (New York: Free Press, 1967), p. 55.

9. *Ethica*, I Cap. I (Land, III, 9).

10. Spinoza, *Ethics*, V, Prop. XLII, Proof. The text is that appearing in *The Chief Works of Benedict de Spinoza*, trans. R. H. M. Elwes (2 vols.; New York: Dover Publications, 1955), II, 270.

11. The "system of synchronization" is another name for Leibniz' pre-established harmony. Its absence figures in Beckett's poem "Cascando":

> . . . . . .
>
> terrified again
> of not loving
> of loving and not you
> of being loved and not by you
>
> . . . .

12. The translation is by Edwin Morgan and is published in *Leopardi: Poems and Prose*, ed. Angel Flores (Bloomington: Indiana University Press, 1966), pp. 127–29.
13. *Ethica*, I, Cap. II, sec. ii, §2, 14; Land, III, 36. The translation is by Gregor Sebba.
14. *The World as Will and Idea*, III, §38; Edman's ed., p. 161. Italics are Schopenhauer's.
15. *Ibid.*, IV, §71; pp. 334–35.
16. *Ibid.*, III, §52; p. 201. Italics are Schopenhauer's.
17. *Ibid.*; p. 206. Italics are Schopenhauer's.
18. *Ibid.*; p. 209.
19. Bergson, *Creative Evolution*, pp. 302–3.

III. The Defeat of the Proto-Zetetic: *Watt*

1. The quotation from Diogenes Laertius is from the *Lives*, IX, 69–70; Hicks, II, 483. The quotation from Empedocles is from Freeman, *Ancilla*, sec. 31, "Empedocles of Acragas," frag. 2, p. 51. The interpolations in parentheses are Freeman's. The quotation from Democritus is from Freeman, *Ancilla*, sec. 68, "Dêmocritus of Abdêra," frag. 156, p. 106. The quotation from Spinoza is from "Epistola L," *Benedict de Spinoza Opera Quotquot Reperta Sunt*, ed. J. van Vloten and J. P. N. Land, 3rd ed. (4 vols.; The Hague: Martinus Nijhoff, 1914), III, 173. The quotation from Kierkegaard is from the *Papirer*, IV, B, 16; included in *Johannes Climacus, or, De Omnibus Dubitandum Est and A Sermon*, trans., with an assessment by T. H. Croxhall (Stanford: Stanford University Press, 1958), p. 101. The quotation from Mauthner ("Pure criticism is at bottom simply an articulated laugh. Every laugh is criticism, the best criticism") is from the *Beiträge*, III, 641.
2. For the dates of these works, see Cohn, *Samuel Beckett*, p. 95, and n. 4, p. 318; and Fletcher, *Samuel Beckett's Art*, p. 148.
3. Claude Fleury, *Histoire Ecclésiastique* (20 vols.; Paris, 1691–1720), V (1697), 2.
4. *Ibid.*
5. *Ibid.*, p. 3.
6. *Ibid.*, p. 5.
7. Hegel, *The Phenomenology of Mind*, p. 87.
8. Kierkegaard, *Johannes Climacus*, p. 104.
9. *Ibid.*, p. 109.
10. Climacus, *The Ladder of Divine Ascent*, Step 29, pp. 258, 260.
11. *Ibid.*, p. 51, n. 3.
12. Berkeley, *Of the Principles of Human Knowledge*, I, 1. I am using the text in *Principles, Dialogues, and Philosophical Correspondence*, ed. with an introduction by Colin M. Turbayne (Indianapolis: Bobbs-Merrill [The Library of Liberal Arts], 1965), p. 22.
13. *Ibid.*, I, 2; Turbayne's ed., pp. 22–23.
14. *Ibid.*, I, 3; p. 23.
15. Leibniz, *The Monadology*, §55; Montgomery, p. 263.
16. "Considerations on Vital Principles and Plastic Natures . . .," in Loemker, II, 955. Italics in original.
17. Hugh Kenner would have the ultimate coincidence of the croaks be the result of the presidency of Malebranche or Geulincx (*Samuel Beckett*, pp. 84–86). Between the doctrine of Occasionalism and that of the pre-established harmony there is not much to choose. The difference lies in the identification of the "efficient cause," to speak in Aristotelian-Scholastic terminology. In the Occasionalist theory God is the immediate efficient cause, whereas for Leibniz the efficient cause is the pre-established harmony created by God, wherefore God is the mediate efficient cause. Cf. Leibniz' "Letters to Nicolas Malebranche," Loemker, I, 320–25, and especially p. 322, where he agrees with Malebranche on certain points (particularly that we see all things in God); but see also the quotation from "On Vital Principles . . ." above (and the letter to Arnauld of April 30, 1687), where Leibniz denies that souls provide the occasions for God's action, the monad being from creation provided of its own conatus.
18. Elwes, II, 264–65.
19. "Epistola L," *Opera*, III, 173; Elwes, II, 370.

20. *Discourse on the Method*, Pt. II; Haldane and Ross, I, 92.

21. "The Principles of Nature and of Grace, Based on Reason," Loemker, II, 1041.

22. Ludwig Wittgenstein, *Tractatus Logico-Philosophicus*, with an introduction by Bertrand Russell (London: Routledge & Kegan Paul, 1960 [first published in English in 1922]), prop. 7 (p. 188): "Wovon man nicht sprechen kann, darüber muss man schweigen." "Whereof one cannot speak, thereof one must be silent."

23. Aristotle, *Metaphysics*, XII, vii. The translation is that appearing in *The Basic Works of Aristotle*, ed. Richard McKeon (New York: Random House, 1941), p. 880.

24. *Ibid.*

25. Malebranche, *Dialogues on Metaphysics and Religion*, trans. Morris Ginsberg (New York: Macmillan, 1923), "First Dialogue," p. 71.

26. Jean-Paul Sartre, *Nausea*, trans. Lloyd Alexander (New York: New Directions, 1964), p. 169.

27. Albert Camus, *The Myth of Sisyphus and Other Essays*, trans. Justin O'Brien (New York: Vintage Books, 1960), p. 11.

IV. Which I Is I? The Trilogy

1. The quotation from Hegel is from the *Phenomenology of Mind*, pp. 530–31. The quotation from Kierkegaard is from *Stages on Life's Way*, in *A Kierkegaard Anthology*, ed. Robert Bretall (New York: Modern Library, 1959), p. 189. The quotation from Heidegger is from *Being and Time*, p. 167. The quotation from Augustine is from the *Confessions*, X, iii and v; Oates, I, 148–49, 150.

2. *Three Novels: Molloy*, p. 3. References to *Molloy*, *Malone Dies*, and *The Unnamable* are to *Three Novels* (TN), the one-volume edition published by Grove Press (1959).

3. Kenner, *Samuel Beckett*, p. 65.

4. Edith Kern, "Moran-Molloy: The Hero as Author," *Perspective*, XI (Autumn 1959), 187ff.

5. *Ibid.*, p. 190. Professor Kern retains this Nietzschean theory of the identity of Molloy and Moran in her *Existential Thought and Fictional Technique*, but complicates it by adding terms and themes taken from Kierkegaard, Heidegger, and Sartre, among others. As will become apparent, I am more in sympathy with the phenomenological-existential interpretation than with Nietzschean or psychoanalytical interpretations. Her basic thesis — that Moran is the hero as author — is incontrovertible, however, and I too begin there.

6. David Hayman, in "*Molloy* or the Quest for Meaninglessness" (*Samuel Beckett Now*, ed. Melvin J. Friedman [Chicago: University of Chicago Press, 1970]), also reads "Obidil" as an anagram for "libido," but goes on to argue for a Freudian interpretation: Jacques Jr. is the conscious mind or ego, and it is by "achieving the proper balance of Molloy (id or libido) and Moran (superego) that Jacques reaches his freedom and maturity" (p. 149).

7. The phrase "finality without end" is presumably Beckett's version of Kant's "Zweckmässigkeit ohne Zweck," "purposiveness without purpose." Kant's explanation of the Beautiful, derived from the third moment of the Analytic of the Beautiful, is: "*Beauty* is the form of the *purposiveness* [Beckett: "finality"] of an object, so far as this is perceived in it *without any representation of a purpose*" (Kant, *Critique of Judgment*, trans. J. H. Bernard [New York: Hafner Publishing Company, 1951], §17, p. 73; italics in original). The point is that, like Watt before him, Moran is not interested in what a thing is or means *in reality* or *in nature*; he is content with what a thing is or means in the realm of art or the imagination. In nature Moran cannot bend over Molloy, whereas in art, in imagination, he can. The difficulty with psychoanalytical interpretations such as David Hayman's (or, in the same volume, John Fletcher's argument in "Interpreting *Molloy*") is that they deal with the characters and events as if they were "natural" and therefore susceptible of "scientific" analysis, instead of dealing with them as "artificial" and therefore susceptible of merely "critical" analysis. In the long run, of course, I would agree that Beckett's art is not just an art about art, as the "Three Dialogues" would have us believe; but is an art dealing with the human condition, with "how it is." Nonetheless, Beckett's work can and must be read as exhibiting the dubious relation between "aliment"

and "manner of dispatch," between writing and the writer; for this "aesthetic" dimension of his work becomes a metaphor for the "natural" event of human consciousness. The way this metaphor gets worked out is the substance of the present chapter, and of Chapter VI. And see n. 11, below.

8. In the original French version the meeting is between A and B, not A and C. I presume that Beckett changed the initials in the English-language text to suggest that the meeting is between Author (A) and Character (C).

9. The passage is also reminiscent of Beckett's poem "Malacoda":

> thrice he came
> the undertaker's man
> impassible behind his scutal bowler
> to measure
>   . . . . .

10. Edith Kern (*Existential Thought and Fictional Technique*) identifies the visitor with Lemuel, the character in Malone's story, and — since "Lemuel" is the Hebraic form of "Samuel" — with Beckett himself. "In this light Lemuel's murders [at the end of the novel] appear rather an author's ridding himself of the characters he has created. They are an author's way of ending a story that has no natural end" (p. 221). Moran's visitor, then, is (1) Lemuel, the murderer of the characters; (2) the undertaker come to measure Malone for his coffin, since Malone too is a character; (3) the Author (in a sense to be explained, the Unnamable); and (4) Beckett himself.

11. The "wild beast of earnestness" padding up and down, "roaring, ravening, rending," sounds rather like Moran's description of Molloy (TN, 151–52): "He panted . . . He seemed to be crashing through jungle. . . . He swayed, to and fro, like a bear." If Molloy is in fact Earnestness and Seriousness, then Moran's task is that of finding and either killing or capturing and taming the beast. Once the beast is dead, Moran-become-Malone is free to "play." What Malone is here confessing, however, is that Moran failed, and therefore Malone has within himself still that quality of the serious he has longed to be rid of.

In other words, *Malone is confessing to the inadequacy of the strict aestheticism expressed in the "Three Dialogues."* Writing about writing is not enough. One must write about the earnest and serious reality called man. Art is not merely a narcissistic or reflexive "playing" — not, at least, for Malone, the creator of Molloy and Moran. Art stands, rather, in a dialectical relationship with grave reality, and the artist who is born grave cannot maintain the playfulness a pure aestheticism requires.

12. I cannot rid myself of the unlikely notion that the story of Sapo is Beckett's version of the childhood of St. Augustine. Augustine disliked school (*Conf.*, I, xii) and was a good athlete (I, x); he sinned by stealing some pears, as did Sapo by flinging his master's cane out of a window; but Sapo was not expelled from school nor Augustine from the city of God for their misbehavior. Both Sapo's father and Augustine's ("a poor freeman of Thagaste") notice that at the age of sixteen the boy is becoming a man (*Conf.* II, iii; TN, 262); and both young men are profoundly introspective. The phrase "marshalling in his mind" may allude to *Conf.* X, xi, in which Augustine explains what it is to think: "But the mind has appropriated to itself this word [*cogitation*], so that not that which is collected anywhere but what is collected [*colligitur*], that is marshalled [*cogitur*], in the mind, is properly said to be cogitated [*cogitari*]" (Oates, I, 156).

13. *Discourse on the Method*, Pt. IV; Haldane and Ross, I, 101. Descartes' admonition to aporia is a revision of the old Sceptical attitude. Cf., e.g., Diogenes Laertius, *Lives*, IX, xi, 61–108. The Unnamable says: "And things, what is the correct attitude to adopt towards things? And, to begin with, are they necessary?. . . The best is not to decide anything, in this connexion, in advance. If a thing turns up, for some reason or another, take it into consideration" (TN, 402). This is his version of the three questions Pyrrho's pupil Timon says every man who wants to be happy should ask. The questions are: What is the nature of things? What attitude ought we to adopt with respect to them? What will be the net result for those so disposed? Cf. Charlotte L. Stough, *Greek Skepticism* (Berkeley and Los Angeles: University of

California Press, 1969), p. 17; or V. Brochard, *Les Sceptiques Grecs* (2nd ed.; Paris: Librarie Philosophique J. Vrin, 1887; reprinted 1959), p. 54.

14. Vivian Mercier, "The Mathematical Limit," *Nation*, February 14, 1959, p. 145.

15. There is an interesting similarity between this and a passage from another "subjective thinker," Soren Kierkegaard. In *Repetition* a lovelorn young man complains as follows: "My life has been brought to an impasse, I loathe existence, it is without savor, lacking salt and sense. . . . Where am I? What is this thing called the world? What does this word [*sic*] mean? Who is it that has lured me into the thing, and now leaves me there? Who am I? How did I come into the world? Why was I not consulted, why not made acquainted with its manners and customs . . .? How did I obtain an interest in this big enterprise they call reality? Why should I have an interest in it? Is it not a voluntary concern? And if I am to be compelled to take part in it, where is the director? I should like to make a remark to him. Is there no director? Whither shall I turn with my complaint? Existence is surely a debate — may I beg that my view be taken into consideration?" Soren Kierkegaard, *Repetition: An Essay in Experimental Psychology*, trans. Walter Lowrie (New York: Harper and Row, 1964), p. 104.

16. The jar is Beckett's second major metaphor for the human body. The first, dominant in *Murphy* and *Watt*, is the machine or automaton-robot or cylinder. The jar becomes, in *Endgame*, the ashbins which Nagg and Nell inhabit; and, in *Play* (1964), the grey urns containing W2, M, and W1. The pile of sand in which Winnie (*Happy Days*) is buried is still another version of the jar, but the grains of sand also represent atomic units of Time. The metaphor of the machine emphasizes the ludicrousness of man's condition — he is mind and body — and is a seventeenth-century image. The metaphor of the jar emphasizes the alienation of one human being from another, as well as the impermeability of the self (none of the persons in the various kinds of "jars" can reach out to or get a hold of any other person), and is a more modern and even "existentialist" image. Both images, however, are profoundly gnostic in their implications for the value of matter, and both express a "horror of the body and its functions," as Moran put it.

17. Hoffmann, *Samuel Beckett: The Language of Self* (Carbondale: Southern Illinois University Press, 1962), p. 115. Cf. the quotation from Pascal at the beginning of Chapter I: "imbecile worm of the earth."

18. *The Ladder of Divine Ascent*, Step 5, §19, p. 103.

19. *Ibid.*, §22, p. 104.

20. *Ibid.*, Step 30, §§29, 30, p. 265.

21. Diogenes Laertius, *Lives*, IX, 108; Hicks, II, 519.

22. *Purgatorio*, iv, 129.

23. John Fletcher explains that Beckett's image is a composite of images taken from Geulincx and Dante. See *Samuel Beckett's Art*, pp. 132–33.

24. Fletcher also points out that the club-bearer may derive from Geulincx: "Another of Geulincx's images for human liberty is that of the dwarf who tries to seize the club in Hercules' hand; the demigod may permit this volition to be put into effect by himself loosing the club." See *Samuel Beckett's Art*, p. 133.

25. Hoffman, p. 3.

26. Although it is all but impossible to avoid the conclusion that the Unnamable is Beckett himself, it should be noted that, if the conclusion is correct or even viable, it is massively ironic, for it means that the fiction (at least) is precisely what Beckett had denied art ought to be — it is "expressive" of the author.

27. *Being and Time*, pp. 152–53.

28. *Ibid.*, p. 164.

V. Time, Ground, and the End: The Drama

1. The quotation from Pascal is from the *Pensées*, II, 72; Dutton's ed., pp. 19–20. The first part of the quotation from Heidegger is from *Being and Time*, p. 306; the second is from the same, pp. 312–13. The quotation from Newton is from *The Mathematical Principles of Natu-*

ral Philosophy, trans. Andrew Motte (2 vols.; London, 1729), I, 20. The quotation from Rudolf Clausius is from *The Mechanical Theory of Heat*, trans. Walter R. Browne (London: Macmillan, 1879), p. 78.

2. Hegel, *Reason in History: A General Introduction to the Philosophy of History*, trans. Robert S. Hartman (Indianapolis: Bobbs-Merrill [The Library of Liberal Arts], 1953), p. 21.

3. Heidegger, *Being and Time*, pp. 315–16.

4. *Ibid.*, p. 314.

5. *Ibid.*, pp. 320, 321.

6. *Ibid.*, p. 318.

7. *Ibid.*, p. 319.

8. *Hamlet*, I, ii, 80–86. The text of this and succeeding quotations from Shakespeare is that appearing in *The Complete Plays and Poems of William Shakespeare*, ed. William A. Neilson and Charles J. Hill (Cambridge, Mass.: Houghton Mifflin, 1942).

9. *Ibid.*, V, ii, 365–67.

10. Quoted in Cohn, *Samuel Beckett*, p. 227.

11. Richard M. Eastman, "The Strategy of Samuel Beckett's *Endgame*," *Modern Drama*, II (May 1959), 36–44.

12. Cohn, *Samuel Beckett*, pp. 226–42.

13. Kenner, *Samuel Beckett*, p. 155.

14. *Ibid.*, p. 160.

15. *As You Like It*, II, vii, 139–43.

16. *The Tempest*, IV, i, 153–56.

17. Cohn, *Samuel Beckett*, p. 239.

18. Anatol Rapoport, *Operational Philosophy: Integrating Knowledge and Action* (New York: Harper and Brothers, 1954), p. 181.

19. Martin Buber, *Between Man and Man* (Boston: Beacon Press, 1961), p. 17.

20. Nathan A. Scott, "The Recent Journey into the Zone of Zero: The Example of Beckett and His Despair of Literature," *The Centennial Review*, VI (Spring 1962), 178.

21. Driver, *Columbia University Forum*, p. 22.

VI. Reduction, Reflection, Negation: Some Versions of Consciousness

1. The quotation from Augustine ("Do not go abroad; return within. Truth dwells in the inward man") is from *De Vera Religione*, xxxix, 72. The quotation from Husserl is from *The Paris Lectures* (1929), trans. Peter Koestenbaum (The Hague: Martinus Nijhoff, 1964), p. 15. The quotation from Sartre is from *Being and Nothingness*, trans. Hazel E. Barnes (New York: Philosophical Library, 1956), pp. 75–76, and 152–53. The quotation from Hegel is from the *Phenomenology of Mind*, pp. 250–51. The quotation from Dostoevsky is from *Notes from Underground*, Pt. One, II; variously translated and published, as in *Notes from Underground and The Grand Inquisitor*, trans. Ralph E. Matlaw (New York: E. P. Dutton, 1960), p. 6.

2. Whitehead, *Adventures of Ideas* (New York: New American Library, n.d.), pp. 12–13.

3. *Ibid.*, Ch. 2, p. 23.

4. Husserl, "Philosophy as Rigorous Science," in *Phenomenology and the Crisis of Philosophy*, trans. Quentin Lauer (New York: Harper and Row [Harper Torchbooks], 1965), p. 146.

5. Husserl, *Ideas: General Introduction to Pure Phenomenology*, trans. W. R. Boyce Gibson (London: George Allen & Unwin, 1958), p. 43. Cf. Beckett's attack on habit in *Proust*.

6. *Cartesian Meditations: An Introduction to Phenomenology*, trans. Dorion Cairns (The Hague: Martinus Nijhoff, 1960), §11, p. 26.

7. *Ideas*, p. 106.

8. Maurice Merleau-Ponty, *Phenomenology of Perception*, trans. Colin Smith (London: Routledge and Kegan Paul, 1962), p. viii.

9. *Ibid.*, p. xx.

10. Herbert Spiegelberg, *The Phenomenological Movement: A Historical Introduction* (2 vols.; The Hague: Martinus Nijhoff, 1960), I, 87.

11. Merleau-Ponty, p. xxi.

12. Joseph Conrad, Preface to *The Nigger of the Narcissus*, variously reprinted, as in *The Great Critics*, ed. James Harry Smith and Edd Winfield Parks (3rd ed. rev.; New York: W. W. Norton, 1951), pp. 912–16. The passage quoted here appears on pp. 913 and 914.

13. *Ibid.*, p. 914.

14. Edward Bullough, " 'Psychical Distance' as a Factor in Art and an Esthetic Principle," in *A Modern Book of Esthetics: An Anthology*, ed. Melvin M. Rader (New York: Henry Holt, 1935), p. 318.

15. *Ibid.*, p. 319.

16. Driver, *Columbia University Forum*, p. 23.

17. *Ideas*, §27, p. 101.

18. *Ibid.*, §79, p. 224.

19. *Cartesian Meditations*, §8, pp. 20–21.

20. The shift is not only from the third person to the first, but from composing in English to composing in French.

21. Bergson, *Creative Evolution*, p. 303.

22. William James, *Psychology: Briefer Course* (New York: Collier Books, 1962), p. 173. The italics are James's.

23. *Ibid.*, p. 167. The italics are James's.

24. *Cartesian Meditations*, §15, p. 35.

25. Kenner, *Samuel Beckett*, p. 106.

26. *Ideas*, §57, p. 172.

27. *Cartesian Meditations*, §31, p. 66.

28. *Ibid.*, pp. 66–67.

29. Jean-Paul Sartre, *The Transcendence of the Ego: An Existentialist Theory of Consciousness*, trans. Forrest Williams and Robert Kirkpatrick (New York: Noonday Press, 1957), p. 38.

30. *Ibid.*, p. 81.

31. *Being and Nothingness*, pp. li–lii.

32. *Ibid.*, p. liii.

33. *Ibid.*, p. liv.

34. *The Transcendence of the Ego*, p. 45.

35. *Being and Nothingness*, p. 21. The last name the Unnamable tries to give himself or the voice is of course Worm (TN, p. 467). "Perhaps it's by trying to be Worm that I'll finally succeed in being Mahood, I hadn't thought of that. Then all I'll have to do is be Worm. Which no doubt I shall achieve by trying to be Jones" (TN, p. 470).

36. *Being and Nothingness*, p. 89.

37. The goal of the for-itself is therefore the aseity which has traditionally been assigned only to God. "Every human reality is a passion in that it projects losing itself so as to found being and by the same stroke to constitute the In-itself which escapes contingency by being its own foundation, the *Ens causa sui*, which religions call God" (*Being and Nothingness*, p. 615). See Ch. VII, below.

38. *Ibid.*, p. 128.

39. *Ibid.*, p. 92.

40. *Ibid.*, pp. lii and 75–76.

41. *Ibid.*, p. 152.

42. *Ibid.*

43. *Ibid.*, p. 153.

44. Hegel, *The Phenomenology of Mind*, pp. 81–83. Baillie's translation must be used with care, and I have inserted the German word or phrase where I thought it would clarify Hegel's use of terms. Walter Kaufmann has a section on Hegel's terminology in his very important and useful study, *Hegel: A Reinterpretation* (New York: Doubleday, 1965). This book has been

re-issued in two volumes as a Doubleday Anchor Book (1966). The volume bearing the original title is a historical and critical study of Hegel's work. The other volume, entitled *Hegel: Texts and Commentary*, is a translation of the Preface to the *Phenomenology*, with commentary; and a translation of Hegel's "Who Thinks Abstractly?"

Sartre took the terms "for-itself" and "in-itself" from Hegel, but what he means by the terms is not what Hegel means by them. The crucial difference, as we shall see, is that for Sartre the for-itself is in irreconcilable opposition to the in-itself, whereas for Hegel the for-itself is or can be congruent and even coincidental with the in-itself. For the present, it is sufficient to warn the reader not to confuse the Hegelian and Sartrean meanings of the terms.

45. *The Phenomenology*, p. 229.

46. *Ibid.*, pp. 229–40.

47. *Ibid.*, p. 243.

48. *Ibid.*, p. 244.

49. "The Manual of Epictetus," §14. The English text is that appearing in *The Stoic and Epicurean Philosophers: The Complete Extant Writings of Epicurus, Epictetus, Lucretius, Marcus Aurelius*, ed. Whitney J. Oates (New York: Random House, 1940), p. 471. The stoic strain sounds uniformly, whether it appears in Epictetus or Geulincx.

50. *The Phenomenology of Mind*, p. 246.

51. *Ibid.*, p. 249.

52. *Ibid.*, pp. 248–49.

53. *Ibid.*, pp. 250–51.

54. Cf. *Being and Nothingness*, p. 162.

55. *The Phenomenology of Mind*, p. 251; Glockner's ed., p. 167.

56. The expression comes toward the end of *Huis Clos* (*No Exit*).

57. C. G. Jung, "On the Psychogenesis of Schizophrenia," in *The Basic Writings of C. G. Jung*, ed. Violet Staub de Laszlo (New York: Random House [Modern Library], 1959), p. 383.

58. David Hume's skepticism is usually tempered by his ironic wit and common sense, but in the concluding section of Book One ("Of the Understanding") of the *Treatise*, he confesses to the *angst* which he has suffered because of his philosophical position. "Methinks I am like a man, who having struck on many shoals, and having narrowly escap'd ship-wreck in passing a small frith, has yet the temerity to put out to sea [i.e., to explore still further the "anatomy of human nature"]. . . . The wretched condition, weakness, and disorder of the faculties, I must employ in my enquiries, encrease my apprehensions. And the impossibility of amending or correcting these faculties, reduces me almost to despair." It is not just a despair for the cause of truth which tortures Hume, moreover, but a despair which brings with it loneliness, and mistrust and fear and even hatred both for others and himself. "I am first affrighted and confounded with that forelorn solitude, in which I am plac'd in my philosophy, and fancy myself some strange uncouth monster, who not being able to mingle and unite in society, has been expell'd all human commerce, and left utterly abandon'd and disconsolate. Fain would I run into the crowd for shelter and warmth; but cannot prevail with myself to mix with such deformity. . . . When I look abroad, I foresee on every side, dispute, contradiction, anger, calumny and detraction. When I turn my eye inward, I find nothing but doubt and ignorance. All the world conspires to oppose and contradict me." And in a remarkable paragraph he expresses the profound anguish, solitude, paranoia, and sense of contingency which we now recognize as "existential" — and in doing so announces the themes which the Unnamable will develop in his monologue. "I am ready to reject all belief and reasoning, and can look upon no opinion even as more probable or likely than another. Where am I, or what? From what causes do I derive my existence, and to what condition shall I return? Whose favour shall I court, and whose anger must I dread? What beings surround me? and on whom have I any influence, or who have any influence on me? I am confounded with all these questions, and begin to fancy myself in the most deplorable condition imaginable, inviron'd with the deepest darkness, and utterly depriv'd of the use of every member and faculty." David Hume, *A Treatise of Human Nature*, ed. L. A. Selby-Bigge (Oxford: Clarendon Press, 1888 [reprinted 1960]), Bk. I, Pt. 4, Sec. 7, pp. 264, 268–69.

59. Husserl, *Cartesian Meditations*, §13, p. 30. The material in brackets was added by Husserl to his original text.

60. Sartre, *The Transcendence of the Ego*, pp. 95–96.

VII. Dialectic and the Absolute Absence

1. The quotation from Diogenes Laertius is from the *Lives*, IX, 76; Hicks, II, 489, 491. The quotation from Pascal is from the *Pensées*, III, 229; Dutton's ed., p. 64. The quotation from Kierkegaard is from the *Concluding Unscientific Postscript*, trans. David F. Swenson (Princeton, N.J.: Princeton University Press, 1944), p. 81. The quotation from Rilke is from the *Sonnette an Orpheus*, I, 3. In a translation by M. D. Herter Norton (New York: W. W. Norton [The Norton Library], 1962), the passage reads:

> A god can do it. But how, tell me, shall
> a man follow him through the narrow lyre?
> His mind is cleavage. . . .
>
> . . . .
>
> Song is existence. Easy for the god.
> But when do we *exist?*

The Hogarth Press publishes an alternative translation by J. B. Leishman.

2. *Metaphysics*, xii, 7; McKeon's ed., p. 880.

3. *Paradiso*, xxxiii, 131. The translation is that appearing in *The Comedy of Dante Alighieri the Florentine*, trans. Dorothy L. Sayers and Barbara Reynolds (3 vols.; Baltimore: Penguin Books, 1964), III, 346.

4. *Ethics*, V, xxxvi; Elwes, II, 264–65.

5. *Pensées*, II, 77; Dutton's ed., p. 23.

6. *The Logic of Hegel*, trans. William Wallace (2nd ed. rev.; Oxford: Oxford University Press, 1892 [reprinted 1959]), §86, pp. 160–61. The quotation is not part of Hegel's text but comes from the additions made to the text on the basis of later notes. The passage does not occur in Lasson's edition of the *Encyclopädie* (4th ed.; Leipzig: Felix Meiner, 1930). See Kaufman's *Hegel* (Anchor Books ed.), pp. 219–20.

7. *Meditations on First Philosophy*, "Meditation III"; Haldane and Ross, I, 159.

8. Hegel, *Logic*, §91; Wallace, p. 171.

9. *Ibid.*, §§93–94; Wallace, p. 174.

10. *Ibid.*, note to §94; Wallace, p. 175.

11. *Ibid.*, §95; Wallace, pp. 176–79.

12. *Being and Nothingness*, pp. 617, 618, 619.

13. *The Logic of Hegel*, note to §94; Wallace, p. 174.

14. *Being and Nothingness*, p. 566.

15. *Fear and Trembling and The Sickness unto Death*, trans. Walter Lowrie (New York: Doubleday [Anchor Books], 1954), p. 146.

16. *Concluding Unscientific Postscript*, pp. 75–76.

17. *The Phenomenology of Mind*, pp. 797–98.

18. *Ibid.*, p. 798.

19. *Being and Nothingness*, p. 615.

20. *The Sickness unto Death*, trans. Lowrie, p. 147.

21. *Concluding Unscientific Postscript*, p. 169.

22. *Ibid.*, p. 171.

23. *Ibid.*, p. 151.

24. *Ibid.*, p. 320.

25. Driver, *op. cit.*, p. 23.

26. Quoted by Alan Schneider in "Waiting for Beckett: A Personal Chronicle," *Chelsea Review*, II (September 1958), and reprinted in Chevigny, *Twentieth Century Interpretations of Endgame*, p. 14.

27. *Concluding Unscientific Postscript*, p. 78.

28. Mercier, *op. cit.*, p. 145.

29. Richard N. Coe calls Zeno "the Gray Eminence" of the plays, since Zeno's theory of time, represented in the "heap of millet," seems to inform the plays (*Beckett* [Edinburgh and London: Oliver and Boyd, 1964], p. 89). In fact, Zeno's four major arguments ("the stadium," "Achilles and the tortoise," "the flying arrow," and "the moving rows," are directed against the possibility of motion and on behalf of the Eleatic concept of the One. Clov calls the heap "impossible" because time, like space, is infinitely divisible; so it is as impossible for time to "pass" as it is for the arrow to move through space. Nonetheless, time does pass, as Clov recognizes, and all he can look forward to is the "time" when the cosmos will have returned to a Zenotic (or generally Eleatic) fullness of the Pleroma, when motion will be no more.

Zeno argues that "If things are many, they are infinite in number. For there are always other things between those that are, and again others between those" (Freeman, *Ancilla*, §29, p. 47). This is an application to time and space of the Pythagorean discovery of the "existence" of irrational numbers. Even though the argument is intended as a *reductio ad absurdum* of the position that being is Many, its effect is to extend the realm of the irrational (or absurd) to include not only numbers (as the Pythagoreans would certainly allow) but also motion in time and space — i.e., to the world itself. For discussions of Zeno and other pre-Socratic philosophers, see, e.g., G. S. Kirk and J. E. Raven, *The Pre-Socratic Philosophers: A Critical History with a Selection of Texts* (Cambridge: University Press, 1960); and Kathleen Freeman, *The Pre-Socratic Philosophers: A Companion to Diels, Fragmente der Vorsokratiker* (2nd ed.; Oxford: Basil Blackwell, 1959).

30. Hegel, *The Phenomenology of Mind*, p. 249.

31. Of the Myth of the Fall, Hegel writes: "Man, created in the image of God, lost, it is said, his state of absolute contentment, by eating of the Tree of the Knowledge of Good and Evil. Sin consists here only in Knowledge: this is the sinful element, and by it man is stated to have trifled away his Natural happiness. This is a deep truth, that evil lies in consciousness. . . . Consciousness occasions the separation of the Ego, in its boundless freedom as arbitrary choice, from the pure essence of the Will — i.e., from the Good. Knowledge, as the disannulling of the unity of mere Nature, is the 'Fall,' which is no casual conception, but the eternal history of Spirit. For the state of innocence, the paradisaical condition, is that of the brute. Paradise is a park [in Molloy's version, a forest], where only brutes, not men, can remain. . . . This existence for self, this consciousness, is at the same time separation from the Universal and Divine Spirit. If I hold to my abstract Freedom in contraposition to the Good, I adopt the standpoint of Evil. The Fall is therefore the eternal Mythus of Man — in fact the very transition by which he becomes man." This passage is from *The Philosophy of History*, trans. J. Sibree (New York: Dover Publications, 1956), pp. 321–22.

32. Scott, *loc. cit.*

33. Kierkegaard, *Concluding Unscientific Postscript*, p. 320.

34. Driver, *op. cit.*, p. 22.

35. *Ibid.*, p. 23.

BIBLIOGRAPHY

This is a list of works which I have quoted or cited. It does not include works by Beckett. For Beckett's works and a checklist of criticism, see *Samuel Beckett: His Works and His Critics*, by Raymond Federman and John Fletcher (Berkeley and Los Angeles: University of California Press, 1970).

Alighieri, Dante. *The Comedy of Dante Alighieri the Florentine*. Translated by Dorothy Sayers and Barbara Reynolds. 3 vols. Baltimore: Penguin Books, 1949–62 (reprinted 1964).

Aristotle. *The Basic Works of Aristotle*. Edited and with an introduction by Richard McKeon. New York: Random House, 1941.

Augustine, Aurelius. *Basic Writings of Saint Augustine*. Edited by Whitney J. Oates. 2 vols. New York: Random House, 1948.

Bergson, Henri. *Creative Evolution*. Translated by Arthur Mitchell. New York: Modern Library, 1944.

Berkeley, George. *Principles, Dialogues, and Philosophical Correspondence*. Edited with an introduction by Colin M. Turbayne. Indianapolis: Bobbs-Merrill (The Library of Liberal Arts), 1965.

Brochard, V. *Les Sceptiques Grecs*. 2nd ed. Paris: Librarie Philosophique J. Vrin, 1887 (reprinted 1959).

Buber, Martin. *Between Man and Man*. New York: Harper & Brothers, 1954.

Bullough, Edward. " 'Psychical Distance' as a Factor in Art and an Esthetic Principle." *A Modern Book of Esthetics: An Anthology*. Edited, with introduction and notes, by Melvin M. Rader. New York: Henry Holt, 1935.

Camus, Albert. *The Myth of Sisyphus*. Translated by Justin O'Brien. New York: Vintage Books, 1960.

Chevigny, Bell Gale, ed. *Twentieth Century Interpretations of Endgame*. Englewood Cliffs, N.J.: Prentice-Hall, 1969.

Clausius, Rudolf. *The Mechanical Theory of Heat*. Translated by Walter R. Browne. London: Macmillan, 1879.

Climacus, John. *The Ladder of Divine Ascent*. Translated by Lazarus Moore, with an introduction by M. Heppel. Harper & Brothers, n.d.

Coe, Richard N. *Beckett*. Edinburgh and London: Oliver and Boyd, 1964.

Cohn, Ruby. *Samuel Beckett: The Comic Gamut*. New Brunswick, N.J.: Rutgers University Press, 1962.

Conrad, Joseph. "Preface" to *The Nigger of the Narcissus*. Reprinted in *The Great Critics*. Edited by James Harry Smith and Edd Winfield Parks. 3rd ed. rev. and enl. New York: W. W. Norton, 1951.

Descartes, René. *The Philosophical Works of Descartes*. Translated by Elizabeth S. Haldane and G. R. T. Ross. 2 vols. New York: Dover Publications, 1955.

Dostoevsky, Fyodor. *Notes from Underground and The Grand Inquisitor*. Translated by Ralph E. Matlaw. New York: E. P. Dutton, 1960.

Driver, Tom F. "Beckett by the Madeleine." *Columbia University Forum*, IV (Summer 1961), 21–25.

Eastman, Richard M. "The Strategy of Samuel Beckett's *Endgame*." *Modern Drama*, II (May 1959), 36–44.

Ellmann, Richard. *James Joyce*. New York: Oxford University Press, 1959.

Esslin, Martin. "Samuel Beckett's Poems." *Beckett at 60: A Festschrift*. London: Calder and Boyars, 1967.

Federman, Raymond. *Journey to Chaos: Samuel Beckett's Early Fiction*. Berkeley and Los Angeles: University of California Press, 1965.

Fletcher, John. *The Novels of Samuel Beckett.* New York: Barnes and Noble, 1964.
————. *Samuel Beckett's Art.* New York: Barnes and Noble, 1967.
Fleury, Claude. *Histoire Ecclésiastique.* 20 vols. Paris, 1691–1720.
Freeman, Kathleen. *Ancilla to the Pre-Socratic Philosophers: A Complete Translation of the Fragments in Diels, "Fragmente der Vorsokratiker."* Cambridge, Mass.: Harvard University Press, 1957.
————. *The Pre-Socratic Philosophers: A Companion to Diels, Fragmente der Vorsokratiker.* 2nd ed. Oxford: Basil Blackwell, 1959.
Friedman, Melvin J., ed. *Samuel Beckett Now.* Chicago: University of Chicago Press, 1970. The volume contains an introduction by Friedman; essays by Frederick J. Hoffman, Bruce Morrissette, Germaine Brée, Edith Kern, Raymond Federman, Robert Champigny, David Hayman, John Fletcher, Lawrence E. Harvey, Ruby Cohn, Rosette Lamont; and a checklist of criticism by Jackson R. Bryer.
Geulincx, Arnold. *Arnoldi Geulincx Antverpiensis Opera Philosophica.* Edited by J. P. N. Land. 3 vols. The Hague: Martinus Nijhoff, 1891–93.
Harvey, Lawrence E. *Samuel Beckett: Poet and Critic.* Princeton, N.J.: Princeton University Press, 1970.
Hayman, David. See Friedman, Melvin J.
Hegel, Georg Wilhelm Friedrich. *Encyclopädie der Philosophischen Wissenschaften im Grundrisse.* Edited by Georg Lasson. 4th ed. Leipzig: Felix Meiner, 1930.
————. *The Logic of Hegel.* Translated from *The Encyclopaedia of the Philosophical Sciences* by William Wallace. 2nd ed., rev. and aug. Oxford: Oxford University Press, 1892 (reprinted 1959).
————. *Phänomenologie des Geistes.* Edited by Hermann Glockner, with a foreword by Johannes Schulze. 3rd ed. Stuttgart: Fr. Frommanns Verlag, 1951.
————. *The Philosophy of History.* Translated by J. Sibree, with prefaces by Charles Hegel and the translator, and a new introduction by C. J. Friedrich. New York: Dover Publications, 1956.
————. *Reason in History: A General Introduction to the Philosophy of History.* Translated, with an introduction, by Robert S. Hartman. Indianapolis: Bobbs-Merrill (The Library of Liberal Arts), 1953.
Heidegger, Martin. *Being and Time.* Translated by John Macquarrie and Edward Robinson. London: SCM Press, 1962.
Hoefer, Jacqueline. "*Watt.*" *Perspective,* XI (Autumn 1959), 166–82.
Hoffmann, Frederick. *Samuel Beckett: The Language of Self.* With a preface by Harry T. Moore. Carbondale: Southern Illinois University Press, 1962.
Hume, David. *A Treatise of Human Nature.* Edited, with an analytical index, by L. A. Selby-Bigge. Oxford: Clarendon Press, 1888 (reprinted 1960).
Husserl, Edmund. *Cartesian Meditations: An Introduction to Phenomenology.* Translated by Dorion Cairns. The Hague: Martinus Nijhoff, 1960.
————. *Ideas: General Introduction to Pure Phenomenology.* Translated by W. R. Boyce Gibson. London: George Allen & Unwin, 1931 (reprinted 1958).
————. *The Paris Lectures.* Translated, with an introductory essay, by Peter Koestenbaum. The Hague: Martinus Nijhoff, 1964.
————. "Philosophy as Rigorous Science" and "Philosophy and the Crisis of European Man," in *Phenomenology and the Crisis of Philosophy.* Translated with notes and an introduction by Quentin Lauer. New York: Harper and Row (Harper Torchbooks), 1965.
Jacobsen, Josephine, and William R. Mueller. *The Testament of Samuel Beckett.* New York: Hill and Wang, 1964.
James, William. *Psychology: Briefer Course.* With a new foreword by Gardner Murphy. New York: Collier Books, 1962.
Jung, Carl G. *The Basic Writings of C. G. Jung.* Edited with an introduction by Violet Staub de Laszlo. New York: Random House (Modern Library), 1959.
Kant, Immanuel. *Critique of Judgment.* Translated, with an introduction, by J. H. Bernard. New York: Hafner Publishing Company (Hafner Library of Classics), 1951.

Kaufmann, Walter. *Hegel: A Reinterpretation.* New York: Doubleday, 1965.

Kenner, Hugh. *Samuel Beckett: A Critical Study.* New York: Grove Press, 1961.

Kern, Edith. *Existential Thought and Fictional Technique: Kierkegaard, Sartre, Beckett.* New Haven, Conn.: Yale University Press, 1970.

————. "Moran-Molloy: The Hero as Author," *Perspective,* XI (Autumn 1959), 183–92.

Kierkegaard, Soren. *Fear and Trembling and The Sickness unto Death.* Translated with introduction and notes by Walter Lowrie. Garden City, N.Y.: Doubleday (Anchor Books), 1954.

————. *Johannes Climacus, or, De Omnibus Dubitandum Est and A Sermon.* Translated, with an assessment by T. H. Croxhall. Stanford: Stanford University Press, 1958.

————. *A Kierkegaard Anthology.* Edited by Robert Bretall. New York: Modern Library, 1959.

————. *Kierkegaard's Concluding Unscientific Postscript.* Translated from the Danish by David F. Swenson. Completed after his death and provided with introduction and notes by Walter Lowrie. Princeton, N.J.: Princeton University Press for American-Scandinavian Foundation, 1944.

————. *Repetition: An Essay in Experimental Psychology.* Translated with introduction and notes by Walter Lowrie. New York: Harper and Row, 1964.

Kirk, G. S., and Raven, J. E. *The Pre-Socratic Philosophers: A Critical History with a Selection of Texts.* Cambridge: University Press, 1957 (reprinted 1960).

Laertius, Diogenes. *Lives of Eminent Philosophers.* Translated by R. D. Hicks. 2 vols. New York: William Heinemann (Loeb Classical Library), 1925.

Leibniz, Gottfried Wilhelm. *Gottfried Wilhelm Leibniz: Philosophical Papers and Letters.* Translated and edited, with an introduction, by Leroy E. Loemker. 2 vols. Chicago: University of Chicago Press, 1956.

————. *Leibniz: Discourse on Metaphysics, Correspondence with Arnauld, and Monadology.* Translated by George R. Montgomery. La Salle, Ill.: Open Court, 1902 (reprinted 1962).

Leopardi, Giacomo. *Leopardi: Poems and Prose.* Edited by Angel Flores. Bloomington: Indiana University Press, 1966.

Malebranche, Nicholas. *Dialogues on Metaphysics and Religion.* Translated by Morris Ginsberg. New York: Macmillan, 1923.

Mauthner, Fritz. *Beiträge zu Einer Kritik der Sprache.* 2nd ed. 3 vols. Stuttgart and Berlin: J. G. Cotta, 1906.

Mercier, Vivian. "The Mathematical Limit," *Nation,* February 14, 1959, pp. 144–45.

Merleau-Ponty, Maurice. *Phenomenology of Perception.* Translated from the French by Colin Smith. London: Routledge and Kegan Paul, 1962.

Newton, Isaac. *The Mathematical Principles of Natural Philosophy.* Translated into English by Andrew Motte. 2 vols. London: For Benjamin Motte, 1729.

Oates, Whitney J., ed. *The Stoic and Epicurean Philosophers: The Complete Extant Writings of Epicurus, Epictetus, Lucretius, Marcus Aurelius.* Edited, and with an introduction by Whitney J. Oates. New York: Random House, 1940.

Pascal, Blaise. *Pascal's Pensées.* Translated by W. F. Trotter, with an introduction by T. S. Eliot. New York: E. P. Dutton, 1958.

Poulet, Georges. *The Metamorphoses of the Circle.* Translated by Carley Dawson and Elliott Coleman in collaboration with the Author. Baltimore: Johns Hopkins Press, 1966.

Proust, Marcel. *A la recherche du temps perdu.* 3 vols. Paris: Bibliothèque de la Pléiade, 1954.

Rapoport, Anatol. *Operational Philosophy: Integrating Knowledge and Action.* New York: Harper & Brothers, 1954.

Rilke, Rainer Maria. *Sonnets to Orpheus.* Translated by M. D. Herter Norton. New York: W. W. Norton (The Norton Library), 1962.

Sartre, Jean-Paul. *Being and Nothingness: An Essay on Phenomenological Ontology.* Translated and with an introduction by Hazel E. Barnes. New York: Philosophical Library, 1956.

————. *Nausea.* Translated by Lloyd Alexander. New York: New Directions, 1964.

————. *The Transcendence of the Ego: An Existentialist Theory of Consciousness.* Translated and annotated with an introduction by Forrest Williams and Robert Kirkpatrick. New York: Noonday Press, 1957.

Schneider, Alan. "Waiting for Beckett: A Personal Chronicle." *Chelsea Review*, II (September 1958), 3–20; reprinted in part in *Twentieth Century Interpretations of Endgame*, ed. Bell Gale Chevigny, pp. 14–21.

Schopenhauer, Arthur. *Essays from the Parerga and Paralipomena*. Translated by T. Bailey Saunders. London: George Allen and Unwin, 1951.

———. *The Philosophy of Schopenhauer*. Edited, with an introduction, by Irwin Edman. New York: Modern Library, 1928.

Scott, Nathan A. "The Recent Journey into the Zone of Zero: The Example of Beckett and His Despair of Literature." *The Centennial Review*, VI (Spring 1962), 144–81.

Shakespeare, William. *The Complete Plays and Poems of William Shakespeare*. Edited with introduction and notes by William A. Neilson and Charles J. Hill. Cambridge, Mass.: Houghton Mifflin, 1942.

Shenker, Israel. "Moody Man of Letters." New York *Times*, May 6, 1956, sec. 2, p. 3.

Spiegelberg, Herbert. *The Phenomenological Movement: A Historical Introduction*. 2 vols. The Hague: Martinus Nijhoff, 1960.

Spinoza, Benedict. *Benedict de Spinoza Opera Quotquot Reperta Sunt*. Edited by J. Van Vloten and J. P. N. Land. 3rd ed. 4 vols. The Hague: Martinus Nijhoff, 1914.

———. *The Chief Works of Benedict de Spinoza*. Translated by R. H. M. Elwes. 2 vols. New York: Dover Publications, 1955.

Stough, Charlotte L. *Greek Skepticism*. Berkeley and Los Angeles: University of California Press, 1969.

Whitehead, Alfred North. *Adventures of Ideas*. New York: New American Library, n.d.

———. *Science and the Modern World*. New York: The Free Press, 1967.

Wittgenstein, Ludwig. *Tractatus Logico-Philosophicus*. With an introduction by Bertrand Russell. London: Routledge & Kegan Paul, 1922 (reprinted 1960).

INDEX

INDEX